Film Out of Bounds

Film Out of Bounds

*Essays and Interviews on
Non-Mainstream Cinema Worldwide*

Edited by MATTHEW EDWARDS

McFarland & Company, Inc., Publishers
Jefferson, North Carolina, and London

LIBRARY OF CONGRESS CATALOGUING-IN-PUBLICATION DATA

Film out of bounds : essays and interviews on non-mainstream cinema worldwide / edited by Matthew Edwards.
    p.   cm.
Includes bibliographical references and index.

ISBN-13: 978-0-7864-2970-7
softcover : 50# alkaline paper ∞

1. Motion pictures. 2. Independent filmmakers. I. Edwards, Matthew, 1978–
PN1994.F439134   2007
791.43—dc22   2007015070

British Library cataloguing data are available

©2007 Matthew Edwards. All rights reserved

No part of this book may be reproduced or transmitted in any form or by any means, electronic or mechanical, including photocopying or recording, or by any information storage and retrieval system, without permission in writing from the publisher.

Cover photographs (top to bottom): Stills from *Intolerance, Boston Kickout, Satan's Playground* and *Forever in Our Memory*

Manufactured in the United States of America

McFarland & Company, Inc., Publishers
   Box 611, Jefferson, North Carolina 28640
      www.mcfarlandpub.com

Acknowledgments

Thanks to my excellent contributors Mark Edwards, Maitland McDonagh, Jasper Sharp and Marcus Stiglegger; a big thank you to Johannes Schönherr for both his articles and the images he supplied; to filmmakers Neil Jordan, Paul Hills, Guy Maddin, Phil Mulloy, Melinda McDowell and Herschell Gordon Lewis for generously giving up a large amount of their time in order to be interviewed for this book; a big thank you to Diarmuid McKeown for organizing the Neil Jordan interview; a big thank you also to Rick Lindstrom for kindly helping out with the *Thundercrack!* images; a special thank you to Dante Tomaselli for kindly writing the opening epigraph for this book and for all the support he has shown during the writing of this book; a special thank you to Steven Jay Schneider.

And thanks for help, encouragement and support to Mum and Dad, my brothers Paul, Mark and Daniel, my sister-in-law Mandy, my nieces Lily and Poppy.

Thanks also to David Jones, Christopher Castle, Nicholas Royle and Jasper Sharp for their advice and guidance, Screen Edge, Kate Ellis, Clare Blakey, Barry Woody, Carrie, Aidan and little Amber Greenswick, Patrick Prescott, Lee Price, David Powell, Scott Baker, Rob Sheeran, Lee Baker, Sue Maitland and to Jackie Scott for allowing me to write this when I should have been working.

Lastly, lots of love and a special *arigato* to Soyoko Kanda for her support and encouragement throughout the writing of this volume. It is to her that I dedicate this book.

Table of Contents

Acknowledgments — v

Introduction — 1
    Matthew Edwards

1. "Don't Stray from the Path": Sexuality, Dreams and Eroticism in Neil Jordan's *The Company of Wolves* — 5
    Matthew Edwards

2. In the Company of the Wolf: An Interview with Neil Jordan — 15
    Matthew Edwards

3. Close to the Bone: An Interview with Paul Hills — 20
    Matthew Edwards

4. The 2001st Maniac: An Interview with Herschell Gordon Lewis — 40
    Matthew Edwards

5. Inside Pink — 50
    Jasper Sharp

6. *Thundercrack!* And a Brief Overview and Appreciation of the Golden Age of Porn — 61
    Mark Edwards

7. An Interview with Melinda McDowell — 67
    Mark Edwards

8. Animating the Extreme: The Animation of Phil Mulloy — 72
    Matthew Edwards

9. Between the Frames: An Interview with Phil Mulloy — 86
    Matthew Edwards

10. Writing Argento — 95
    Maitland McDonagh

11. Requiems for Abandoned Souls: The New Wave of 103
    Spanish Mystery Thrillers
    Marcus Stiglegger
12. The New Throwback: The Films of Dante Tomaselli 112
    Matthew Edwards
13. *Godspeed You! Black Emperor* and the Japanese Underground 126
    Biker Phenomenon
    Matthew Edwards
14. A Permanent State of War: A Short History of North 135
    Korean Cinema
    Johannes Schönherr
15. Godzilla Goes to North Korea: An Interview with 205
    Kenpachiro Satsuma
    Johannes Schönherr
16. The Winnipeg Wonder: An Interview with Guy Maddin 221
    Matthew Edwards

About the Contributors 239
Bibliography 241
Sources and Resources 243
Index 245

Introduction

Operating outside the commercial boundaries of Hollywood cinema, alternative and independent cinema flourishes. But these features must fight for the few scraps of coverage that will elevate them into the psyche of the movie-going public. Since they are largely ignored by mainstream press and television, the best source of promotion for these films comes from the Internet (notably *Senses of Cinema* and *Film Threat* and through more specific websites, such as *Midnight Eye*, a seminal and comprehensive site dedicated to the promotion of Japanese Cinema). While this acts as an influential tool in generating discussion and interest in alternative and world cinema, as well as reaching out to a greater potential number of readers, it doesn't solve the problem of lack of critical writing on the subject in print.

Through important journals like *Headpress* and *Creeping Flesh*, magazines such as *Sight and Sound* and maverick publishers such as Fab Press, coverage has been given to the obscure and weird titles that would have been ignored had it been left to the more highbrow papers or commercialized magazines. The current climate indicates that we have a situation whereby independent and alternative cinema is championed by independent and underground publishers. Aside from the aforementioned journals, there has been a rise in the number of academic books discussing cult, alternative and world cinema. Featuring comprehensive essays on diverse topics (from the work of Takashi Miike to the sexploitation flicks of Radley Metzger), they are useful critical guides; however, they also have a tendency to alienate their intended audience with their lofty philosophical theories. This book therefore aims to bridge the gap between fan-boy fanzines and serious film criticism as seen in a wide range of contemporary film books.

This book is dedicated to World Cinema, on both a cult and art-house level. Its aim is to provide a critical and in-depth look at some of alternative cinema's more obscure titles, with a strong emphasis on British Cinema.

The book's intention is to promote a spectrum of films that receive little critical commentary, while remaining accessible. Featuring in-depth articles by such esteemed writers as Maitland McDonagh, Jasper Sharp, Johannes Schönherr and Marcus Stiglegger, the book also includes interviews with filmmakers who work at the very heart of this medium, therefore giving the reader a better insight into independent filmmaking and the struggles and pitfalls indie filmmakers face. Realizing the necessity of promoting both established and rising filmmakers, this book give its readers a diverse range of interviews, including conversations with critically acclaimed filmmakers such as Neil Jordan, Guy Maddin and Herschell Gordon Lewis, contrasted with some of independent cinema's most exciting young filmmakers like Dante Tomaselli, Paul Hills and Phil Mulloy. Last, but certainly not least, this book includes an interview with infamous actress Melinda McDowell of *Thundercrack!* fame.

The evolution of cinema is discussed, particularly the rise of digital filmmaking and the impact this has had on independent filmmakers, as well as the global DVD boom. With Hollywood features dominating the multiplexes, the majority of alternative cinema titles premiere on the retail market, albeit a lucky percentage manages to receive a limited theatrical release. This monopolization has prompted the independents to seek new avenues of distribution. Festivals, retrospectives, DVD, video and cable have now replaced the theaters these films once graced. Yet, as the filmmakers reveal, the desire for their movies to have a theatrical run is still their motivating force.

This book is a marriage of new cinema and old, as it is particularly interested in looking back on old classic films that have revolutionized cinema and their respective genres. In the collection of interviews and essays complied for this edition, we are proud to include a twentieth anniversary retrospective on the cult classic British film *The Company of Wolves*, along with an exclusive interview with Neil Jordan. *The Company of Wolves* is unquestionably one of the best British films to have emerged within the last thirty years, and is fondly remembered by cinephiles and critics alike.

Matthew Edwards

Why do I make experimental horror films? I'd like to whisk the viewer off to another dimension. I want to escape from this plane. There's another place, a layer ... I see the images and sounds when I close my eyes ... like slides projected in my mind. When I was a little boy and all through my teens and early twenties, I had re-occurring nightmares. I can't keep them inside. I have to replicate those places I've visited. I've done it three times now ... and I can't stop. I'm addicted. It's an addiction. —Dante Tomaselli, August 2004 (from an interview with editor Matthew Edwards)

1

"Don't Stray from the Path": Sexuality, Dreams and Eroticism in Neil Jordan's *The Company of Wolves*

MATTHEW EDWARDS

Neil Jordan is one of British-Irish Cinema's most respected and visionary filmmakers. Alternating between mainstream Hollywood features and more independently driven projects, Jordan's impressive résumé includes such works as *The Crying Game*, *The Butcher Boy*, *Interview with the Vampire*, *Michael Collins*, *Mona Lisa* and *The End of the Affair*. His independent features tend to be more controversial and confrontational. Jordan's skill as a director is most evident during his indie projects, or Irish-Anglo co-productions, where his dark and unnerving creative vision is most fully realized.

Jordan's films cover a wide spectrum, from comedies and thrillers to more personal projects like politicized works revolving around the IRA and Ireland. Jordan holds a certain affinity for the horror genre, by his own admission: "I love the horror genre and I haven't made enough horror movies."[1] From watching the lavishly produced *Interview with the Vampire* and the offbeat and darkly delicious *The Butcher Boy* (not to mention the psychological horror of *In Dreams*), it becomes obvious that Jordan revels in making disturbing features. The vastly underrated *The Butcher Boy*, an adaptation of the novel by Patrick McCabe, held many of the motives and themes associated with horror cinema. Jordan points out that he feels that *The Butcher Boy* "was too brutal for audiences,"[2] before going on to sing the praises of Eamonn Owens, who played the lead role of Francie Brady. "He's a great, great actor. He's grown up and he's now in his twenties. It's shocking when you work with these young actors, and you see them two years later and they're nothing like you remember them—he's a big guy now."[3]

Jordan's first horror foray *The Company of Wolves* would become one of British-Irish Cinema's most treasured and influential horror films, and justifiably termed a cult classic by critics and film aficionados alike. Jordan's 1984 film was proof that British Cinema was still capable of producing innovative horror features.

Since its release, *The Company of Wolves* has had the misfortune of being overshadowed by Robin Hardy's *The Wicker Man* and Nicolas Roeg's *Don't Look Now*. *The Company of Wolves* has slipped a little out of the limelight, yet it still has the power to shock and enthrall audiences.

Upon its initial theatrical release, *The Company of Wolves* succeeded in crossing over to both art-house and mainstream audiences, taking in over $2 million on its opening day in the US. In both Europe and the UK the film was a box-office hit. Funded by IPC and Palace Pictures, *The Company of Wolves* was adapted from a collection of short stories entitled *The Bloody Chamber* by novelist Angela Carter. Based mostly on Carter's stories *The Company of Wolves* and *Wolf-Alice*, the film's screenplay was written by Carter in tandem with Jordan. The final result was a strange hybrid of fantasy and horror, oozing with eroticism, symbolism and sexuality.

Essentially an adult reworking of *Little Red Riding Hood*, the film is told through the dreams and nightmares of a young adolescent girl. The death of a girl (ravaged by wolves) triggers the development of a close relationship between her sister Rosaleen and their eccentric grandmother (played superbly by Angela Lansbury). Constantly telling cautionary tales about strange wolves and stranger men whose eyebrows meet in the middle, Granny relishes spinning the grim tales for impressionable Rosaleen. When walking through the forest, Rosaleen is repeatedly told by Granny to not "stray from the path." Temptation leads her to stray. Though it brings dangers, Rosaleen realizes it opens up a new and enticing world. Here she meets a seductive huntsman, who is not all that he seems. As the story crosses into the familiar territory of *Little Red Riding Hood*, Rosaleen reaches her grandmother's home only to discover the huntsman has beaten her there. As the huntsman transforms into a wolf, the film is given license to use the infamous fairy tale lines of "oh Grandmother, what big teeth you have." The ending sees Rosaleen taming the wolf—differing from the ending in Angela Carter's short story wherein Rosaleen removes her clothing, ending up in the arms of the wolf.

Interpreting the film simplistically, it is recognizable as a modern retelling of *Little Red Riding Hood*; though in the twisted Angela Carter-Neil Jordan version the land is plagued with werewolves. A detailed analysis of *The Company of Wolves* reveals that the film is open to interpretation on various levels, notably with its Freudian symbolism and the return to traditional fairy tale ethics by fusing a sense of the macabre into the narrative. Further examination reveals the intelligence behind Carter and Jordan's work, most notably in the overall structure: Tales within tales within tales form the backbone of the film, where dream and reality collide, blurring what is real and what is not.

The modernizing of fairy tales, and relating them to a more contemporary viewpoint, seems rather passé now, as the last decade saw a glut of films inspired by classic stories. Writers and directors became fascinated with the wicked and bloodier aspects of fairy tales and myths, notably American director Matthew Bright. Bright's 1996 effort *Freeway*, like *The Company of Wolves*, was a radical and dark reworking of the *Little Red Riding Hood* tale. He followed up *Freeway* with the violently deranged *Confessions of a Trickbaby*, a weirdly revisionist version of *Hansel and Gretel*.[4] Like Bright, Jordan returned to fairy tales for inspiration with the disturbing *In Dreams* (1999).[5]

Back in 1984, this concept was seen as remarkably fresh, and immediately identified *The Company of Wolves* as an important piece of cinema. A study of fairy tales reveals that they are far removed from their cinematic counterparts. History shows that they have been debased by both modern literature, Hollywood and corporations like Disney, who stripped away most of the dark and disturbing undercurrents that lie within these works, replacing them with cuddly characters, talking animals, woeful adventures and friendly trolls and dwarves. The whole notion of the term "fairy tale" implies goodness, such as a "fairy tale wedding." *The Company of Wolves* eschews this reading of fairy tales in favor of exploring the subconscious themes omnipresent in these works (themes connected with sexuality and adulthood) and tapping into the stories' more grisly aspects.

The readings of texts like *Hansel and Gretel* and *Snow White* from *The Brothers Grimm* support this theory, revealing them as nasty and cruel works of fiction. Gruesome imagery of crows pecking out the eyes of witches fill the pages, creating a brooding sense of horror that is conspicuously absent from mainstream and animated adaptations. When assessing *The Company of Wolves*, it is clearly noticeable that Jordan and Carter's agenda was to faithfully capture the spirit of these fairy tales.

Regarded as one of Britain's best female writers, Carter frequently took hold of classic fairy tale writings and reworked them, giving them a contemporary and feminist facelift.[6] As detailed in her book *The Bloody Chamber* (1979), Carter set out to modernize such widely established tales as *Little Red Riding Hood*, *Alice in Wonderland* and *Puss in Boots*, among others; she also translated the fairy tales of French author Charles Perrault.[7] Fascinated with both fantasy and the Freudian unconscious, her work was a successful marriage of post-modern literately theories and feminist politics, resulting in a series of uniquely original novels[8] and short story collections. Focusing specifically on Carter's contribution to *The Company of Wolves*, having taken into consideration the fairy tale aspects that underline her work, further discussion is centered on the Freudian symbolism and philosophy at the heart of Carter and Jordan's screenplay.

The key ideas of sexual awakening and the passage into womanhood are defined through the clever amalgamation of cryptic symbols. Thematically, the most obvious is the recurring use of the color red within the film. Rosaleen is given a red shawl by her grandmother; when out in the forest, she discovers red lip-gloss; and Jordan utilizes red lighting (the full moon is tinged in a red glow). Red is used to symbolize danger, passion and sex, but more explicitly menstruation. Dissection of the menstruation theory reveals a distinct correlation between menstruation and werewolf folklore. The werewolf myth is structured around the idea of a monthly cycle, in this case the full moon; during this part of the month, the transformation from human into wolf takes place. Relating this to menstruation is simple, for menstruation is also governed by a regular monthly cycle with the discharge of blood from the uterus. While the full moon is used to represent the passing from human to wolf, Carter uses this myth to comment on the hidden subtext at play involving the female menstrual cycle, and the idea that the beginning of this cycle is the first recognition for many women that they have passed from their childhood self into adulthood. (Or, expressing this in more accessible terms, the transformation from a child into an adult.) Here Carter displays an uncanny knack of probing beneath the surface of these texts, picking out startlingly original links, thus making her loss from British literature even more profound.

So what is the importance of the shawl? Given to Rosaleen by her grandmother, it is designed to keep Rosaleen safe. The grandmother comments that the shawl is as "soft as a kitten," and is intended to bring Rosaleen comfort and security. The use of the phrase "soft as a kitten" indicates that, in the grandmother's eyes, Rosaleen is still a child, and must be protected from the horrors and corruption of the adult world, keeping her pure and innocent. The demise of Rosaleen's grandmother and the shawl frees Rosaleen from the shackles of childhood, allowing her to mature and pass into the adult world. This is eventually achieved when the huntsman persuades Rosaleen to abandon the shawl, advising her to throw it in the fire. By doing so, she not only disposes of the shawl but her former childhood self, allowing her to progress into adulthood.

Again the subtext here draws parallels with the previously detailed menstruation theory, but in this instance it is presented in a far more discreet fashion; this theory stems from Rosaleen's comments that the shawl is as "red as blood." The shawl is open to various degrees of interpretations and readings, with one example being that the shawl has been knitted by the grandmother so that it can cover Rosaleen's body. The grandmother's intention is to stop men lusting over her granddaughter.

Some discussion should be focuses on the underlining meanings connected to the wolves-werewolves. If Rosaleen is intended to represent female sexuality, then correspondingly Carter uses Lycanthropy as a metaphor for the horrors of puberty, menstruation, sexual awakening, and male virility.

In attempting to decipher the correct reading, it becomes somewhat apparent that Carter is casting her net far and wide, allowing for numerous interpretations. Perhaps the best reading of this idea would be to consider that the wolves-werewolves represent the fear of male sexuality, or the beast in man. The wolves are never depicted as evil in the conventional sense, and at points they are revealed to be vulnerable; they display gentle qualities and have moments of tenderness. Rosaleen's fear stems from the unknown and from the stories her grandmother spins. These myths act as a warning for Rosaleen, fueling her fear evermore; Granny advises that men are not what they seem, and tells Rosaleen to beware of handsome strangers whose eyebrows meet in the middle and men who are hairy on the inside. It is clear that Rosaleen's grandmother despises men, and tries to steer her granddaughter away from the corruption men bring—notably sex. The stories Granny tells are designed to make Rosaleen fearful of men, presenting them as seductive and untrustworthy, capable of transforming into beasts. Rosaleen's mother dismisses them as merely Old Wife tales. Instead Rosaleen learns that "if there's a beast in men, then it meets its match in women." From the comforting words of her mother and the advice she has been given, Rosaleen begins to learn that wolves/men are not as fearful as she believed. Evidence of this emerges in the film's key scene when Rosaleen is confronted with the wolf; she is seen as no longer afraid, and ultimately takes pity on the wolf. The idea here is that there is a need for the reconciliation between male and female sexuality.

Throughout the film, Rosaleen is frequently told not to stray from the path that runs through the forest. The path is used to symbolize an allegoric path of virtue; off the beaten path are danger, corruption, temptation and sex. By straying, Rosaleen discovers a new, enticing world, and in many respects this is the first catalyst that triggers her to abandon her childlike self, in favor of the curiosity and seductions of adulthood. Immediately her grandmother's advice seems both hollow and shallow, and reveals that the grandmother wanted Rosaleen to live her life by this regimented path of goodness. By ignoring that advice, Rosaleen is no longer weighted down by the burden that has been placed on her, at once freeing Rosaleen to explore herself, the world and her sexuality.

The ending of *The Company of Wolves* has been the subject of countless critical studies and theories, with various interpretations and ideas being put forward. This has played a significant role in the film's lasting appeal and critical acclaim. The ending depicts a wolf crashing through Rosaleen's window, as reality and dream collide. In her dream world, Rosaleen is reflecting in her newfound liberation, independence and sexuality, before awakening to find wolves invading her room. The most sensible and plausible theory is that the ending implies that through the loss of childhood innocence there comes the corruption of adulthood. Therein, the younger Rosaleen "must be destroyed to make room for her adult"[9] self. Note that Rosaleen's room is filled with childhood toys, and when the wolf first crashes through the window, the toys are the first things to be knocked over. The idea here is that the wolf is trying to destroy the room, allowing Rosaleen to fully abandon her childhood self. In fact we don't see, or ever know for that matter, what the wolf does from here, or whether it would hurt Rosaleen. This ambiguity is less important, to the overall centralized idea, and a key theme in Angela Carter's work "that the corruption of adulthood is absolute"[10]—the loss of innocence and security that adulthood brings.[11]

While it is intriguing to reflect on the Freudian aspects, equal weight should be administered when scrutinizing its narrative structure. Functioning inside a dream, *The Company of Wolves* is cleverly composed of a set of interlinking vignettes that collectively form its backbone. Though the tales are connected purely on a thematic level, each episodic story recounts a myth relating to lycanthropy, with the stories having little bearing or impact on each other when placed together. Each story has its own separate identity, and consequently the film defies the traditional forms of plot structure, ripping down the boundaries normally associated with genre cinema. This non-linear approach had the potential to catastrophically diminish the impact of the film, severely undermining the excellent script and ideas. This eventuality was prevented from happening, as *The Company of Wolves* successfully weaves these stories together, fused in part to the irrational dreams of a young pubescent girl, confirming this as the film's greatest achievement. This lyrical storytelling binds the film together, creating a sense of wonder and dreaminess.

Jordan deliberately set out to make a movie that did not follow a distinct narrative path, opting instead to construct a film that tried to function as dreams do. According to Freud, dreams as a rule are very symbolic and can be representative of repressed or subconscious thoughts; he believed dreams to be the "royal road" to understanding the unconscious. Skeptics argue that dreams have no meaning, and through analysis a false tabulation is established. Such is the complexity of Freud's theories, relating to the Ego, Super-Ego and Id, that further observation is unwarranted.[12] It is critical to consider the idea that Jordan was attempting to replicate lucid dreams, along with the meanings of what we dream—effectively, their importance.

The term "lucid dreams" is descriptive of the state when the dreamer is aware that they are dreaming, and they become immersed in the imaginary world they are experiencing, believing it to be totally real and believable. In this instance, Rosaleen believes herself to be Little Red Riding Hood. We have established that during Rosaleen's dream she liberates herself and progresses into adulthood. Upon waking, as the wolves crash through her window, Rosaleen realizes the horror of what she is going to lose. The resulting screams may signify the fear of losing her childhood self, as opposed to the fear of the wolf.

The one weak aspect of *The Company of Wolves* is the rather stifled and wooden acting. Even actors like David Warner and Stephen Rea fall into the trap, delivering below-par performances. Taking into consideration the film as a whole, citing the minor acting flaws come dangerously close to nitpicking. In fairness, the acting may seem substandard when compared to Angela Lansbury's sublime performance. Clearly enjoying herself in the role, Lansbury seems to have walked straight out of one of the Grimm fairy tales, perfectly characterizing the wise motherly figure the stories depict. In her screen debut, Sarah Patterson also delivers admirably as Rosaleen. Her performance would hint at the emergence of a promising young actress, with the potential to develop a solid movie career. This never materialized, as Patterson has only made two on-screen performances since, in Michael Brezs' *Snow White* (1998) and in Lisa Gornick's *Do I Love You* (2003). One story that is frequently bandied around is that Patterson, attending the audition to provide moral support for a friend, was spotted by Jordan, who immediately cast her. Whether there is any truth in this story remains debatable, but the small number of movies Patterson has made since *The Company of Wolves* does give credence to the notion that Patterson fell into acting, as opposed to her pursuing a dream of becoming an actress.

Aside from the narrative and film structure, a major strength of *The Company of Wolves* is the rich gothic visual style. Owing much to the Hammer horror films of the sixties and seventies, the overall look and feel holds many similarities to Hammer's output. Instead of merely replicating this "look," Jordan used it as a template in order to fully maximize his vision. Ninety percent of *The Company of Wolves* is set during the Middle Ages, when superstition, folk tales and beliefs in witches and the devil were commonplace. Similarly, a large majority of Hammer's films were period pieces, set either in Old England or Victorian Britain. Shooting on location proved decidedly more expensive, so in order to rein in the costs the best strategy was to shoot the film within a studio, with a small number of exterior shots edited in. This practice didn't always work seamlessly, as represented in Terence Fisher's classic *Dracula: Prince of Darkness*, as continuity suffered glaringly (scenes set during the night were frequently interrupted by a single shot that was obviously filmed during the day, making the viewer wonder whether the scene was actually set during the dead of night or during the afternoon).

Such continuity gaffe were absent from *The Company of Wolves*. Jordan's decision to shoot within the confines of a studio had its rewards and merits—

as well as keeping the budget down. Relating back to the fairy tale aspect of *The Company of Wolves*, the tale is set in a fictional forest, so the chance of finding a specific location that had all the necessary qualities was remote. Shooting within a studio gave Jordan license to create a place that matched how he had visualized the forest looking and feeling. This in turn gave the creative department more opportunities to create the nightmarish and fantastic world both the story demanded and fairy tales generally evoke.

Jordan, seizing on the creative possibilities at his disposal, conjures up a world that is claustrophobic and unearthly, laced with the sense of the unknown, where strange beasts lurk in the darkest recesses of the forest. Swirling mist lingers around drooping trees, their bony branches resembling skeletal fingers, and twisted vines seem ready to snatch any unsuspecting passerby. At night, the forest is portrayed as a place of horror, a place to be fearful of. In stark contrast, the daylight scenes reveal the forest to be a magical and mysterious place, a place of discovery for the adventurous. Jordan's camera glides through the forest, like a bird in flight, or observes from a distance, peeping like a wolf hiding within the undergrowth. This serves to heighten the otherworldly feel created by the rich atmospheric texture of the film.

Presented with the opportunity to design his own imaginary world, Jordan exploited this fully, in relation to Angela Carter's subconscious themes of sexuality and eroticism. The forest Jordan envisaged would assume strange qualities, with the trees and giant mushrooms resembling phallic symbols, while potholes and portals took on womb-like features. Cleverly recognizing that the landscape could take on sexual symbols as expressed in the script, Jordan accordingly set about populating the landscape with exaggerated objects that could be seen to have sexual connotations. Multiple viewings, and a more analytical approach, reveal levels of eroticism that may slip past casual viewers. Jordan's decision therefore to shoot within a studio was immediately vindicated.

The visual effects of Christopher Tucker[13] were perceived as revolutionary at the time, but some modern critiques make reference to the "out-of-date" transformation effects, pointedly saying that they have a detrimental effect on the film. With the advancement of CGI and digital effects, the effects used in *The Company of Wolves* are bound to seem primitive compared to what is presented in 21st-century Hollywood sensation. *The Company of Wolves* rewards the viewer in so many ways that quibbling about the visual effects seems totally irrelevant. It would be like criticizing Fritz Lang's *Metropolis* (1927) on the grounds that the effects didn't stand up to newer sci-fi works like George Lucas' latest *Star Wars* episodes.

Examination of the transformation scenes reveals that Jordan and his effects team opted to use the latest developments in animatronics, similar to effects used in John Carpenter's *The Thing*. Admittedly, the effects certainly look unrealistic—unreal—but such is the nature of the film, that it seems appropriate. During Stephen Rea's transformation into a wolf, we first see him ripping his flesh from his face, before contorting into a bloody pulp; and strangely Rea's head begins to resemble a pepperoni pizza. The remnants include an animatronic head that slowly metamorphoses, by way of a number of animatronic tricks, from a human head into a wolf's. Repeating this formula, the film's end transformation scene again utilizes animatronics, most infamously with the image of the wolf's snout jetting out of the huntsman's screaming mouth.

Jordan's decision to use animatronics may have been slightly forced, when you consider that *The Company of Wolves* had come off the back of two werewolf features that had broken new ground in the visual effects field. Joe Dante's *The Howling* (1981) and John Landis' *An American Werewolf in London* (1981) both featured satisfyingly realistic transformations (courtesy of Rob Bottin on the former, Bottin's mentor Rick Baker on the latter) that no CGI effects could ever replicate. Both morphing scenes were generally frightening and revolutionary (they used real-time air bladder transformation effects), giving the viewer a sense that this was "real," as opposed to CGI where the effects never truly resemble reality. Jordan may have decided that it would be hard to surpass the groundbreaking effects of Bottin and Baker, signaling the alternative approach the filmmakers finally undertook.

There is something timeless about *The Company of Wolves* that has always kept it floating on the fringes of popular cult cinema, but never reaching the giddy plateaus the film warrants. Its magical qualities, and the sheer enjoyment in storytelling, combined with the wickedness of old fairy tales, and subconscious themes of sexuality, Freudian symbolism, dreams and eroticism, have left an everlasting impression on countless cinematic spectators. *The Company of Wolves* is a cauldron of delights, mixed perfectly to convey a story that depicts the horrors of puberty, and of a girl who abandons the shielded world of childhood and passes into adulthood.

Notes

1. Neil Jordan, interview with Matthew Edwards, March 2004.
2. Ibid.
3. Ibid.
4. Bright's *Freeway* and *Freeway 2* were contemporary re-workings of classic fairy tales and marked him as one of American cinema's most interesting new filmmakers. Unfortunately, his subsequent films, the awful *Ted Bundy* and the lackluster *Tiptoes*, made Bright's reputation plummet dramatically.
5. *In Dreams*, interpreted as a loose reworking of *Snow White*, failed to find its targeted audience and barely made an impact with cinemagoers. A flawed work certainly, the film did feature elements that were compelling, but ultimately failed to deliver, or fully develop, most of its stronger features.

6. Carter died in 1992 of cancer, aged 51.

7. Perrault is best remembered for his fairy tales *Le Petit Chaperon Rouge* (*Little Red Riding Hood*), *La Belle au bois Dormant* (*Sleeping Beauty*) and *Le Chat Botté* (*Puss in Boots*). His work is still widely published today and many of his stories have been adapted into feature films, most successfully by Walt Disney.

8. Carter's wrote a number of critically acclaimed novels, including *The Infernal Desire Machines of Doctor Hoffman* and *Heroes and Villains*

9. Part of a quote taken from the website www.geocities.com/za5tar/the companyof wolves.html.

10. Ibid.

11. This paragraph, and some themese explored in this essay, was inspired by the excellent analysis of The Company of Wolves at www.geocities.com/za5tar/thecompanyof wolves.html. Author unknown.

12. For further reading, consult Sigmund Freud's The *Interpretation of Dreams*. London: Penguin, 1991.

13. Christopher Tucker is a special effects artist who has worked on many high profile feature films, including *Star Wars*, *The Elephant Man*, *Dune* and Neil Jordan's *High Spirits*.

2

In the Company of the Wolf: An Interview with Neil Jordan

MATTHEW EDWARDS

The following interview was conducted in March 2004 to tie in with the 20th anniversary of *The Company of Wolves*.

MATTHEW EDWARDS: *Are you surprised by the impact* The Company of Wolves *still has on audiences?*

NEIL JORDAN: Does it still have any impact on audiences? Well, I'm pretty gratified. It was made so long ago, and it has since become somewhat of a cult movie. It was very successful in Britain and Europe. Cannon released it in America and they did a trailer that made it look like *Friday the 13th*. So it missed its audience in America, but I think it has regained it through the years. There is something obviously universal in the fairy tale aspect of *The Company of Wolves*, which I took from Angela Carter's story. When I was making it I was just trying to reach an area of enchantment that a lot of horror movies seem to miss. I'm really glad that it's still being seen.

Though The Company of Wolves *is in the horror-fantasy genre, its key themes deal with the issues of sexual awakening and the corruption of adulthood. Is it fair to conclude that an element of eroticism runs through a lot of your work?*

Yes it is, and more so in *The Company of Wolves* than in anything else that I've done. I think that's because Angela Carter wrote the story and the script. When a lot of horror films deal with eroticism, they don't often deal with the idea of it directly. The fact that Angela Carter had written this post-modern spin on a fairy tale enabled me to address the issue in a much more direct and questioning way than you would normally get in horror-fantasy movies. Often in horror-fantasy movies the sexuality is subdued and it's not overt. It's more unconscious than it is in *The Company of Wolves*.

The Company of Wolves *was financially successful for Palace Pictures, wasn't it?*

Yes it was. It was one of the first few films Palace Pictures released. They had previously released *Diva* and *Evil Dead*. They released it in the Odeon on Leicester Square, which was a very bold thing to do at the time, because release patterns were much different than they are now. They needed to get an enormous audience to make a success of it in any way, and they actually managed to do that.

I thought Angela Lansbury was great in her role as the grandmother. Throughout the film she tries to make sure her granddaughter stays innocent, but ultimately, it is through her death that Rosaleen eventually matures, passes into adulthood.

Absolutely. Angela Lansbury is a unique actress. She is most unusual among British actresses, in that she went to Hollywood and she made a career for herself quite independently. I was just lucky enough that she agreed to do *The Company of Wolves*, because she hadn't at the time begun the TV series *Murder She Wrote*. She was someone who had appeared in critical films like *The Manchurian Candidate*. Angela had been in some marvelous films, and played some wonderfully offbeat roles, but she hadn't become the motherly figure that we now all know. I think I got her at the perfect time, really.

Tell us how you came to collaborate with writer Angela Carter.

I was at a festival in Dublin to celebrate the centenary of writer James Joyce, and Angela Carter was there, among many other writers that were invited from around the world. I got to know her, we got to talk, we were speaking at a panel together, and she showed me a radio play that she had written based on the story *The Company of Wolves*. She had published a collection of stories called *The Bloody Chamber*, which dealt with a whole string of fairy tales, and *The Company of Wolves* was just one of them. I read the radio play she had written, and she wanted to make a film, but it was too short. So when I read all of her stories I said, "We should come up with a structure whereby stories are being told within stories." In other words, someone would be telling a story, and within the story that they're telling, someone else tells a story, and somebody else tells a story, and we could come up with a structure that could include all the other stories she made reference to in her collection. That was basically it. So we sat down and began to write the script together, to see if this concept worked, and it did work.

You shot the majority of the film in a studio. Why was that?

First of all I couldn't find a forest with the depth and dimensions that we needed. We checked out some locations, but we would have probably needed to go to Brazil or somewhere, to get the atmosphere we needed. Secondly, when I came to think about it, the script was set in an imaginary forest, so it made much more sense for us to construct a forest—an impossible

Opposite: Rare Brazilian poster of Neil Jordan's *The Company of Wolves*.

forest, where the trees were like skyscrapers, and the trees almost begun to assume human and animal shapes. I worked with a brilliant designer called Anton Furst, and once we made that decision to shoot the entire film in a studio it liberated the design and visual possibilities of the film for us.

The visual style is very reminiscent to the sixties Hammer horror pictures and early German Expressionism. Was that deliberate?
Absolutely. It was the first horror-fantasy film that I had made, and I kind of looked at everything I possibly could as a reference point. Because it was set in a dream and an imaginary space, I could pick and choose images from all sorts of films that I had seen from my childhood. I could reference a lot of things from Murnau to Hammer films.

A key scene is when Rosaleen's mother tells her, "If there's a beast in men, it meets its match in women too." This explicitly comes to the fore in the film's climax as Rosaleen ends up taming the wolf. Critics have argued that this implies the need for reconciliation between male and female sexuality. Do you agree with this?
Yes of course, because the whole theme of Angela's story was about how the young girl needs to learn that what she has been told to fear is not fearful at all, it's part of her, it's part of nature and part of the process of growing up. That symbolically comes to the fore when Rosaleen embraces the wolf. So the movie, if it's about anything, should be about abandoning preconceptions, in particular, abandoning the fears one has of the unknown.

The Company of Wolves is open to a lot of critical analysis and discussion, in relation to the Freudian themes and symbolic nature of the imagery involved. What are your thoughts on Wolves being debated on such a level?
It's not a narrative movie, we consciously set out to make a film that was about dreams, and about the impact of dreams and the symbolism of what we dream, actually emotional wakes. So, I'm not surprised that people see all sorts of readings into the film. I was conscious when I made it; I'm not making an allegory, I was trying to make a film that functioned as a dream, and I included the elements of the irrational that also happen in your dreams. I was writing it with Angela, and we would always try and find an image, or an event, that was unexpected in a strange way that could only be explained on an emotional level. It's quite easy to make an allegorical movie, but it's more difficult to make a film that operates in the way dreams do. I haven't read a lot of the stuff that has been written about *The Company of Wolves*, but I'm not surprised that people do want to see those meanings in it.

Do you think the ambiguity of the film's ending has played a significant part in the film's lasting appeal?
When the wolves crash through the window? Do you think it has played a part?

2. Interview with Neil Jordan (Matthew Edwards) 19

Yes, I believe so...

Actually, I wanted the film to have a different ending, but I couldn't do it at the time. We didn't have the technical or digital resources available, not like we have now.

What was originally intended?

Basically the girl wakes up and she bounces up and down on her bed, and she dives into the floor, and the floor just ripples like water. It's an image that would be so familiar to you now—out of advertising—but at the time it was impossible to realize. So I thought about it, and I came up with this other ending, with this symphony of wolves, and it turned out quite well.

The Company of Wolves saw you work with producer Stephen Woolley for the first time. How important has he been to you, throughout your filmmaking career?

Very important. We have made about ten movies together, and they were quite successful. The producers, writers, cinematographers that I collaborate with are all very important to me. If you get to make movies with the same people, then you're very lucky. And sometimes you just get tired of each other. You say, "Give it a break for a while." It's a bit like being in a rock band.

Lastly, should we heed Grandmother's advice and stick to the path, or do you advocate that we stray from it?

Oh, I think you should stray from the path. I think you should let your eyebrows grow too, and meet in the middle.

3

Close to the Bone: An Interview with Paul Hills

Matthew Edwards

I seem to be drawn to individuals who have the desire to get out there and make a film, despite budgetary restraints and obstacles faced by the lack of proper resources and/or equipment. Films like *Man Bites Dog, Tetsuo, Eraserhead, Begotten, Evil Dead* and *Pi* are all unique and distinct despite minuscule budgets, and display more flair, invention, style and substance than your average Hollywood popcorn flick. Financed in most cases out of the filmmaker's own pocket, or from friends and family, their idiosyncrasies are allowed to flourish and their particular styles emerge.

In the early nineties, thanks to UK independent distributor Screen Edge, a new variety of cutting edge cinema titles hit the high-street shelves. Screen Edge's blunt motto read simply: "Nothing like Hollywood," an accurate description, for the label promoted and championed a new generation of filmmakers, many of whom have now gone on to forge successful film and television careers.

The UK is not a hot basin for underground cinema; in fact, finding an alternative cinema here in Britain is extremely difficult, partly due to lack of funding and support for new filmmakers. With the British film industry so wrapped up in financing Cockney gangster films, period dramas and lightweight romantic comedies, it's no wonder that British Cinema is devoid of talents such as David Lynch, Abel Ferrara, Werner Herzog, Takashi Miike, Ringo Lam and David Cronenberg. (Film Four has subsequently funded Lynch, Herzog and Cronenberg films, though that is largely due to their reputations as icons of World Cinema.)

One of the early titles to emerge from the Screen Edge label was a British film called *The Frontline*, directed by Paul Hills. Shot for a paltry £8,000, *The Frontline* is a fine example of what can be achieved through the pure desire to make a feature film, despite all obstacles. It's a great British film, and one that has fallen into obscurity. Much credit should go to Hills that the feature was even completed in the first place, as the production was plagued with countless problems.

After the awful experience making *The Frontline*, Hills went on to make the autobiographical film *Boston Kickout* (1997), a feature that succeeded in crossing over to a more mainstream audience. This was partly due to Danny Boyle's *Trainspotting*, as an emphasis on British features was very much in vogue during this era. *Boston Kickout* cemented Hills' reputation as one of the most interesting new voices to emerge in British Cinema, and the film received numerous plaudits. And just when it seemed that he was going to become a major player, circumstances took a cruel twist and his intended follow-up to *Boston Kickout*, *Raving Beauties*, was grounded for numerous reasons.

Paul Hills has returned to feature filmmaking, after a stint making commercials and episodes for the British Television series *Urban Gothic*. His new film, *The Poet*, was released in Germany in late 2003, and the following interview was arranged to tie in with its release and to discuss his work and the state of British Cinema. I arranged to meet Hills in the Berners Hotel in Oxford Street, London. When recording of this interview commenced, the hotel lobby was quiet, though relatively busy. Two questions in and we were then treated to a blast of cheesy lounge music, kind of like jazzed-up instrumental interpretations

Do you want to come with me? John Simm and Emer McCourt in Paul Hills' *Boston Kickout* (courtesy Paul Hills).

of classic songs. If I recall correctly, we both went "Oh, fuck" before we decided to carry on.

MATTHEW EDWARDS: Boston Kickout *was greeted with much critical acclaim when originally released, and you were then all set to shoot the film* Raving Beauties. *What happened to that project? I thought it was a given that you were going to shoot the picture.*

PAUL HILLS: Yes, so did I, maybe because *Boston Kickout* wasn't such a trauma in terms of raising the money, partly of course because it didn't cost that much. We shot it very cheaply. With all the naiveté in the world I envisaged that *Raving Beauties* would be shot immediately after *Boston Kickout*, in 1995–1996. We tried to do it in 1995, and we got incredibly close in 1997; we got nine days away. We got a few weeks away in 1999, and we nearly did it again in 2001, before I did *The Poet*. But on all those occasions the project fell through for one reason or another. The first time it fell through in 1995, it fell through because of an actor who was going to play an important role—he had a conflict in his schedule. In 1997 it fell through because of a sales agent who reneged on the commitments they had made to us. In 1999 we had a problem with a distributor pulling out, and in 2001 we had another problem with a different distributor.

It's either the most cursed project ever, or, it's the project I am going to spend my whole life trying to make and never do. Or, it's one of these stories, you know, triumph over adversity like John Madden's *Shakespeare in Love*, a film that takes twelve or fifteen years to eventually come out. So who knows? It's not a film I originated, it's a film that came to me, and it's a film that I have made my own and believe in utterly. It's a comedy set in the North of England chasing the dreams and aspirations of six working class women who all enter a beauty contest for very different reasons. In a way, you could now call it *The Full Monty* meets *The Calendar Girls* if you wanted to spin it. But the problem you also have with a project that has been around the track a little bit is that you have to change people's perceptions of it, because people know it, they have heard of it, and they have heard it hasn't happened. It's unfortunate, but it's still a project I want to do. It's still on my slate. We will see.

You have recently returned to directing feature films with The Poet. *What can you tell us about the picture? What can we expect?*

It's a film that I read because the German producers sent me the script, basically. They sent me the script after I had been away in Cuba, and while in Cuba a mystic told me to expect a surprise upon my return. On my return I got a message from a producer asking me if he could send me the script. And I read it, and I liked it. Basically, to me, the story of a killer who kills for money is the ultimate capitalist metaphor: money over human life, money over humanity. And the story of the lead character Andrei, played by Dougray Scott, is the story of someone who regains his humanity, and sees the error of his previous endorsement of capitalism, let's say. It has the veneer of a very commercial film; it's the story of a killer. In a way that's the lowest common dominator, commercial brief for a film. But for me it had more important values and metaphors at its heart.

How did I become involved? I read the script in early 2002 and I became attached to the project around April 2002. We did some more work on the script with a brilliant English writer called Robert Hammond and we started shooting in August 2002 and finished October 2002. The film was finally completed in 2003.

You worked with Scottish actor Dougray Scott, on The Poet. *What was that like?*

Dougray is an amazing guy, he's a wonderful guy. I have known his work from *Twin Town*, that was the first film I saw of his, and of course I have seen *Mission Impossible 2* and *Enigma*, etc., etc. He's a joy to work with. He's very professional, very amenable, and good-natured, you know he doesn't have any of the traits you'd expect from someone who has done a number of big Hollywood films. He doesn't have that kind of egotistical preciousness that you expect. You would characterize him as a method actor, but he has great professionalism at heart. If you take the simile of *Marathon Man*, Hoffman or Olivier, in a way he's a great marriage of both. He also has such a good sense of humor, he's such a good laugh that he has this great thing where he can fool around and then as soon as you shoot, he's right there and right in it. He does a lot of preparation of his roles, which I like a lot as well. He also loves accents, which I'm also keen on.

In the six years that have lapsed since you made Boston Kickout, *do you think your directing style has evolved in any way? Do you feel* The Poet *is a more mature piece of filmmaking?*

That's an interesting question because you are always evolving and changing as a filmmaker, and there are many things that you do at one stage in your career that you wouldn't do at another. Having said that, I recently had to do the audio commentaries on the DVD of *The Frontline* and *Boston Kickout*, and I re-viewed those films and certainly with *The Frontline*, I hadn't seen it in years, really years, and I had not wanted to see it. And sometimes you're surprised by the similarities in the way you've done things. I mean, for instance, I hadn't even noticed it, but there is a scene in *The Frontline* that takes place in a club and then goes outside, which is similar to a scene in *The Poet* which takes place in a club, and then goes outside of it. I suppose there are things that I am now more interested in and keen to pursue in filmmaking, than I was when I first started.

Paul Hills in Ireland during the making of *Boston Kickout* (courtesy Paul Hills).

It's complicated. Basically, the answer is a mixture of the both. Certainly I have changed and evolved, and there are things and shots I would say, watching *The Frontline* again, I wouldn't do. But subconsciously there are things that I'm still doing. There's a certain amount of evolution and a certain amount of taking the same view. But, I think people watching *The Poet* would probably, I don't know, consider *The Poet* a departure from *Boston Kickout* and *The Frontline*. *The Poet* is, in a way, slicker. You know I hate that word *slick* and I don't at all aspire or feel an influence by American Cinema, especially not Hollywood Cinema. I like European filmmakers, but, I suppose looking at *The Poet*, people will think it's more American, unfortunately. It's probably because *The Poet* has more of a polish and slickness. I took the view on *The Poet* that there would be certain things that were right for that story, and certainly they would not have been right for *Boston Kickout* or *The Frontline*. Although, on *The Poet*, I tried to do a number of sequence shots in it. It's the first film that I have extensively used Steadicam on. Even saying that, there is an amount of hand-held camerawork at a certain point in *The Poet* which there was a lot of in *Boston Kickout*, and even more so in *The Frontline*. On my next film I won't come to it with a preconceived idea of how I am going to shoot it. More importantly, the function of what you're trying to do with the film influences the style and I don't see *The Poet* as the only style that I could do.

It is often wrongly stated that Boston Kickout *is your debut film, for prior to this you directed the rarely seen but impressive* The Frontline.

Have you seen it?

I have seen it ...

Fucking hell, you've seen *The Frontline*. You are one of such a small number of people.

You went through absolute hell to make that feature, didn't you?

God, did I. I went through unbelievable things on that film. When I started making that film, in the end of 1989, start of 1990, I had made a couple of student films, one of which was for the National Film School and one was directed for Bournemouth & Poole College of Art and Design. And, pretty much, I just took the principles of how we made those films at the film schools and just applied it to a bigger film. In retrospect, I did all the things that you probably shouldn't do on your first film. Your first film, if you're smart and take the Tarantino model, you would set it in one location with a cast of five or six. Stupidly, with *The Frontline* I set it in about four different locations with a cast of well in excess of twenty, excess of thirty really, and I started shooting that film when I had £2,000 in the bank. In the end it had a raw cost of about £8,000, with umpteen amounts of deferments, etc. That movie was a beg, borrow, steal and credit card movie, in the style of *Clerks* and later *Leon the Pig Farmer* and *I Brought a Vampire Motorcycle*. That experience was a great experience, but it was a hell of a fucking experience, a terrible experience. Basically with £2,000 I pretty much hitchhiked up to Manchester and thought, "I will start making this film," and tried to get a load of people on board who could get behind the film. But somehow the naiveté I had was a great bonus because I didn't really understand all the pitfalls and problems that I was going to face. I had no prior knowledge of that, so the problems came up and they had to be conquered.

But at the start it was tough. I was sleeping on park benches, and I was doing everything I could to save money. I was living on a budget of £1.88 a day, which sometimes meant I had to nick food out of fucking shops in order to survive. The most important thing at that time was the money for the film stock. To eat was less important than money for film stock. That was the priority. Many times during the shoot we ran out of film stock. Most films are shot on a ratio of 10 to 1, some 20 to 1, some 400 to 1. *The Frontline* was shot at a ratio of 4 to 1. When you've got a normal scene of two people talking, you would expect in that scene to do one angle on one guy, and one angle on another guy, and inter-cut the two. If you do one take on either one of those,

3. Interview with Paul Hills (Matthew Edwards)

then that is 2 to 1 for starters. If you are going to do a wide shot, okay, then that's another set-up, and if you only do one take on that, then its 3 to 1. That excludes the idea of complicated camera moves, or even the idea of having to do a second take, because it's not right. Jesus, we were close to the bone. But we were close to the bone on everything on that film. I remember the instance where famously the location manager Callum Watson at one point opened the back of his car to get some files out and in amongst the dirty rags and tires there were a couple of cheese sandwiches that were two weeks old. And people really dived on them, like locusts, to try and get these sandwiches because the level of hunger, exhaustion and insanity was at that level.

You had people throwing syringes at you as well.

When we were shooting in the Hulme housing estate, they didn't like us there. They thought we were actually making a documentary about the estate. They thought the idea of us doing a film was a cover, and that we were working for Granada, or somebody trying to do an exposé of how bad the estate was, which wasn't the case. Because of that, they wanted to chuck us out. They bashed down a door at one point with a sledgehammer and they did throw syringes off the thirteenth floor of a building at us ... that's quite serious. When someone is going to fucking throw a syringe at you, it's more than enough to get you paranoid, quite honestly.

If it were not for Screen Edge, who picked up the UK distribution rights, The Frontline would have remained unseen. As you will probably agree, it's a disgrace, the amount of British films that get made and then end up unable to secure a distribution deal. American independent features fare a lot better.

The truth of the matter is that a mediocre American film will have more chance of being released in the UK than a mediocre British film. The American film will probably have an actor in it who is more well known and they will probably have the backing of a major studio that is going to pay a fortune on P&A and it's not going to make any difference if the film is good, bad or indifferent. It's harder now than it was ten years ago, or even seven years ago, when *Boston Kickout* came out theatrically. When *Boston Kickout* came out in the cinemas here, it was a film that had kind of broken through. It had been made independently, totally independently, and it got distribution through a proper distributor. To achieve that now is probably harder, and you're right, I know a lot of people who have made good British films and they can't get a theatrical distribution. To come out straight to video isn't as hard, so that's what happens to a lot of these underachieving British films.

In relation to *The Frontline*, in Cannes 1993 I bumped into John Bentham

Opposite: UK DVD sleeve of Paul Hills' low-budget masterpiece *The Frontline* (courtesy Paul Hills).

PAUL HILLS DIRECTOR

At the age of eighteen, during an interview for a place at film-school in Plymouth Paul Hills was asked what he wanted to do in the business. "Direct feature films" he replied. He was promptly informed by the lecturer he had more chance of being struck by lightning twice. Two years later he started making 'The Frontline'.

Paul Hills describes the making of the film as "absolute hell!" With no money to finance the project he arrived in Manchester in search of cast, crew and locations, all of which he had to get for free. He slept on the streets until he found actors who's floors he could sleep on; he posed as a member of staff and slept in the local nurses dorm. They were filming in the notorious Moss Side and Hulme housing projects. The crew suffered constant harassment from - drug addicts throwing used syringes from tower blocks, smoking heroin in phone booths next to the shoot - and gang members after a bit of quick profit, the threat of violence never far away.

Paul begged borrowed and begged again. Hitch-hiking up and down the M1 over a hundred times to buy film stock one reel at a time or attempt to raise some cash to continue. After twenty four days shooting spread over several months the film was completed. It was edited over the next nine months in Manchester, Leeds, Sheffield and London. Anywhere they could use for free and finally after three years and a £12,000 budget 'The Frontline' was in the can.

Above and Opposite: Inlay card from Screen Edge's DVD release of *The Frontline* (courtesy Paul Hills).

3. Interview with Paul Hills (Matthew Edwards)

writer, producer, director, and editor
Paul Hills

principal cast
Vincent Phillips
Amanda Noar
Geoffrey Leesley
Renny Krupinski
Leroy Cooper

executive producer
Tedi DeToledo

co-producer
Neil Molyneux

director of photography
Martin Parry

art director
Dennis Strode

music
Nicolas Roy
David Barron

production and location manager
Callum Watson

sound recordist
Erik Ollson

makeup designer
Joceline Andrews

focus puller
Michael Riley

boom operator
Paul Lord

assistant editor
Steve Marles

production company
Bluebell Films

Paul Hills had all but sold his soul to make his debut feature film but nothing could prepare him for the disappointment to come. In his own words: "Financed by friends, my family, my girlfriend, by selling my possessions - my books and records, a bank loan and a grant, the film was finally finished. Everyone in any distribution company you care to name wouldn't give the film the time of day."

Available now on DVD 'The Frontline' is a shining example of what can be achieved for very little money and is all the more remarkable because of the conditions under which it was made.

FILMOGRAPHY

The Harry Allen Mystery	1987	short
Until We Sleep	1990	short
Lost	1991	short
The Frontline	1993	feature film
Boston Kickout	1996	feature film
Mad In Tokyo	1997	short
Villefranche	2000	short
f2point8	2002	short
The Poet	2004	feature film
Secrets	2004	short

3. Interview with Paul Hills (Matthew Edwards)

of Screen Edge when he was just about to put together his titles to put out on the Screen Edge logo. And he actually complained of having a problem finding good British independent films. But that was in 1993, and that was at the start of this impetus to make low-budget British films. Since 1993 there have been more and more of them being made, especially now when you have digital technology. The bottom line figure to make a film has dramatically decreased. The problem is that a lot of these distributors have got on their shelves thirty or forty of these digitally made feature films and it's very Darwinian, the amount that have a chance of being released. In fact, if you add up the number of UK–based DV feature films that have got a theatrical release, and if you exclude the ones made by prominent filmmakers like Michael Winterbottom, it's actually incredibly tough.

What's your take on features shot digitally? I am personally not convinced by digital features. I find some filmmakers are becoming too pretentious with the medium. Take Mike Figgis. He made the great Leaving Last Vegas, *but now he makes unforgivable films like* Hotel.

Funnily enough I visited the set of *Hotel*. My girlfriend was the production manager at the time. Do you like *Time Code*?

Yes, I didn't mind that film ...

Time Code is an interesting concept, a great concept. The good thing about *Time Code* is that the stories are completely linked, and it's all taking place at the same time, at four places simultaneously. That has a great connectivity in it. It is a final piece. With *Hotel* he went away from that, didn't he, and tried to combine the two things, and he lost some of the power of *Time Code*. The good thing about Figgis is that he is experimenting in those films; he's experimenting with the form, by having the four parallel stories going on. I think the problem with digital filmmaking is actually also the strength of it. The strength of it is its open access to anyone. But that's also a problem because there are thousands and thousands of people shooting digital feature films around the world and the space for distribution, as I said before, has got less and less. So, it's a difficult one. The thing is that some kid on the streets of Nairobi, who would never get a chance otherwise, will have a chance. We may get the discovery of a great filmmaker we wouldn't have had without that accessibility. In truth, only the films made by directors with some profile, or with a great banner, like the *Dogma* films, have performed and found an audience. We will see.

I find The Frontline *a very bleak film. The tone is oppressive, downbeat and grim. When there seems to be a sign of hope, between Marion and James, it is ultimately*

Opposite: James King says goodbye to Ronnie in Hills' *The Frontline* (courtesy Paul Hills).

Photograph of the *Frontline* crew. It was taken at the end of the shoot; the crew seems surprisingly upbeat despite their grueling experience (courtesy Paul Hills).

quashed by Marion's death. Yet, in Boston Kickout, *the ending offers some degree of hope, in that John Simm's character Phil manages to escape his banal life, in pursuit of something he is passionate about [photography]. Did you deliberately set out for a more optimistic ending with* Boston Kickout?

You're right, The Frontline is bleak, very bleak. Actually, that's one of the reasons why the film has underachieved. It's hopeless; in the ending of the film, James is sent back to the mental institution he was originally released from. The cycle is downbeat. Funnily enough, in all three of my films, and this goes back to what I was talking about earlier, about the similarities and differences, all three of my films have a kind of tragedy to them. I am not saying that I get up in the morning and go boom, I'm going to do the third part of ... I am only thinking about this in retrospect, certainly with The Frontline, which I hadn't seen in seven years, until last month. At the end of The Frontline, when James goes back into the mental hospital, on the way in he meets his friend from before, who is on the way out. In that, there is a seed, the tiniest, tiniest, tiniest little bit of hope within that. I know it's tentative, I'm sorry about that. The function really for me as a writer in that was that the character was given another chance, another ray of hope. I think realizing how downbeat, depressing, stark and negative The Frontline was in its portrayal of life, was one of the reasons that made me have a more optimistic ending to Boston Kickout. But somehow I still managed to subvert the ending of Boston

Kickout by ending the final shot on the roundabout. Phil gets out and goes to pastures green in Scotland, to study photography, but the pessimist in me, I suppose, puts the shot of the roundabout in as a symbol of going around and around and around and getting nowhere for the people left in Stevenage. Also, even before Phil goes away, I have the Steve character in the hospital talking about how everything is sorted now, because he has realized that space is his dream. Of course it is deliberate that this dream is the most futile, impossible thing ever. I am deliberately trying to mix tragedy and optimism. In Phil's journey, in *Boston Kickout*, he has to have these real "coming of age" moments, with Shona in Ireland and the argument with his father. Both those moments are in a way quite autobiographical. In *The Poet* the ending is, again I'm afraid, quite tragic. But, I suppose, I have manufactured another upbeatness ... I don't want to give away the ending. You haven't seen it, have you?

No I haven't.

It would have been a miracle if you had seen it. You would have to go to Germany and you would have had to learn German. Do you speak German?

No ...

Don't worry, it's not good to watch the movie in German. It's better to see it in English. I try and manufacture an upbeat ending, but my point of view really is that life continues. You have very bad experiences sometimes, but that is a very good learning principle in life. These things make you stronger. Making *The Frontline* for me personally was like that. There are similarities in the journeys of James King, Phil and Andre. All three of those characters have that kind of journey where they have to overcome certain things.

Vincent Phillips was exceptional in The Frontline, *especially during the climactic scene, when he sticks the revolver to his head. That is such a great piece of cinema.*

I am very proud of that scene, because of the nature of the making of that film. I'm not as happy with *The Frontline*, as I am with *Boston Kickout*. And understandably it was a mistake on my behalf to write, produce, direct and edit. That was a mistake, and not one I have repeated since, because physically, on that film, it was just too much. But that scene is a scene that I am very pleased with. I am also very pleased with the discourse between the two actors. The idea of that scene is that James King is going into William Armstrong's world by talking about the self-belief stuff and he turns it around on him, at that moment. In the script it was one of the braver moments in the film, to actually try and conceive a scene where you get a guy who's got a gun on you and you convince him to put the gun on himself. Jesus Christ, that's ridiculously tough. So, I was quite pleased with that scene.

It's very funny, but when we were shooting that scene, we had to shoot it in the house of the art director. This was his own personal house, where he lived, and that was the last scene we were shooting, and I wanted to shoot

Paul Hills directing Vincent Phillips and Amanda Noar in *The Frontline* (courtesy Paul Hills).

all those scenes chronologically. What the art director had not told anyone, and in fact he didn't know himself, was that his girlfriend had just got out of a mental hospital. And he had not told her that we were filming in the house, taking it over. When she came back and found twenty scruffy, dirty guys and a few gals of course, she took a bit of an exception to it. Actually, when I was trying to direct that scene, the art director was trying to restrain her in the next room. So, it was an interesting scene, that siege part of the film is the crux of the film in a way.

One thing I am very pleased of in that scene: I made the decision to shoot a lot of it very close, in close-up. I recall this; even though most of it was done between these two close-ups, I had two pivotal moments that I wanted to treat in a different way. The moment where the gun is taken from James' head and put on William Armstrong's, I did this solid two-shot that is only on screen for one second. That was deliberate. Also, I did this close-up of James' eyes at the moment when Armstrong pulls the trigger. Somehow, and talking about cinematic style and how it changes, I still would like to do something like that. To have a scene that goes on for four minutes and there's a shot in it that only has one purpose. Sometimes when you get a repetition of a scene, close-up, close-up, close-up, close-up, close-up, and boom, you do something different, that gives that moment more impact. If I repeated that two-shot from the side beforehand or after, it would have somehow dissipated that shot. That shot has a function for that one moment. That's still something I am keen on doing. Funnily enough and going back to what we were discussing earlier about tragedy, that moment in retrospect and even though I did it intuitively then, I would now call that moment, and I done similar things in *The Poet*, a kind of Dionysian scene. The great thing about cinema is that it has the propensity of the change of perspective. When you're in the theater you don't get a change of perspective, because you sit in the same seat all the time. Within a film you can cut from Peru to China in one frame. That change of perspective is one of the great strengths of cinema, not just in terms of scenes, but also in terms of locations.

You have said that Boston Kickout *is 95 percent based on personal experience. It's therefore a very autobiographical piece of work. What are you reflections on the film now, looking back?*

My reflection is that I am still very proud and lucky ... I feel lucky to have been able to tell such a personal story, and even more lucky that people liked it, and critics liked it, and people went to see it. It's the most natural thing in the world for a director to make a personal film and for it to turn out to be a right old self-indulgent piece of bollocks.

But it wasn't, was it?

Thank God it wasn't. I'll tell you what I really love in cinema. I love the truth. I love that word—truth. I always try and tell the truth, but it's a very misunderstood word. What is truthful filmmaking? I think you're truthful and honest if you put things in a film that you know are true and that have happened, i.e., to you, or can happen, even if it's little details of characterization or things that have happened. In *Boston Kickout*, even though I have combined characters and incidents ... you have to do an amount of work to make something presentable, accessible and interesting. For me, *Boston Kickout* is still a very truthful and personal film about my experiences in growing up in an English New Town.

The four lead characters were very much based on my friends and myself at that time. And the relationships with the families, as such, were very much like my friends and mine. You could take the view that just because it happened, it doesn't mean that it's relevant to anyone and they want to see it. In a way, *Boston Kickout* is a universal story; the story of four guys growing up isn't a new one, you could probably go back five hundred years and find a story very similar. The truthfulness comes from the details in it that are true.

Am I right in thinking that the making of Boston Kickout *was also beset with problems?*

No ... *The Frontline* had umpteen problems, caused by a lack of money.

John Simm in *Boston Kickout* (courtesy Paul Hills)

Boston Kickout didn't have anywhere near those difficulties. The difficulties on *Boston Kickout* occurred when we were shooting in Stevenage, and the council did not want to support us, because they perceived the film as a damagingly negative film. When we started shooting, they had just spent two million pounds on a PR exercise to promote Stevenage. So it was bad timing for them. We had a couple of council stooges following us around, reporting, and turning up to locations, before we shot, and cleaning it. There was a time when we were going to shoot in Stevenage town center. We were shooting near this little pool, and normally the pool was filled up with fucking gunge and supermarket trolleys, everything. We turned up and it was immaculate. I said, "What's happened here then?" The council had turned up during the night and cleaned it up. In terms of the making of *Boston Kickout* there was no serious problems. But the funny thing is that you can have a terrible shoot but have a great film. You can have a great shoot and have a terrible film.

Director Danny Cannon helped finance Boston Kickout, *and is credited as an executive producer. You are good friends, aren't you? You originally worked with him on the Channel 4 drama* Play Dead *that subsequently became* The Young Americans.

When I started making films in Stevenage, when I was young, I came across this workshop called 33 Video. When I arrived there to edit a film of mine, I met Danny there. Danny was the hotshot of this workshop. Danny's father, Roy Cannon, had been a prop master on a lot of big films and Danny was steeped in the industry and making short films out of 33 Video, using their facilities. We worked together on a number of projects, like I worked on his and he worked on mine, and we worked on the projects of another guy, a guy called Andrew Saunders, either recording the sound or shooting them, etc. Danny was a little older than me and went on to the National Film School, and in his second year there he had fallen out with all the producers on the course, and he needed someone to produce a film for him. He asked me to go around and produce *Play Dead*, which was a crazy endeavor at that time, but was one of the crazy endeavor's that allowed me to believe that I could make *The Frontline*.

He had a bad experience making Judge Dredd, *didn't he?*
On that movie he didn't have final cut. The film we all saw was not the film that he envisaged. Unfortunately, people who thought that they could edit, i.e., Sylvester Stallone, had a bit of input.

Didn't Danny Cannon say he would rather stick pins in his eyes than work with Sylvester Stallone again?
Did he say that? If he said that, then I can believe it. The thing was, for Danny that was the perfect film. When I knew Danny as a young lad, I remember going on the bus from Marylebone station to the National Film School, every morning for eleven months. Every Thursday he would be reading 2000 A.D. He was a fan of *Judge Dredd*. So, *Judge Dredd* was the perfect film to end up at his door. The problem is that you have someone like Stallone in it. In the comic strip, Judge Dredd never takes his helmet off, for five hundred episodes. As soon as you get Stallone he's got to get his fucking helmet off, so that we can see his ugly mug.

During your hiatus from feature films, you have been directing commercials, pop promos, short films, documentaries and episodes of Urban Gothic. *Did you enjoy working in these media?*
I want to make films. The problem I have had is that it has taken time to do them. Doing short films, and other things like commercials, is good to do in the meantime to keep your hand in. It's not as good as making a film and never will be. I have had some fun doing commercials, in particular this crazy Japanese commercial in 2000. I had good fun doing the *Urban Gothics*, for Channel 5.

Since the demise of Film 4, has there been a downturn in the funding of British films?
Over the last three or four years the number of different avenues, gatekeepers, organizations that you can go to fund your film in the UK has shrunk. There are fewer distributors who have enough money to pre-buy the UK

territory rights. In fact, pre-selling the UK territories is probably one of the hardest territories to pre-sell in the world. The broadcasters has less amounts of money to spend on film, and the state finance has been brought together under the Film Council, which there are two gatekeepers, but only one is ever going to be appropriate to you. We are seeing, possibly with the three film franchises coming to the end of their remit, or at least two of them, it's getting harder and harder to finance a film in the UK.

This is part of the trend that we have now. Five or six years ago, when we had a lot of lottery money in films, there was a perception from a lot of people, who now have quite important roles, that this money was just pissed away. The general perception is that the movies made were a load of old bollocks, and that they shouldn't have been made. This has allowed things to change now to the degree where the idea is not "Let's support filmmakers, and make lots of films, and maybe a few of them will be good." That's not the attitude now. The attitude now is that your film will be made if it's good enough. This deliberate Darwinian philosophy that is at work in the hierarchy of the film industry is that they want to make less films, but make better films. This is especially true in lower budget films. To make a lower budget film, the kind of film that might be funded by the BFI or the British Screen, etc., they are harder to make now, because there are less people to go to. But what people tell you though is that with section 42 and section 48, sell and lease back, that there's actually more money. The thing is that these section 42 and section 48 films, they can go into any film. What we are making now is a lot of co-productions. That money that is between 10 and 18 percent of the budget means that a lot of people will want to be partners with British producers, so that they can access this 10 to 18 percent. These films that are normally 10 to 20 percent British are now under the banner of British films, even if really they're not. There's a false tabulation, I feel, when it comes to British films being made now. American producers can access this section 42 and section 48 sell and lease back. It has become a normal part of any budget, rather than additional. Also, you always have the discourse between commercial ambitions and artistic ambitions, and there's always a kind of battle between the two. At the moment, if not least, because we are not making art house films, commercial films are in.

Do you think we lack an alternative cinema, here in the UK?

There's no real support for alternative cinema here in the UK, unfortunately at the moment. Possibly the occasional short film may get funded like that, without the BFI and the British Screen, what you got is the New Cinema fund, though that's not particularly experimental.

How do we expect to produce filmmakers like David Lynch?

I don't know how David Lynch would get on producing films in this country. It would be very tough. David Lynch had a nightmare on his debut film *Eraserhead*. There's a sequence in *Eraserhead* where the second shot was eighteen months after the first shot. He had a similar experience trying to get the money, and then shoot a bit more, like I did on *The Frontline*. I would say that to have a David Lynch–style person to come out of the UK would be very tough now with the Draconian views of the British film industry.

Part of the reason I have great respect for you, and other filmmakers of your ilk, is that you have shown that you can make a movie with very little funds, as long as you have the drive and ambition to succeed. A lot of filmmakers today are delusional. They think they need x amount of money to shoot a film. You shot The Frontline *for £8,000 for Christ sakes ...*

Yes, and it nearly killed me, but I proved it! The industry has its ups and downs. It goes in circles. In the eighties, after the fall of Goldcrest, everyone was sitting on their arse for the very few places that could fund their films to give them the green light. Then in the early nineties, with films like *The Frontline* and *Leon the Pig Farmer*, learning from the credit card movies of the States, like *Clerks*, people started making films again off their arse. Apart from the people doing DV films, possibly it has gone back again. I meet new emerging filmmakers filled with enthusiasm and hope. I meet them at the New Producers Alliance. I can't see any reason now, with digital technology, why people don't get off their arse and make films. The problem with filmmaking generally is that making a film is like climbing a mountain. You have to be courageous enough to say, "Right, I am going to do it," and stick to it. Everyone dreams of having their film made properly by a big studio with the best cast. And you can chase that dream forever. Personally, to be honest, I have had that problem with *Raving Beauties*. *Raving Beauties* is a period film; even though it is set in the eighties I can't make it for fuck all. Because of that, I have been trying to make it properly, for a long time. That's a common seduction for people.

4

The 2001st Maniac: An Interview with Herschell Gordon Lewis

Matthew Edwards

Regarded as the Godfather of Gore, most notably for his twisted trilogy *Blood Feast, Two Thousand Maniacs* and *Color Me Blood Red*, Herschell Gordon Lewis' contribution to horror and exploitation cinema is without measure. Along with producer David F. Friedman, Lewis revolutionized filmmaking with *Blood Feast*, introducing a new genre of blood-soaked mayhem to the drive-ins and sleazy theaters of yesteryear. Some audiences were repulsed, others lapped it up gleefully; the splatter film was born.

Through the transgression of cinema, or, more explicitly, the horror film, the desire to commit the most outrageous imagery onto the screen has been at the forefront of many filmmakers' agendas. Yet, Lewis undoubtedly set the mold; many have imitated, with varying degrees of success. Although critics remain divided on the quality of Lewis' work, and his impact on the progression of cinema, it's key to point out the importance of the splatter film and the subsequent influence Lewis has had on filmmakers. The splatter film tore down the boundaries of what was deemed acceptable on screen. The splatter film challenged the censors, and has given rise to a cinema more daring in the portrayal of violence. Although the splatter film is generally presented in comic book fashion, provoking laughs more than disgust, it's interesting to point out that the graphic nature of the violence did eventually cross over into the ethics of filmmakers more interested in more serious and realistic filmmaking.

Lewis reveled in the prospect of making films that were seen to be dangerous and perverse, and took the brunt of the censors wrath. In contrast, with films like *Kill Bill*, even Hollywood seems intent now on cashing in on a little bit of splatter. Funnily enough, now the major players have caught on and it is deemed acceptable, an irony that is not lost on Lewis, who is still unfairly vilified in some quarters.

4. Interview with Herschell Gordon Lewis (Matthew Edwards)

In 1972, after the completion of *The Gore Gore Girls*, it was assumed that Lewis had retired from filmmaking, concentrating instead on his marketing career. Not so, for in 2002 the horror fraternity rejoiced with the news that he had again saddled up in the director's chair and completed a follow-up to his most infamous film *Blood Feast*. Released directly to DVD, *Blood Feast 2* was seen as a welcome backlash against the shoddy product that horror cinema had been churning out. One of our most notorious filmmakers was back and lovingly spraying red crimson across the screen.

You would be forgiven into thinking that Lewis was a sordid and depraved sicko. Far from it: Lewis is a true gentleman, kind, accommodating, as well as possessing a great sense of humor (anyone who has followed his career will testify to this). When I originally contacted Lewis about the possibility of interviewing him, he promptly replied that he was scheduled to visit the UK the following week and he kindly arranged time during his busy itinerary so that I could meet up with him.

I was scheduled to meet Herschell at 1 pm, at Earls Court, London, in the guest speaker kiosk. When I arrived I was greeted with a large deserted room, two elevator attendants, and some chap loitering in the corner. I convinced myself that this wasn't the right place, so I wandered around for five minutes before making my way back to the deserted room. Upon my return I suddenly realized the chap loitering in the corner was Herschell Gordon Lewis.

Dressed immaculately, Herschell introduced himself and commented on how perplexed he was by the lack of a reception. We shuffled off somewhere quiet, where we could conduct the interview. The venue was undergoing a facelift at the time, in preparation for the forthcoming lecturers, though the organizers found us a small room away from the builders and their noise. Shut away in a tiny room, with only one chair, thus forcing me to crouch and shove my Dictaphone in Herschell's general direction, we proceeded with the interview.

MATTHEW EDWARDS: *I understand you're here in the UK to give a series of talks and lectures on marketing.*

HERSCHELL GORDON LEWIS: Yes, I am here for what is called European Catalogue and Mail Orders days. I have spoken at this event before, and it has nothing to do with film, this is my other career, direct marketing, in which I have some position. In film, as you know, I've always been considered something of a hack.

People seem surprised when they find out that you're now a leading marketing guru, though to me it seems a natural progression.

It's strange, because until the Internet exposed me, on occasion I would be giving a speech on marketing and someone would come up to me and say "Do you know there's some crazy fool who has the same name you do, who used to make these screwball movies"? I would say "Obviously an impostor." Or they would show up with a poster or a still photograph, or something to be autographed, and we would get a big chuckle out of it, because I had thought that was a matter of history ... dead history, for that matter, which shows how cloudy the crystal ball can be.

It was the excellent marketing you used on Blood Feast *and* Two Thousand Maniacs *that made the films so successful and infamous in the first place.*

That's a very astute remark, as I had always felt that any fool can aim a camera ... I'm proof of that. To get bodies into the seats of theaters requires a different kind of talent. And I became the master of campaigns, to the point at which other producers were bringing me their movies to do their campaigns. Because, today especially, there's such a glut of product, in that everyone is shooting a digital film. What has happened is that a movie called *The Blair Witch Project* broke open a floodgate for people who thought that they could do that, and get away with it: "I can do better than that." And so, the market is simply flooded with films, many of which will never see any release at all. Some go directly to video or DVD, some, if they're very lucky, will open in theaters and then quickly close. And some just sit in someone's closet. So marketing is the key, especially for horror movies, which seems to be the destination for so many beginning filmmakers.

You have recently returned to filmmaking with Blood Feast 2, *after a long hiatus. Was the desire to shoot another feature partly a reaction against the current trend of horror movies?*

Yes, I think so. I hadn't really analyzed it to that extent. I felt there is a certain sameness to contemporary horror films, they're derivative, and I watched movies like *Scream* and I felt I knew what was going to happen next. And when someone is watching a movie and knows what is going to happen next, without fear, without hair-raising on the base of the neck, without some feeling of "Oh my goodness I'm terrified," it's time to have a different approach to it. So, over the years various people have said, "Let's make *Blood Feast 2*." I've heard that, I would guess, at least 500 times, since we made the original *Blood Feast*. I developed a defense mechanism, which was "Put your deal together, and call me." And that effectively dismissed them, because they just wanted to talk about it. A fellow called me and said, "I want to make *Blood Feast 2*." I said, "Put your deal together and call me." The next thing I knew I got sent a hundred-page script, professionally written. And I said, "Great heavens, this man is serious." And that was the beginning of a negotiation that wound up in *Blood Feast 2* being made.

Was that Jacky Lee Morgan?

Yes. In fact, when Jacky sent me the script he phoned me to ask what I had thought of it. I didn't know what to tell him. I wanted to make this movie, but I thought the script was dead, that is in the sense that it was a 1980s type of script. So I said, "Jacky, it's certainly a professional job, but I feel the industry calls for a slightly different approach, in the twenty-first century. We need some dark humor in this movie." So Jacky said, "Send me over some suggestions." Feeling like a complete idiot, I e-mailed Jacky a gigantic memo with suggested scenes. A month and half went by, and I then got sent a 120-page script. I then realized that this movie was going to be made. Subsequently, Jacky and his screenwriter, a fellow named W Boyd Ford, arrived in Fort Lauderdale where I live, and we hammered out a deal, and we shot *Blood Feast 2*. I had the time of my life and it couldn't have been easier. It was shot on film by the way, we did not shoot it digitally. We shot *Blood Feast 2* in 35mm color with a big beautiful Panavision camera. God, what I would have given for that camera when I shot my early movies. I had an old Mitchell, which weighed I am guessing 35 tons, and there was a rack-over, that used to say you can look through the lens and the camera can look through the lens, but not the two at the same time. So, you would set up the shot, rack it over, and then pray that you have the scene centered, and there's no light revolt in the picture. For those movies I was the director, cameraman, lighting technician, I was the editor and I did the advertising campaign. In *Blood Feast 2*, I was the director. I sat in a canvas chair, I said, "Roll sound." I could watch the action on a television monitor, so if there was a microphone in the picture I could see it at once, and play the scene back immediately, instead of waiting for the dailies that night to see what mistakes we made. The film is infinitely faster than it was when I shot my early movies. Subtleties in lighting are possible, which they weren't with the antique equipment I used to have. With *Blood Feast 2* we had a crew. In fact, I didn't know what half those people were supposed to do. In the early days, with my partner David Friedman, I was a director and cameraman, and he was the producer and soundman, and when we shot movies like *Lucky Pierre*, we were it. The actors had to work their own clap sticks, and then push them aside and start acting. So, *Blood Feast 2* was a truly luxurious experience for me. In fact, I had an assistant director.

How did that feel, having an assistant director?
Uneasy, because every assistant director I have seen, and that's the first one I had ever dealt with, but I have been on other film sets ... they're power-mad and they have this imperious attitude that infuriates both the cast and the crew. My assistant director was no exception, by the way. I am sure he felt he was doing a service for me, but I would have been happier if I had no assistant director.

You have always cited Two Thousand Maniacs *as your personal favorite film. I would have thought the long mooted 2001 Maniacs would have seemed the more likely project to get you back into filmmaking.*

There is a group that is making *2001 Maniacs*. I have nothing to do with that movie, but I have been told, by a third party, that I am listed as executive producer on that movie. But that may be a title I have not sought out, nor exploited, nor in fact had any activity in connection with. *Two Thousand Maniacs* was and is my personal favorite. Of all my movies I didn't want to remake, that's the one. If they want to remake *The Wizard of Gore*, I'd be delighted. If they want to remake *The Gruesome Twosome*, then I'd be thrilled. That it was *Blood Feast 2* that we made was Jacky Morgan's decision, he came up with a script, he came up with the money to make the picture. I was really, in a sense, a hired hand on this movie. I was the director. I didn't even cut the movie. I have some reservations about the way the movie was cut, but it was not my decision to make. I'm just delighted that I had that opportunity.

Were you pleased with the final cut of Blood Feast 2?

I feel we have a lot of movie, for the amount of money that was in it. I certainly would have been happier had we had major company backing, in that some of the things we short-changed ourselves on, because of budget limitations, could have been done in a more profound and maybe more professional manner. Considering what we had, and that of course is no excuse for an audience, the audience doesn't care, they don't care if you spent many millions, look at that movie *Gigli*, whatever it was called, with Ben Affleck ... died ... *Ishtar*. The amount of money in a movie has nothing to do with the success of it. Compared with the original *Blood Feast*, we have an epic, we have *Ben-Hur*. I would have liked to have been a little more exploitive, but I'm not unhappy at all with the results. And people who have seen *Blood Feast 2*, they react in the way the movie was intended to generate a reaction.

You worked in a golden era of cinema, whereby exploitation films were frequently seen at drive-ins and in sleazy theaters that dared to exhibit material that deviated from the norm. Do you think it's sad that such venues no longer exist?

We are fighting for our lives on the mainstream. But there's a balance, just as the drive-ins have disappeared, and the sleazy theaters have vanished, in favor of multiplexes. We do have videocassettes, we do have DVDs, we have cable, we have satellite, and we have areas of distribution and exhibition that didn't exist then. It's a mixed blessing. Some films that go directly to DVD are almost hidden, because they don't have the benefit of the theatrical release, which means the reviews don't appear, so they are not really released, they are *excreted*, I guess is the better word. They just slowly disappear into the mainstream. Like pouring paint into water—it just dissipates. That's simply the nature of the marketplace at this time.

Blood Feast 2 *came straight out on DVD, didn't it?*

Yes, there are in fact two versions of *Blood Feast 2*, and that's another area in which my own personal desire was overruled. I had always intended for this movie to be released unrated. The reason being, how does an independent film compete with major company product? The answer: by being more outrageous than the major company product. There's a lot of blood and gore in major product, there's *Kill Bill*, and movies of this sort. So, we did over-the-top gore in *Blood Feast 2*, and I was delighted with what we did there. For distribution I got a phone call one day from Jacky Morgan saying that he was getting an R rating, so that Blockbuster Video would carry the movie. I said, "Please don't," and Jacky said that he couldn't turn the deal down. Now, I understand the nature of business. The result was that he had the film ... I won't say cut, *massacred* is a better word, to get the R rating. In exchange they had also agreed to release, what is called, the Special Edition, but unfortunately the typical person doesn't know what is going on. The typical person goes into Blockbuster, rents this movie, and says, "What's this?" The R-rated version is somewhere between six and ten minutes shorter than the un-rated Special Edition, and those six to ten minutes are what *makes* the movie in my opinion. So we have this dichotomy, we have this split, we have this confusion. Whenever I have the opportunity, and I know I am being disloyal, but that's my nature, I warn people against the R-rated version. My reputation such as it is, and I grant you it's a checkered reputation in the film business, is for making the most God-awful movies anyone ever made, and the R-rated version is not one of those, the Special Edition is. So I have tried to protect my natural bastard child.

You are probably aware that Blood Feast *was originally condemned as a Video Nasty, here in the UK.*

I know that, it had to appear in film clubs. There's a certain amount of hypocrisy there, as I've been here in the UK where the theater for the night would become a film club. It struck me as very, very strange. About a year ago I was in Edinburgh, at the Dead By Dawn film festival, and they showed a whole bunch of my movies, and apparently that era has come to an end, and the reason it has is not because of me but because the major companies now are making the same kind of movie, and that gives it legitimacy. And to me that's hypocrisy too.

A lot of your work has now surfaced here on DVD, and the majority have been passed uncut. However, due to legal reasons, Blood Feast *was released with thirteen seconds of cuts ...**

I did not know that.

Does that annoy you?

Yes, very much so. I am fervently opposed to censorship. I feel that's a family proposition, obviously no one can control what an individual family does, but apparently the government wants to. Now, you say 13 seconds have

---

**Blood Feast has since been re-submitted to the BBFC, and has now been passed uncut—05/04/2005.*

been cut out ... that will be the tongue scene ... I'm guessing, I don't know ... what 13 seconds would anyone regard as that detrimental to someone's development? The entire film has thirteen seconds cut out of it ... do you know what those thirteen seconds are? Of course you wouldn't, if you haven't been able to see it.

I refuse to buy it.
Attaboy.

I bought the Something Weird DVD from America, instead.
Isn't that NTSC though? Have you got it in a Pal version?

I have a multi-region DVD player.
You're my kind of person.

On the subject of Something Weird Video, were you happy with the editions of your movies they have so far released on DVD?
Yes, very much so. A Mike Vraney, who owns Something Weird Video, is a true gentleman first of all. There aren't a lot of gentlemen in film distribution; most of them are scoundrels. So, in that respect, we were very lucky to have these things wind up that way. I lost control of these movies years ago. I felt I had a good time, it was over, and I had the good fortune in my other career, which was fortunate for me. If I had been a career film director, I'd be on the dole, instead of living in a penthouse on the 26th floor, overlooking the ocean in Florida.

A young chap called Jim Maslon wound up buying up all these old movies and he in turn made this arrangement with Something Weird Video for releasing the movies, originally on [VHS] and now on DVD. I have absolutely zero complaints about the way Something Weird Video has been in operation.

Are they still planning to release Year of the Yahoo? *That has been mooted for sometime now.*
Yes, in fact Mike Vraney sent me, much to my astonishment, a copy that's chopped. Apparently, what happened was that it was made off a print, and the print had some wear and tear, but it is still like watching one of your children coming home from war, missing a limb, dragging one foot and blind in one eye, but it's your child and it's come home. *Year of the Yahoo* is apparently now available, and that leaves only a few that has apparently vanished into the woodwork forever.

Hopefully Something Weird Video will dig them out.
They're good at doing that. A fellow from North Carolina, the distributor of *Moonshine Mountain*, called me, oh, this must have been five or six years ago, and said, "I have a print of *Moonshine Mountain*, in pretty good condition," and he was retiring from the business, and he said, "Should I send it to you?" And I said, "Send it to Jim Maslon." I got a call from Jim, who said, "I have in my hands what has to be the worst print I have ever seen, of any

movie ever. It must have two thousand splices in it. I will give it to Mike, to see what he can do with it." That's the last I heard of *Moonshine Mountain*, which is one of my favorites by the way, next to *Two Thousand Maniacs*.

I will tell you a story out of school: As recently as four or five days ago I had a call from this fellow who is making *2001 Maniacs*, and he said, "Who owns the music to *Two Thousand Maniacs*"? Now therein lies a tale, because when these films passed from my possession I did not know that music is a separate set of rights. I had forgotten about it, until one day Jim Maslon called me and said that John Waters was making a movie, and John is an old and dear friend—in fact, he is in *Blood Feast 2*. John was making a film called *Serial Mom*, and he wanted to use the opening of *Blood Feast*. I'd said, "That's very nice," and Jim said, "John wants to use the music," and I said, "Let him." Jim said, "I don't own that, you do." Big mistake, as I didn't know I still owned it. Now I got a call a few days ago, from the fella who was making *2001 Maniacs*, and he said someone called Johnny Legend wants to rerecord the opening theme from *Two Thousand Maniacs*. And I said no. Now that may cost me, but I don't care. I don't want that done. I don't know Johnny Legend, but I do know that this is the one proprietary thing that I don't want tampered with. It's my voice on there, I wrote that music, and it's my voice and I don't want that changed. It's like someone saying that they want to put a moustache on the Mona Lisa, not that it's of that caliber, but this is mine, and I want to play with it.

On the subject of music, you worked with a band called Southern Culture on the Skids. How did you wind up working with them?

When you make a movie of this type and word appears in the trade publications, the phone rings, and e-mails come in, and you get samples and you get CDs. I don't get it myself. I don't think there's a garage band between here and Bangkok, that hasn't said, "We will do the music for you." The ultimate relationship was set up by Jacky Morgan and I'm not the least bit unhappy with that. It's the kind of background that we wanted for this music. I wrote the opening theme lyrics only, not the music, but I am not credited with it, that was part of the deal with Southern Culture on the Skids. Anyway, who cares?

I liked the performances of Thomas Wood in Blood Feast *and* Two Thousand Maniacs. *He starred in a lot of your early nudies, didn't he, under the name William Kerwin?*

His real name was William Kerwin, and he used the name Thomas Wood because the Screen Actors Guild would have given him all kinds of problems. He was in a great number of my pictures. On some of the films where he wasn't in the cast, he was in the crew. Tireless fellow, he was my kind of actor. First of all he knew his lines, and secondly he showed up on time. Thirdly, at the end of the day when I was picking up cables, he was there alongside me. He died about seven or eight years ago, and it was something of a loss. He never quite connected the way he should have. He was quite a good actor. I was thrilled to have him on the cast and crew.

You made a lot of nudie films, early in your career. Was the sudden shift towards splatter brought about by the soft-porn industry becoming somewhat stagnated, ultimately redundant, with the sudden rise of hard-core pornography?

Here was the problem. The movies that I made were harmless, I felt. I thought that kind of movie was going in a direction I didn't want to take; and that's one reason why David Friedman and I split up. He was very comfortable with that, and I wasn't. I had small children, and he didn't. And I felt, first of all, that this kind of film was becoming very crowded, just as the horror film genre is becoming crowded today. It was time to go in a different direction. So when we made *Blood Feast*, I knew we were breaking down some walls. After we had made *Blood Feast*, *Two Thousand Maniacs* and *Color Me Blood Red*, I went off with that kind of film, with *The Gruesome Twosome* and *A Taste of Blood*. David went back to California and continued making sex films. I wasn't the least bit unhappy that I had gone in the other direction. And looking back now at what has happened, I am very pleased that I didn't continue in that line of filmmaking.

How important has David Friedman been to you throughout your career? You worked well together, didn't you?

Yes we did. David was the perfect partner for me; in fact, he has often referred to us as the "perfect partnership." He brought with him a sense of showmanship that I thought was very instructive. I brought with me a technique of filmmaking he found instructive. So the partnership worked out very, very well. We trusted each other implicitly too, another rarity in a film partnership. After we shot *Color Me Blood Red*, which was the third film of the Blood trilogy, we had two other partners. One was a man named Sidney Reich, who lived in a city called Rochester in New York, and owned a paint factory, or something. The other was a man called Stanford Kohlberg, who was a film exhibitor, and owned some theaters in Chicago. And we all wound up suing Kohlberg. That's why I was in a hurry to make *Moonshine Mountain*, because Kohlberg had the money in his control. That's why we were suing him. We had no income, so we thought we better make a movie in a hurry. At that point, David Friedman settled with Kohlberg unilaterally, and moved to California. David didn't even tell me he was doing that, and I phoned him one day and his phone was disconnected. We didn't speak for two years. I was furious because I had this movie to be made, and here was my partner gone. Luckily, *Moonshine Mountain* was a big success, thank goodness. Through the cooperation of the film's distributors who at that point knew who I was, they were willing to take on the product. And then, a couple of years later, David and I ran into each other at some theater-convention, and embraced, and have been close ever since.

David's health is not good these days. I sent him an e-mail about a month and a half ago, and it came back saying "undeliverable." So I phoned him and said, What's wrong with your e-mail? And he said that he can't see the screen any more. His eyesight has gone.

Now that you have made Blood Feast 2, *has your passion for filmmaking been re-kindled?*

My dear friend, filmmaking is like malaria. You think you're over it. But it's in your blood. It explodes when you don't expect it to explode. I have a script called *Herschell Gordon Lewis' Grimm Fairy Tale*, which is the film I wanted to make. That would have been preferential for me over *Blood Feast 2*. But up came someone with the package for *Blood Feast 2*. If some production facility said yes, let's make *Grimm Fairy Tale*, then I would jump into the saddle.

Is that likely?

I could not have predicted we would have made *Blood Feast 2*. The phone is ringing, I'm getting e-mails, but that means nothing. The motion picture business is loaded with phonies, with posers. I'm not anticipating anything. *Grimm Fairy Tale* either happens or it won't. Those are the only two possibilities.

Are you surprised by the amount of interest that is still generated in your work?

It is surprising on this level: The films that I made had almost no budget. They had no star names. They had effects that are rather euphemistically described as primitive. Yet they have survived. I noticed on Halloween that a number of theaters were showing *Blood Feast* and *Two Thousand Maniacs*, decades after they had been made. So many contemporary films strut themselves on the stage for an hour, and are never seen again. Yet films like *Blood Feast* and *Two Thousand Maniacs* have endured. I am delighted my films have endured. Hey, I am delighted *I* have endured. I appear occasionally at horror film festivals, and people say, "Are you still alive?" People now know I am still alive, that helps too.

5

Inside Pink

Jasper Sharp

Discreetly tucked away under the stretch of train track known as the Yamanote line, a mere stone's throw from Shimbashi Station, lies the Roman Gekijô (or Roman Theater). Wedged next to the Bunka Gekijô (Culture Theater), a discount second-run cinema with which it shares the same management, the Roman Gekijô is but one of little more than a dozen similar venues in Japan's capital that still manages to stay afloat through the commercial exhibition of soft-core sex films.

Since the early sixties, erotic films known as *pinku eiga* (pink films) have been gracing national cinema screens, making up an estimated 50 percent of all film production during the late seventies and eighties. This decade marked something of a watershed for the Japanese movie industry, and the Roman Gekijô is proof that this deluge has yet to dry up.

With most countries' sex film industries eschewing celluloid in favor of videotape, the continued production and theatrical distribution of the pink film in Japan makes for a small phenomena. They are a distinct entity from the thousands of titles churned out every year for the ever-burgeoning, cheaply produced hardcore Adult Video (AV) market, and Tokyo and a number of other regional Japanese cities still boast numerous cinemas exclusively devoted to their screening. Around 100 pink films are shot on 35mm for the big screen every year before going on to circulate more widely on video and cable TV. Given the bizarre fan culture and critical discourse that has built up around this underground sexy sub-genre over the past 40 years, it's safe to say that, in the early years of the 21st century, there's nothing like it in any other part of the world.

The Roman Gekijô can be described as a typical Tokyo pink cinema. For a reasonable 1300 Yen (around £6), customers extract their ticket from a battered vending machine, allowing them entrance into this gloomy chamber of unearthly delights. It is like stepping into a time warp. There are no previews for other films, no adverts, and definitely no popcorn. Vending machines containing bottles of cold green tea and Pocari Sweat sports drink provide the only home comforts one might expect from a modern movie-going experience in Japan.

What you do get, however, is a standard triple-bill of films, each around an hour in length, playing in a continuous loop without breaks. Usually this program consists of two newer works followed by something dating from the seventies, the Golden Age of the Japanese sex film, when Nikkatsu's high-budget *Roman Porno* films* meant that, in terms of the national cinematic output, onscreen copulation represented more of a rule than an exception.

The label "pink film" derives from the worldwide cultural association of the color blue for boys and pink for girls. If there is any difference between the Western "blue movie," however, it is that the Japanese product places more emphasis on the girls in front of the camera than the viewers on the other side of it. If the patrons of the Roman Gekijô are anything to go by, this may not be such a bad thing. It is described on one Japanese website as "a resting place for the salaryman"; jaded white-collar workers in their fifties or sixties pass the time shuffling distractedly in their seats, pointedly ignoring the non-smoking signs and barely engaged by the action taking place up onscreen. The auditorium is probably less than a third full.

Director Takahisa Zeze cut his teeth in the genre, and now takes part in mainstream filmmaking with big budget sci-fi action movies like *Moon Child* (2003). He once revealed that the now standard one-hour running time of the pink film was so that the screenings could fit into a salaryman's lunchbreak. But aside from acting as a home away from home for the beleaguered metropolitan office worker, pink theaters also have a reputation for functioning as gay pick-up joints. To discourage less-salubrious activities from their all-male patrons, the lights are barely dimmed down and the sound system is kept sufficiently low for the moans and groans and cries emanating from the actors to be periodically drowned out by the sound of trains rumbling overhead. If, as early cinematic surrealist Jean Cocteau once said, cinema is "a dream we all dream together," then there's small chance of this motley assortment of dreamers even remotely approaching REM state.

Is the pink film pornography? Certainly by Western standards, for those looking at erotic film solely in terms of a basic visual trigger, the sexual content of these films comes across as almost endearingly coy. Japanese films may have picked up a reputation for their excesses of sex and violence over the years, mainly because such works as the *Guinea Pig* series, Nagisa Ôshima's *In the Realm of the Senses* (*Ai No Corrida*, 1976) or the films of Takashi Miike are the ones that are primarily showcased abroad. But as is the case with all Japanese movies, the pink film is still encumbered to some extent by the strange

---

*Short for "roman pornographique," to lend it more high-brow associations with the genre of French erotic literature of the same name.

cultural anomaly imposed by the censorship board Eirin—the no-pubic-hair boundary.

With any portrayal of male or female genitalia buried beneath enough obstructive digital mosaics and optical fogging devices to ensure that not so much as a tuft makes it onto the screen, pink filmmakers have attempted to come up with newer and ever more inventive ways to deliver the goods. As hardcore AV videos began to seriously threaten the pink film's existence in the eighties, it was this one strict no-go area that arguably prevented the terminal slide of Japanese eroticism into the realm of zero-budget straight-to-video filth, as happened in so many other countries, with the selective editing of the early days of the sixties and the convenient draped kimonos and strategically placed vases in Nikkatsu's *Roman Porno* films subsequently giving way to more audacious forms of artistic license.

But there are other factors contributing to the pink films' current anachronous existence, factors that exist outside the scope of the sexual content. Whereas all you need for AV is a girl and a camcorder, the very manner of the pink film's theatrical presentation has a lot of bearing on its style. The AV is for the home, and its use is purely functional. There's no fast-forward button in the cinema, so the pink film has to maintain interest between the sex scenes by other means—namely, a plot.

While it would seem that these plots are of little interest to the viewers who trudge at whim in and out of the Roman Gekijô, it is for this reason that the pink film has won over the interest of an entirely new audience of viewers on video, DVD and retrospectives in Tokyo's arthouse theaters; a number of its leading directors have been invited to high-profile international film festivals such as Rotterdam and Udine Far East Festival. Given the nature of their original forum of exhibition, it is a remarkably diverse audience and one that counts a surprising number of female viewers amongst its numbers.

Rather than treat this facet of domestic film production with embarrassment, filmmakers, fans and critics alike celebrate its continuation with a mixture of nostalgia and pride. Steamy, sultry, kinky, cute, violent, grotesque or just plain weird, the plethora of titles that spill from the shelves of local video shops are considered a vital part of the country's cinematic legacy.

During the sixties and seventies the mass-production of sexploitation cheapies was a major aspect of most national film industries. In countries such as America, France, Italy, Germany and Britain, these years marked the heyday of independent film production, and the promise of bare female flesh was a guaranteed seat-filler. Japan was no different, except for the fact that the immense popularity of these films also saw the major film studios following the independents' lead.

In 1971 Japan's oldest studio Nikkatsu decided to switch their production *exclusively* over to a new line of glossy, high–production value sex films marketed under the label of *Roman Porno*. Cinemas all over Japan, from the frozen wastes of Hokkaido to the balmy sub-tropics of Okinawa, were soon filled with titles such as *Rope and Breasts* (*Nawa To Chibusa*, Masaru Konuma, 1983), *Catholic Nun Runa's Confession* (*Shûdôjo Runa No Kokuhaku*, Masaru Konuma, 1976), *Tokyo Emanuelle* (*Tôkyô Emanieru Fujin*, Akira Katô, 1975) and *Lovers are Wet* (*Koibito-tachi Wa Nureta*, Tatsumi Kumashiro, 1973). Several of these films, including Chusei Sone's *Hellish Love* (*Seidan Botandoro*, 1972) and Noboru Tanaka's *Watcher in the Attic* (*Yaneura No Sanposha*, 1976) have been released in the UK by Pagan Films.

Nowadays, many of these films are considered classics, mirroring the retro-affection for European "porno-chic" films of the mid-seventies like Just Jaeckin's *Emanuelle* and *The Story of O* (both 1975). While sex was obviously the selling point, a good deal of artistic liberty was granted to directors and scriptwriters. Budgets, while not quite up to the levels of mainstream movies of the time, were comparatively high when compared with those of the independently produced sex films. If the end requirement was to deliver a given number of nude or sex scenes within a running time of around seventy minutes, then there was a considerable amount of leeway with what the rest of the film could consist of. The diversity of Nikkatsu's product was amazing, ranging from traditional period dramas, ghost stories, melodramas, thrillers, and literary adaptations, all packed with lashings of the requisite coupling scenes. For a decade, the Japanese film industry *was* sex.

The Roman Gekijô often plays *Roman Porno* films from the seventies or eighties alongside newer pink offerings. The title playing this time translates rather awkwardly as *Extreme Indulgence Woman—Pleasure Deep Within* (*Inzetsu Fujin—Kairaku No Oku*). It was directed in 1976 by Shogorô Nishimura, one of Nikkatsu's more interesting in-house directors (the following year he made a respectable *Roman Porno* version of *Gate of Flesh*—Seijun Suzuki's version of the tale in 1963 is considered a classic of Japanese cinema). The story concerns a woman just released from prison after being put away for seven years for brutally braining her university professor husband with an iron after she caught him indulging in extra-curricular activities with a student. Immediately after her liberation, the ex-jailbird is raped by a porcine truck driver she hitches a lift with, from which point her fortunes go from bad to worse. After she has her life savings stolen by an acquaintance and gets embroiled in an ill-advised liaison with a wet-behind-the-ears student with severe emotional problems, she eventually comes face to face with her husband's ex-mistress again in a bar, which is where the fun really begins.

Like so much *Roman Porno*, the appeal of Nishimura's film stretches beyond the sex scenes, which are more stylized than graphic, though the production is marred by a particularly brutal and gratuitous rape-murder scene that roots this squarely within the very extremes of seventies excess and is strong enough to ensure that there's little chance of it being met with open arms by Western audiences nowadays. The film's chubby starlet Rumi Tama also went on to become a prolific pink film director in her own right, highlighting the fact that women are often just as active behind the camera in the Japanese sex industry as they are in front.

Roman Porno films are not, strictly speaking, the same as pink. As Nikkatsu was a major studio, these lavishly produced erotic spectacles utilized far higher budgets, a skilled in-house technical staff, and were shown in the company's own network of theaters across Japan. They were highly influential for future pink directors and well-regarded by critics, but due to the aforementioned reasons, a distinction must be made between these and conventional pink films, made independently on short shooting schedules and shoestring budgets. We should also differentiate pink films, which are shot on film for theatrical presentation, from soft-core erotica shot on video and released to video (the vast output of the TMC/Total Media Corporation label, for example), *V-cinema* productions shot on film and released to video, and erotic films that achieve brief theatrical releases before going straight to video.

There's a deeper history behind the pink film, of course. Its impetus was born out of the turbulent counter-cultural movement of the sixties, when the streets echoed with the cries of students protesting against growing class inequalities, the Vietnam War and the renewal of the Japan-American Security Pact, or Ampo Treaty, which allowed the US to keep their bases on Japanese soil in order to maintain a military presence in Asia. Independent directors such as Kôji Wakamatsu, Masao Adachi and the late Takechi Tetsuji lured audiences into cinemas with promises of sex, which they combined with tub-thumping political messages and images of riots and left-wing revolutionaries.

One seminal work was Wakamatsu's *Skeleton in the Closet* (*Kabe No Naka No Himegoto*, 1964), set in a cramped modern housing development in the suburbs of Tokyo. A young student tries to revise for his university entrance, alternating between studying the pages from his secret stockpile of pornographic magazines and the activities of his apartment block neighbors through a telescope. He eventually sexually assaults his sister and then breaks into the house of a female neighbor to rape and murder her.

The film created a stir when it was picked for the 1965 Berlin Film Festival, completely bypassing the official Committee of Japanese Film Production whose job it was to sanction films for foreign exhibition. Shown shortly after the Tokyo Olympics, at a time when all eyes were on this country that had so rapidly risen from the ashes of post-war defeat to the ranks of the major industrial nations, its appearance in the West caused much consternation back at home, with domestic dailies bemoaning "the shame of Japanese cinema spread out on a global level." Wakamatsu went on to make dozens of features for his own production company Wakamatsu Pro, including *Violated Angels* (*Okasareta Byakui*, 1967), which features a murderer-rapist let loose in a nurse's dormitory. It is still making films to this day, but none of then fall under the pink category.

Takechi Tetsuji's *Black Snow* (*Kuroi Yuki*, 1965) tells the tale of a disturbed youth who, after spying on his prostitute mother and a black American GI, finds himself unable to attain sexual arousal unless fondling a loaded pistol. Later that night, he stabs and murders the soldier before running amok through the building and finally slaying his mother. The film is famous for a long sequence of a naked woman running along the fence of the US military base at Yokota. "I admit there are many nude scenes in the film, but they are psychological nude scenes symbolizing the defenselessness of the Japanese people in the face of the American invasion," Tetsuji said when he went to trial on charges of obscenity.

In the early seventies, Wakamatsu's scriptwriter and contemporary Masao Adachi moved away from pink filmmaking, traveling to the Middle East to direct a documentary-cum-propaganda piece entitled *The Red Army / PFLP: Declaration of World War* (1971) showing the Palestinian liberation movement and the Red Army's participation in it. The move cost him several years of his liberty when he was later arrested in connection with alleged terrorist activities. He came back to Japan two years ago, at the age of 61, and is currently planning a return to filmmaking. His works such as *High School Guerrilla* (*Jogakusei Gerira*, 1969), *Gushing Prayer—A 15 Year-Old Prostitute* (*Funshutsu Jûgosai Baishunpu*, 1971) and *A.K.A. Serial Killer* (*Ryokushô Renzoku Shashatsuma*, 1969) are some of the most fascinating pieces of avant-garde Japanese filmmaking of their time, energetically establishing a connection between sex and violence as a form of underground resistance and youth rebellion.

With over a hundred films in the pink category still being released every year, obviously not all are as worthy of closer interest as these early iconoclastic offerings. Indeed the vast majority are complete tripe. The film currently playing on the screen of the Roman Gekijô certainly fits into this category. A bored housewife and a bespectacled office worker stand in a kitchen, both stripped down to their waists, passing a slimy raw egg yolk between their mouths in a messy scene seemingly inspired by Jûzô Itami's cult comedy *Tampopo* (1985). The film is called *Omorashi Okusan Noopan Kappôgi* and, like most pink titles, it is virtually impossible to put into satisfying English, with a literal translation rendering as *Moistening Housewife: Panty-less Apron*. The plot involves the comings and goings of a group of four who meet for cooking lessons over a series of weekday lunch times. The tone is light, the production values virtually non-existent, and the end results ultimately no more than perfunctory, as they labor over the perfect stroganoff and indulge in the inevitable whipped cream scenes. The film seems destined to go no further than specialist sex cinemas before the print wears out and it evaporates into just a mere catalogue title without even making it up to the next grade on video, as is the case with so many titles.

Out of the five companies who currently run the erotic film market, the one whose output seems ensured the most longevity on video is also one of the longest established. Kokuei began in the mid-50s, originally making educational shorts for the government before deciding nudie films were a more profitable prospect. Because of his experience in filming animals, Kôji Seki, an in-house specialist in wildlife documentaries, was assigned the task of directing one of their earliest titles, the now-lost *Valley of Lust* (Jôyoku No Tanima, 1963), which featured a topless female Tarzan.

Kokuei's long-serving producer and current company president Daisuke Asakura has been responsible for bolstering the reputation, both at home and abroad, of many of pink's best-known directors, including Adachi in the sixties, and a group of young mavericks—Hisayasu Satô, Toshiki Satô, Kazuhiro Sano and Takahisa Zeze—who caused a stir at the beginning of the nineties, earning themselves the name *Shi-Tennô*, or the Four Devils.

Similar to the directing of the sixties, the work of the Four Devils was born out of a particular place and time. The downturn of Japan's economic fortunes in the early nineties coupled with both the rise of AV video and the vacuity of much of Japan's mainstream film in the eighties saw a swing back to the filmmaking convictions of the Japanese Nouvelle Vague, with directors using the pink film to tackle true-life problems such as social alienation in the big modern metropolis of Tokyo and the changes in class structures due to a growing polarization of wealth during the Bubble Years.

These directors used the relative flexibility and freedom of the medium, where the main guideline is to deliver a given number of sex scenes within an hour-long running time and to deliver their individual philosophical, political and social critiques of post-Bubble Japan, breathing fresh air into an increasingly hermetic filmmaking culture. Zeze later stated, "The pink film was very much in danger of extinction, so that was what made me think that if they're disappearing anyway, then we can get to do what we want."

It is because the interest of Kokuei's films stretches beyond the sex scenes that, while they are the best known to cult specialists, they were also the least popular with regular pink theatergoers. The label of the Four Devils did not originally come about due to any shared filmmaking philosophy of the directors, but was coined by the theater owners and *ojisan* (old men) patrons who had come to watch sex films only to be confronted with opaque and subversive political allegories and New Wave–style technical experimentation. The tag was a stigma, not a compliment. Fortunately mainstream movie critics caught up a little later when the work of the Four Devils was showcased

5. Inside Pink (Jasper Sharp)

at the Athénée Français Cultural Centre in Tokyo in 1993 as part of a series entitled Biographies of New Japanese Filmmakers.*

The work of each of the Four Devils, though dwelling on similar subjects, was startlingly different in its aims and approach. The oldest of the four, Kazuhiro Sano, worked primarily as an actor, mainly in pink films but also in other independent productions. His works, with titles such as *Adultery Mother Daughter* (*Furin Haha Musume*, 1993) and *Don't Let It Bring You Down* (*Hentai Telephone Onanie*, 1993), are more conventionally structured and dramatic than most in the genre, with the director himself usually playing the leading role of an outsider around whom the action revolves.

Toshiki Satô, who in 2002 delivered a disappointing live-action version of Satoshi Kon's psycho-horror animation *Perfect Blue* (1998) named *Yume Nara Samete*, is considered the most accessible for viewers, and especially so for the

UK DVD sleeve of Toshiki Sato's *Tandem*. *Tandem* explores the well-known myth of sexual gropers who molest young women on rush-hour Tokyo commuter trains. The problem became so severe that commuter trains now carry women-only carriages. *Tandem* is widely regarded as a key entry in Japanese pink cinema.

The program also featured the early 8mm film diaries of arthouse director Naomi Kawase long before she won the prestigious Camera d'Or prize for new directors from the Cannes Film Festival in 1997 for Suzaku.

ladies. Films like *Tenement Wife Midday Adultery* (*Danchi Tsuma Hakuchû No Furin*, 1997) and *Tandem* (*Chikan Densha Hitozuma-Hen: Okusama Wa Chijo*, 1994), an entry in the long-running *Train Pervert* (*Chikan Densha*) series, are marked by a greater attention to structure and story-telling than most erotic filmmakers, as well as a warmer approach to character and a perky sense of humor.

With films such as *Tokyo X Erotica* (2001), *Anarchy in Japansuke* (1999) and *Raigyo* (1997) to his credit, Takahisa Zeze is by far the most successful of the four, over the past few years proving himself to be a rather versatile director with the supernatural teen horror *Kokkuri* (1997), the lovers-on-the-lam road movie *Hysteric* (2000), and the romantic fantasy *Dog Star* (2002). Even his pink work is marked by the same artistic aspirations and filmmaking philosophy as his more mainstream independent contemporaries Shinji Aoyama (*Eureka*) and Kiyoshi Kurosawa (*Cure, Pulse, Charisma*).

With titles such as *Lolita Vibrator Torture* (*Rorita Baibu Seme*, 1987), *The Bedroom* (*Shisenjô No Aria*, 1992), *Night of an Anatomical Dummy* (*Jintai Mokei No Yoru*, 1998) and *Naked Blood* (*Megyaku: Naked Blood*, 1997), Hisayasu Satô's films at first seem to straddle the extreme nature of eighties *ero-guro* with the demands of standard soft-core. Using a discomforting range of experimental

UK DVD sleeve of Sato Hisayasu's seminal pink film *The Bedroom*. The film starred infamous real-life killer Issei Sagawa, who in 1981 murdered and then ate Dutch student Renée Hartevelt.

techniques, in his explorations of the connections between flesh and technology he takes us into the darker realms of weirdness pioneered by directors such as David Cronenberg. Utilizing a variety of different visual medias as diverse as 8mm film, video and even photocopied material as mediating devices between reality and the viewer, his films are more about dis-communication than straightforward titillation. As such, Satô remains one of the most idiosyncratic and interesting directors of Japanese cinema in the late eighties and early nineties, regardless of genre. Those who have reduced the focus of his work entirely to the images of rape and violence have done him a great disservice.

Takahisa Zeze and Toshiki Satô are still very active agents in pink filmmaking, balancing their work in the field with more commercial productions. They highlight the fact that, with the collapse of the long-running studio apprenticeship system during the seventies that previously offered a stable career path in the industry, the pink film has provided one of the few routes for filmmakers to hone their skills and experiment within the format of the feature film. A large number of today's established commercial directors, including Hideo Nakata (*Ring*, *Dark Water*), Masayuki Suô (*Shall We Dance?*), and Yôjirô Takita (*The Yin Yang Master*, *When the Last Sword Is Drawn*), all cut their teeth working in the erotic film. In looking at modern Japanese cinema,

UK DVD sleeve of Tajiri Yuji's *No Love Juice: Rustling in Bed* (*Fuwa-fuwa to Beddo no uede*).

particularly independent productions, to ignore this world would be a grave oversight.

So what is the future for the pink film? With the Four Devils having now been superseded by a new group known as *Shichifukujin* (Seven Gods of Fortune), who count such names as Mitsuru Meike, Rei Sakamoto, Toshiya Ueno, and Shinji Imaoka amongst them, pink film now appears to be retreating further from politics into the realm of the interpersonal, where women are as often as not seen as the stronger partner. In 1999, Yûji Tajiri's *Rustling in Bed* (*OL No Rabu Jûsu* a.k.a. *No Love Juice*) depicted the relationship between an Office Lady (OL), just dumped by her long-term boyfriend, and the younger man she meets one night after he falls asleep on her shoulder on the train, missing his stop. Tajiri's film points to one of the new directions being taken in the field. As the legions of director swell with an increasing number of female directors such as Yumi Yoshiyuki and Moe Sakura (both former pink actresses), and women in Japanese society become more open about sex, an increasing large number of female viewers now claim an interest in this once "men only" domain, with housewives apparently making up one of the largest audience sectors when the films air on cable TV.

This softening of style has not been without its victims. With much of the revenue of the pink film now being earned back from TV sales, where the images of rape and bondage so prominent in the eighties are strictly taboo, the reputation of the most notorious of the Four Devils, Hisayasu Satô, was for many years enough to bar him from further work in the genre, relegating him to the seamier, more déclassé underworld of AV production.

No longer playing the role of agent provocateur, the work of the next generation of pink directors has failed to impress older hands such as Takahisa Zeze: "If you look at the films of the younger generation of pink film directors, the *shichifukujin*, they don't have this sense of struggle. They make films that relate to themselves and to a very tiny world that surrounds them. They don't try to present a new vision of society or ask questions relating to broad topics, but work on a more personal level. The framework is getting smaller."

Personal politics aside, with such a long and colorful history and the genre currently showing no immediate sign of slowing down its levels of production, the legacy of the pink film provides a rich seam of startling visual images that remain virtually unknown outside of Japan. The films themselves should prove enough of a lure, but given the wealth of history and sociological context behind them, and the sheer eclecticism of those directors and actors drawn to their production, it is indeed a subject that literally screams out for a closer look. Because whether viewed artistically, commercially or as a mirror to the society in which it is made, the pink film represents an aspect of contemporary Japanese cinema that is, for the foreseeable future at least, most definitely here to stay.

6

Thundercrack! And a Brief Overview and Appreciation of the Golden Age of Porn

Mark Edwards

In the early seventies, following the box office success of Gerard Damiano's *Deep Throat* (1972), the porn industry took off. No longer confined to the underground, a slew of XXX features became available to theater going audiences.

Despite its reputation, *Deep Throat* wasn't the first triple X feature of its type (the first narrative-driven porno is said to be 1970's *Mona, the Virgin Nymph*, directed by Bill Osco and Howard Ziehm, who would go on to create the classic *Flesh Gordon* in 1974), and it is certainly not the best. What *Deep Throat* did do however was kick off the Golden Age of porn, a decade which would see some of the wildest XXX action ever to be played on screen. (The last classic of the Golden Age is generally regarded to be Stephen Sayadian's *Café Flesh* (1983).

The seventies produced a number of popular and well known names: Gerard Damiano, Annie Sprinkles, Harry Reems, Henry Paris (AKA Radley Metzger), Jamie Gillis, John Holmes, Linda Lovelace, Marilyn Chambers, the Mitchell Brothers, Terri Hall, Vanessa Del Rio and Zebedy Colt, who between them starred in, and were responsible for, some of the most fascinating, challenging and entertaining XXX titles ever to be poured out to the jaded masses.

Damiano's *Deep Throat* may have kick-started the golden era, but technically the film is seen as something of a mess, especially when compared to his next feature, *The Devil in Miss Jones* (1973), which would go on to spawn several sequels. Meanwhile, the Mitchell Brothers were vying to become the leaders in adult film entertainment, directing Marilyn Chambers in *Behind the Green Door* (1972) and *The Resurrection of Eve* (1973). The Mitchells would go on to produce the entertaining *Autobiography of a Flea* (1976), directed by

Sharon McKnight, while Marilyn Chambers continued to appear in XXX classics such as *Insatiable* (1980).

It was during this period that Radley Metzger directed his critically acclaimed porno offerings under the pseudonym Henry Paris; his *The Opening of Misty Beethoven* (1976) is regarded by many critics as the greatest porn film of all time. Zebedy Colt helmed, and starred in, some of the most twisted porn films during this eventful era. Appearing as a sex maniac in *Sex Wish* (1976), Colt directed (with Howard North) the infamous *The Devil Inside Her* (1976), a film that was so rough it is alleged that Annie Sprinkles quit the porn industry for two years as a result. Colt was also the genius behind *Terri's Revenge* (1976), starring Terri Hall, perhaps the strongest XXX feature I've ever sat through, featuring rape (both male and female), urination and a tear-inducing testicle torture climax, which you simply have to see to believe.

As indicated by films directed by the likes of Colt, the seventies were also the time of the hardcore roughie: a major bone of contention for women's libbers and the late Ronald Reagan. These were films that centered on violent themes of rape, degradation and murder. Titles that fell into this category included *A Dirty Western* (1973), *The Defiance* (1974), *The Taking of Christina* (1975) *Little Orphan Dusty* (1976), and *Expensive Tastes* (1978). *Water Power* (1975), starring Jamie Gillis, was based on a real crime case. *Forced Entry* (1972), perhaps the most notorious roughie from this period, starred Harry Reems (under the pseudonym Tim Long) as a deranged Nam veteran who runs a gas station, but who also enjoys raping and murdering women in his spare time. Just to give the reader an idea as to how strong the film is, in one scene we see Reems' ejaculation intercut with actual images of Vietnam War atrocities, including bomb blasts and dead babies, before his terrified victim is knifed to death. Extremely brutal and disturbing, *Forced Entry* is actually a very good film and well worth checking out ... if you can find it.

The films from the golden age were able to cross genres in a way that is unthinkable nowadays. One genre that seemed to suit the porno format in the seventies was the horror genre, with its themes of possession, demons and devil worship. Of the horror-themed XXX titles during this era, *Horror Whore* (1974) is of particular interest, as it is very possibly the goriest porno movie of all time. The aforementioned *The Devil Inside Her*, *The Devils Playground* (1974), *Devils Ecstasy* (1974), *The Possession* (1976) and *Sex Séance* (1975) also deal with the devil and possession themes. But Jonas Middleton's *Through the Looking Glass* (1976) is without doubt the best of the bunch, another title starring the talented Jamie Gillis, this time as an evil demon lurking behind an old mirror. Boasting superb production values, *Through the Looking Glass* works well as both a porno and a horror movie. Also worthy of note is *Night Dreams* (1981), directed by F.X. Pope and produced by Rinse Dream (AKA Stephen Sayadian). This film contains a sex scene in Hell amongst other disturbing

6. Thundercrack! The Golden Age of Porn (Mark Edwards)

and bizarre sequences, the funniest being a woman fellating a guy who is dressed as a cereal box while another man—dressed as a piece of toast—dances in the background and plays the saxophone!

As weird and as wonderful as all these films may be, none of them can quite compare to the art-house porno classic that is Curt McDowell's hilarious *Thundercrack!* (1975). Quite unlike anything else, this sprawling 156-minute XXX epic, wittily written by and starring George Kuchar, was shot in black & white and uses the "old dark house" horror film set-up, tossing in a mad gorilla for good measure.

Thundercrack! stars Marion Eaton as Mrs. Gert Hammond, a drunk, crazy old woman living alone in an isolated house on a hill (the house is depicted by a cheesy drawing, which only adds to the film's charm). Her only company—apart from the bottle—is the pickled remains of her late husband Charlie that she keeps in the wine cellar (he was chewed to death by locusts on a hot summer's day, after getting covered in wheat powder!). Mrs. Hammond's lonely existence is about to change, as a violent storm results in a group of strangers becoming stranded and seeking refuge at her old house. Amongst the collection of freaks and oddballs are the homosexual Toydy (Rick Johnson), Bond (Ken Scudder), hippie chicks Roo (Maggie Pyle) and Sash (Melinda McDowell), Willene Cassidy (Moira Benson) and Chandler (Mookie Blodgett), another tormented soul who was on his way to destroy Phillips Unlimited, girdle makers in "Dr. Pepper Country" whom he blames for his ex-wife's fiery death.

The group of strangers are taken to the room of Mrs. Hammond's son, who they are told "no longer exists." The room is full of sex toys, which the guests immediately put to good use, leading us to the first of many outrageous hardcore moments. They include Toydy humping a male blow-up doll while forcing a dildo into his anus, as Mrs. Hammond watches through a peephole, masturbating with a cucumber (later to be eaten by Willene: "Boy, does this taste odd!").

As the night progresses, we get to see more carnal encounters, in between sequences involving lots of bickering, fisticuffs, a mysterious locked door and pork chops. But as if all this wasn't enough to deal with, along comes Bing—to whom we have been briefly introduced in the film's prologue—played by the writer George Kuchar. Bing works for a traveling circus and has just crashed nearby, and is also seeking refuge from the storm. However, the house is now surrounded by escaped circus animals, which include an elephant, a lion and a gorilla called Medusa ("Pamela Primate"). It is soon revealed that Medusa is no ordinary primate—she craves young men just as much as she craves bananas! After another mouthful of pork chop, Chandler quizzes Bing as to why the creature craves men, and Bing reveals the whole sordid truth: On his 30th birthday, while blind drunk, Bing was tricked by some fellow carnies into having sex with the gorilla in one of the tents. Waking the next morning, Bing found himself being masturbated by the chained and shaved gorilla. He was later found by the maintenance men singing "I love you truly" in his madness: "It took four men from the loony bin to carry me away," Bing says sadly. After a week of observation, he was released and went back to work, only things had changed—the gorilla was in love with him. Its love repressed, the beast tried to make love to its trainer instead, only to tear the man limb from limb and throw his bits into a terrified crowd and a tub of popcorn. When asked why the gorilla wasn't put down, Bing explains that the circus owner Mr. Harlan couldn't have Medusa destroyed, because his wife loved her too much, having looked after her all her life and even at one stage having gone so far as to "donate her mink coat" to the gorilla so she wouldn't die of pneumonia.

As a result of this care and attention, Medusa learned to love and obey only Mrs. Harlen ... until the 59-year-old woman started to climb into the ring wearing only a bikini. The audience reacted badly to the sight of this saggy bloater, and Mrs. Harlen began taking her frustration out on the gorilla. It was at this point Medusa killed again: Stripping Mrs. Harlan before a terrified crowd, the creature strangled her with her own whip before whirling her bloated body around and tossing it into the arena of dancing hippos, where she was crushed to death! Bing explains how Medusa was once again spared from being put down: Mr. Harlen made a fortune on the insurance money from his wife's death, so the gorilla had done him a favor. However, its act was to be down graded to hula hooping. Despite all this, Bing could tell through the creature's eyes that it still pined with love for him.

Eventually Bing comes completely clean, revealing he hadn't just crashed in the storm: He deliberately took the vehicle off the road in order to kill himself and the animals. "I couldn't see those animals suffer any more, and me along with them!" he shouts. When asked why the animals suffer, Bing explodes into a rage, telling the others how he was on his way to St. Barnabies school for crippled children: "Have you ever been there when the circus was in town? Did you ever see the kids poking at the animals with their crutches? Have you ever seen an ostrich run down by a wheelchair? Did you ever hear what it sounds like to hear a tiger's head crushed by a broken arm in a cast!?" Bing breaks down, finally blurting out, "I have the hots for that gorilla! No one ever satisfied me the way she has!" The others react sympathetically: "Easy, kid, easy! They say all is fair in love and war. Take it from there!"

Meanwhile, Toydy offers Bond a way out, telling him he has access to a crate of bananas, which he will give to him at a price. This leads to the film's infamous gay sex scene. Once that's over with, Bond learns he has been well and truly shafted as the others are going to let the gorilla into the house any-

6. Thundercrack! The Golden Age of Porn (Mark Edwards) 65

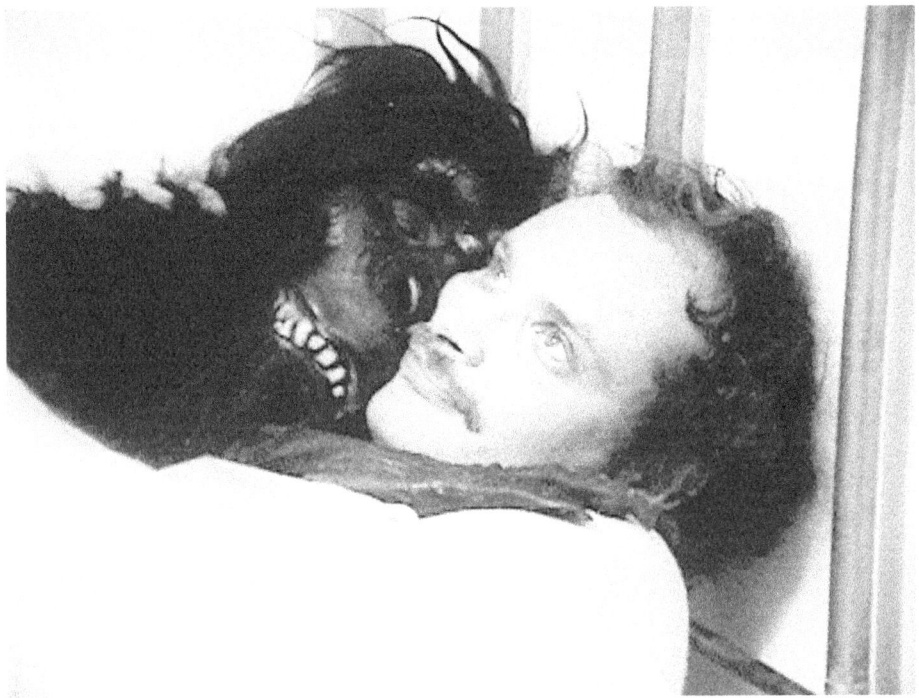

Bing and Medusa plan for the future ... together! (courtesy Melinda McDowell).

way, so it can marry Bing. Roo and Toydy meanwhile have discovered the keys to the locked door and unravel the mystery of Mrs. Hammond's son. As they are locked in the room, screaming for their lives, the gorilla bursts into the house. The others flee, leaving Bing and Mrs. Gert Hammond, who in a tremendous and hilarious moment shouts to her trapped guests: "You see he does exist, behind this door! But not out here in the world of sanity!" as Bing enters the shot, shouting wedding vows at the gorilla while wearing a white wedding dress. The beast follows Bing into a bedroom where they both leap into bed. Bing has finally tamed the wild creature: "The parasites that have sucked the juices from your body have not all belonged to the insect population." He continues: "Many fat businessmen have fattened their wallets by exhibiting your animalism. But it's not my wallet I want fattened. It's you. Fattened with our first child, our first newborn child. The first of a race of supermen."

Thundercrack! is the perfect example of seventies porno—a time of unpredictability, when filmmakers were willing to break taboos and show us gratuitous sex. At the same time filmmakers aimed to deliver films with a fun or interesting storyline, and made them with impressive production values.

The films made during the Golden Age of porn were not just wank videos. Many of them were good movies in their own right, and if they happened to turn you on in the process, then great, you got the best of both worlds!

The Golden Age of porn is gone, but thanks to video and, increasingly thanks to DVD, it is not forgotten, and many of these classic films are becoming available for new generations of fans to enjoy.

7

An Interview with Melinda McDowell

MARK EDWARDS

MARK EDWARDS: *Your brother Curt directed* Thundercrack! *(1975). What can you tell us about him, both as your brother and a director?*

MELINDA DOWELL: Curt had a way of making each person feel so attractive, talented, or sexy ... his kindness and honesty were such an integral part of both his personal and his film lives. Actually, one and the same, weren't they?

George Kuchar, who also gives a very entertaining performance as Bing, wrote Thundercrack!*'s original screenplay. What was George like to work with, and how did the idea for* Thundercrack! *come about?*

George is pure entertainment—working with him was a joy. Curt and his friend Mark Ellinger originally concocted the characters and storyline of *Thundercrack!*, but it was George who then wrote the screenplay incorporating all of Curt's hardcore ideas and injecting some of his own, including the lustful gorilla.

Before starring in Thundercrack! *you appeared in George Kuchar's* The Devil's Cleavage *[1973], and Curt's* Nudes—A Sketchbook *[1974]. Could you let us know a little more about these?*

The Devil's Cleavage? I barely remember my own brief appearance in that film, but Curt had a starring role, which met with enthusiastic reviews! I consider *Nudes—A Sketchbook* one of Curt's most artistic and sophisticated films. It does resemble a sketchbook of a number of his friends (and me) in small vignettes. Some of us were nude, literally, others not—but the film is so lovingly and beautifully shot, people seem quite moved by it.

You also starred in Curt's Taboo: The Single and the LP *[1980] and Sparkle's Tavern [1985]. Have you had any other roles since appearing in* Thundercrack!*?*

I believe all the films I did were in a three-year period (1974–1976). The very first was a short film called *Beaver Fever* featuring George and me as paramours, "Hunk" and "Goldenrod." There were a few other films, but the last one that I remember doing was *Sparkle's Tavern*. After that, my days of husband and babies and domestication.

In Thundercrack! *you played the part of Sash. What are your memories of working on the film?*

The very first scene that was shot was Sash and Chandler's bus depot sex scene in the wine cellar. So, no easing into the hardcore parts! Filming was great fun, with laughter between almost every take. Curt was such a wonderful director—each time he'd say, "Cut!" it would be followed by, "Perfect!" Even if it wasn't, he would only suggest trying it a different way, thus sparing the actors' feelings. What a sweetheart!

You appear in a couple of the hardcore sequences. Did you find it easy to perform sex scenes in front of the camera?

A little *too* easy, perhaps? Picture all the sex scenes with the crew members just outside the frame. Not everyone would feel comfortable in that situation, but I seemed to have adapted rather quickly!

Sash, as played by the excellent Melinda McDowell (courtesy Melinda McDowell).

7. Interview with Melinda McDowell (Mark Edwards)

How long did it take to complete Thundercrack!, *and what was the budget?*

The actual filming was done in about ten days, the editing took about eight months. I believe $10,000 was the amount that got us started, and a little more was needed to completely prepare it for release.

Where was the film shot?

Two houses in San Francisco were used, one for the interior shots, and the other house mainly for the film's car and rain scenes. The exterior shots of the Gert Hammond house were cardboard cut-outs drawn by Curt!

Through its unique use of lighting, tight camera shots and some very eccentric acting (particularly Marion Eaton's character), the film creates a great sense of madness and claustrophobia. Was this the intention?

I think any time Curt, George, and Marion were together, madness would ensue! I can't say what their intentions were, but George's lighting and Curt's camerawork were the perfect collaboration, to be topped off with Marion's maniacal (and yet, genteel) performance.

How well did the film perform at the box office on its initial release?

Its very first showing, in New York, sold out. It was presented again, one week later, and was sold out once more! It took awhile, but the film eventually found itself comfortably seated in the midnight movie time slot, where it stayed for many years.

On a personal level, I find Thundercrack! *to be a very witty and entertaining film. What was the critical reaction at the time of its release?*

Horror or delight, but indifference was never an option! Curt saved any reviews of *Thundercrack!* in his scrapbooks, and I believe he thought the few that were negative were much better than no review at all.

One of the most talked-about aspects of Thundercrack! *is the inclusion of a gay sex scene. How did this go down with audiences of the time?*

Audiences entered the theater never dreaming they would be subjected to close-up man on (or, in) man scenes. A thrill for many, a reason to make a mad dash from the theater for others.

There is a funny scene where the gorilla, Medusa, masturbates George Kuchar's character Bing. However, the tight close-ups and the way the scene is edited suggest that maybe a double was used. Was that really George being pleasured, or did he prefer not to appear before the camera in such scenes?

That absolutely *was* George. The person who was portraying Medusa for that particular scene remained uncredited!

The film has met with some censorship troubles—how do you feel about this? And what are your thoughts on the issue that pornography degrades women?

Yes, *Thundercrack!* has had its share of troubles. It was banned in England

and wasn't allowed into the country the second time Curt escorted it there. The first time, he managed to slip it through by placing an additional label on it: *Thundercrack!—Weather Conditions in the Southwest United States.* It worked! Appearing in pornography is a choice, just as viewing it is. Exactly which factions of society are proclaiming degradation? I just can't go along with that way of thinking.

Most prints of the film available in the past have had a running time of about two hours, whereas the DVD will be the complete uncut version. Who was responsible for cutting the film and for what reasons were the cuts made?

The original producers, the Thomas Brothers, thought that a two-hour version would be more commercially marketable. Perhaps they thought 2:00 am would be late enough for midnight moviegoers to stay out? Curt never accepted the butchered version, and didn't want it to be seen by anyone. That's why I've been so determined to present the full version in all its glory—the director's cut.

You are personally involved in releasing Thundercrack! *as a special edition DVD. Why did you decide to do this?*

After doing plenty of research online I discovered two things. One, that there were people selling poor quality, unauthorized versions of the film, and two, that there has been an unflagging fascination with this film for all these years. People are still talking about it, searching for it, hoping to find a good quality version to purchase. My goal is to preserve, protect, and present Curt's work in a way that would honor him.

You will be selling the DVD through your website, but do you have plans to distribute it through other channels (e.g., on-line stores)?

We haven't made decisions yet about distribution from outside of the website. We'll start there, and see what happens. I'll try to keep everyone updated as to the progress of the DVD on the website [www.thundercrackthefilm.com].

How do you feel about the cult following Thundercrack! *has attained? Are you surprised at this?*

When I was a 23-year-old, having such fun doing this film, I never once imagined it would be this notorious nearly thirty years later, nor did Curt, I'm sure.

As your website and involvement in the DVD shows, you are obviously very proud of the film. Can you give us your personal opinion of the film Thundercrack! *and what you like most of all about it?*

For me, there was a time lapse of many years without seeing it, and when I finally did see it again, I realized I love it more now than when it was new. Seeing it in a different light, I think. I was never an actress, so my "non-acting" was always hard to watch. Maybe I see the character of Sash now, and not myself, which makes it much easier to accept! Even though *Thundercrack!* is seen, among other things, as a comedy, the actors did not deliver their lines as if they were supposed to be funny, and that is one of the main things I love about it. That and the original score written and performed by Mark Ellinger. I consider the *Thundercrack!* title theme to be the sexiest element of the entire film!

Finally—have you eaten a cucumber since the filming of Thundercrack!?

Hah! No, I haven't. I never liked them in the first place, and after having to take bite after bite shooting the dinner table scene, that was quite enough for me. As far as the "used" cucumber that "Gert" tosses into the fruit bowl—few people realize that it was, indeed, the actual one she'd used in her ... er ... "peephole" scene, and the other actress [Moira Benson as Willene] did take a bite of it. She was the only one who was unaware it was the used one, and it was all the crew could do to keep their laughter contained until the end of the shot. I may not be the only one who has sworn off cucumbers forever!

8

Animating the Extreme: The Animation of Phil Mulloy

Matthew Edwards

Animated short film remains an area of cinema that has received so little critical analysis and commentary that it has become marginalized and largely ignored by cinematic commentators and establishments. The precarious climate arising from this indicates that very few avenues remain open for the filmmakers willing to experiment in this medium. With regard to its place in cinema, we can consider short-film animation as a valid expressive art form and its development and transgression as equally important as feature filmmaking. Yet, it has to crawl out of the dark underbelly of cinema in order to be noticed.

British Animation once had an unparalleled reputation for producing some of the most innovative, groundbreaking and distinctive films. But such is the wisdom of the British film industry, that funding and support has been radically streamlined, making it increasingly difficult for filmmakers to get their projects developed and produced. This treatment, namely by such commissioning bodies as the Film Council, has led British animators to seek foreign investment, and they have been more readily welcomed. Therein lies the paradox: The impact of such a move will undoubtedly have a detrimental effect on British cinema, resulting in our talented animators migrating overseas. Diversity has been abandoned in favor of pursuing more commercialized projects that are consequently force-fed to today's generation of cinephiles. Taking this into consideration, it is unsurprising that the noose around experimental cinema is slowly tightening.

Inevitably, and characteristically for films of this type, the tendency with short film animation is for it to be relegated and consigned mostly to film festivals or to feature on late night television. Tapping into the psyche of a wider audience remains frustratingly difficult, but there is some degree of comfort in the knowledge that such festivals across the globe actually promote and

8. The Animation of Phil Mulloy (Matthew Edwards) 73

engage in animated short film. This rule generally applies, but there is interesting evidence that some animators have managed to attract a small, but highly dedicated following, successfully exploiting a niche in the system. In this increasingly competitive age, getting your work exhibited and watched remains decidedly difficult. In adversity there is hope, whereby there seems to be a tried and tested method that seems to provoke interest: explicit violence and sex (coupled with a large dose of bestiality, blasphemy and downright plain weirdness). This accurately defines one of British Cinema's most innovative animators. Welcome to the surreal world of Phil Mulloy.

Phil Mulloy is not concerned with detail. That's the first thing that strikes you about his films. The animation he employs is far removed from the Disney school of art; a far more accurate description would be that they're galaxies apart. The artwork is crudely drawn, with Mulloy's characters etched primitively and simplistically—both the male and females display the same characteristics, tall, skinny, with a jarring expression across their face. With a set of monstrous teeth and white piercing eyes, they are invariably only distinguishable by their genitalia. Drawn using only black paint on paper, the films become easily recognizable as Mulloy's. His style complements his stories and rightfully sets the tone for his anarchic films.

The American Dream—Phil Mulloy's *Cowboys* series (1991) (courtesy Phil Mulloy).

Animation is, to some degree a murky minefield. Predominantly, it is a medium that is specifically targeted towards children or is family-oriented, and is deliberately designed to be cute and sentimental, with a strain of light-hearted humor attached. Equally, it's naïve to think that animation cannot be a source of adult entertainment. With shows like *The Simpsons, South Park, Family Guy*, Japanese Anime, Ardman Animation, and the films of Hayao Miyazaki, animation has infiltrated adult popular culture. Mulloy's work is supportive of this theory. His films are the polar opposite of the traditional and certainly mainstream style of animating. By commenting on human nature and contemporary values within the framework of his outrageous and unique tales, his animation effectively highlights, and pokes fun at, the society in which we live. His films are both satirically funny and scathing in equal measure. Mulloy's animation is also raw and uncompromising, his cynical worldview and punk ethics working in harmony with the fables he creates.

Those of a sensitive disposition will find Mulloy's crude fables perverse and sickening, and will write to *The Daily Mail* accordingly to voice their abhorrence. Mulloy, like the best of all contemporary artists, never censors his own work, and presents his material without apologies. Erections, masturbation, buggery, murder, nudity and torture: These images comprise of much of the films' highly entertaining running time. Such is the importance of his work, that his key films deserve further discussion and observation.

Mulloy's films tend to be structured around a common theme or idea. Take Mulloy's 1991 film *Cowboys* to illustrate the point: The film is comprised of six short animated features that deal with a particular theme. In this case, the Wild West is used as his narrative device. By doing so, Mulloy maximizes the potential of his film by exploring some of the clichés connected with the genre, and by commenting on the absurdities he feels are evidently apparent. Mulloy's films are reflective of the problems infecting society generally today, and an all-out attack on male masculinity. In *The Ten Commandments*, the opportunity to offer his particular perspective on the Ten Commandments set out by God, makes for hilarious viewing but, more importantly, a definitive narrative his audience can easily relate to. Mulloy's films are like movements in classical music. Each has its own separate identity, but when combined, they become part of a whole collective piece of work.

Though effective, this specific style of filmmaking doesn't always apply, for upon closer inspection of Mulloy's overture it becomes immediately apparent that his body of work is also represented by a number of longer individual pieces. Accordingly, they represent his more extreme, if not provocative work, like *The Sound of Music* and *The Sexlife of a Chair*. They are seemingly more experimental, not just in terms of the artwork, but also in the marriage of imagery and music, an essential component that underpins most of Mulloy's work. The power and intensity of Mulloy's imagery reveals that he is an insightful critic on the inequalities, hypocrisy and conflict that has infected contemporary life.

Key Films 1991-2004

Cowboys

Mulloy's first major film, commissioned by the British Arts Council and Channel 4, consists of six animated features, loosely tied together under the theme of the Wild West. Unlike Hollywood's interpretation of the Western genre, Mulloy illustrates a place without glamour, infested with greed and male dominance. The violent nature of the Wild West is exposed, and the landscape is constantly drenched in a sea of crimson splatter. Infanticide and bloodlust are commonplace in a community driven by revenge and retribution, and any perpetuators of violence are publicly hung. Here a horse is a man's best friend, and although the Lone Ranger and Silver may have been companions, in Mulloy's version of the Old West they would also have been fuck buddies.

Mulloy's *Cowboys* episode 6: *Outrage!* (courtesy Phil Mulloy)

In the short film *That's Nothin*, male masculinity is ridiculed by way of highlighting the competitive tendencies that emerge in an all-male environment. The perception that we are seen to be better than our fellow man is a characteristic that undoubtedly affects the male psyche. This is revealed to maximum effect in *That's Nothin*, as we witness males arm-wrestling as a way of exhibiting their physical strength, through drinking, or jostling for the attention and appreciation of the group (who goad and gleefully lap up the competitive rivalry) by announcing their sexual achievements. Placing this outside the boundaries of the Wild West, evidence concludes that this is an inherent feature that is ingrained into the genetic makeup of males, as the same characteristics are recognizable and apparent when exploring social trends in male culture in today's society.

In the short film *High Noon*, Mulloy chooses to explore the concept of the duel. Here Mulloy further attacks the notion of male superiority through violence. To settle disputes, arguments and feuds through such a potentially fatal act distinctly exposes the lunacy behind them, and at the end of the feature they are literally revealed to be the "clowns that they are."[1]

In *The Conformist* the idea that we need to comply with that of the rest of society's way of thinking is examined. Concluding that individuality is eventually smothered out by our desire to "fit in" and adhere to a set of rules governed by those dictating what is acceptable and what is not, Mulloy demonstrates this theory in typical fashion. When riding through the plains, our protagonist stumbles across a horse unlike his: It has hoofs, as opposed to wheels. Giving chase, our cowboy eventually captures the beast, then returns home, justifiably proud. Yet his supposedly triumphant return is greeted with hysterical laughter and sneers. Ashamed, the

Mulloy's first notable collection *Cowboys* demonstrates the wicked sense of humor that has enthralled audiences the world over. This scene is taken from the segment entitled *That's Nothin* (courtesy Phil Mulloy).

cowboy decides to cut off the legs of the horse, and fits a set of wheels in their place. His return is met with cheers, and he is accepted back into the group. As he mingles into the group, he has become indistinguishable from anyone else. Mulloy ends the film with a shot of a faceless procession riding across the plains.

The *Cowboys* series is representative of Mulloy's early work, in that the animation is not rich in detail, with background artwork at times negligible. With such a short running time (around three minutes), the narratives tend to be less focused, but more importantly, they address the ideas and themes that reoccur in Mulloy's later work. By assuming that the audience is familiar with the conventions of the Western genre, Mulloy is able to manipulate some of the clichés readily associated with it, and in doing so relates them within a wider and more contemporary viewpoint.

The Ten Commandments

Religion is a recurring theme that presents itself in Mulloy's work. It is important to acknowledge that Mulloy was educated at a Catholic school, and this has greatly impacted on his work as an animator. *The Ten Commandments*, Mulloy's most direct attack on religion, questions the beliefs and the rudimentary way we structure our lives around a set of ten principles supposedly decreed by God. Mulloy is given license and free rein to embark on a tirade of blasphemous imagery all at God's expense, as well as targeting fanatical religious groups, who forcibly execute the writings in the Bible onto their followers as the gospel truth.

Mulloy is playing on

Our hero finds a novel way to play the piano! Mulloy's *The Ten Commandments*, episode 1: *Thou Shalt Not Adore False Gods* (1994–1996) (courtesy Phil Mulloy)

Is that Jesus or a Zog? More blasphemous imagery from Phil Mulloy in *The Ten Commandments*, episode 3: *Remember to Keep Holy the Sabbath Day* (courtesy Phil Mulloy).

the idea that if God created himself in his image, then he must be a pretty inhuman God. Mulloy comments that the characteristic flaws we have as humans must have been inherent from him. During the ten features, Mulloy portrays God as both ruthless and harsh towards his people, and far removed from the Christian portrayal of a loving God. In *Thou Shalt Not Adore False Gods*, we are shown a God that is deeply jealous of others, while in *Thou Shalt Not Commit Blasphemy*, God is seen to revel in inflicting pain and suffering on his people. At one stage in the latter, Mulloy treats us, if that's the correct description, to the sight of God's cock, when pissing. This will certainly anger anyone with even the remotest religious beliefs.

In the excellent *Thou Shall Not Kill*, our character Josh has a severe case of bad luck. After a drought wipes out his crops and then his wife is stuck by lightning, you would have imagined that Josh was due a change in fortune. Apparently not so, as his three children accidentally fall off a cliff when picking berries and then the family dog dies of a broken heart. Naturally distraught, Josh commits suicide. In light of the circumstances, this seems a justifiable act, but it is soon revealed that there is some logic in his actions. In Heaven, Josh meets his creator and decides to dish out a spot of retribution.

8. The Animation of Phil Mulloy (Matthew Edwards) 79

Above: **Burnt sausage! Outrageous imagery from *The Ten Commandments*, episode 6: *Thou Shalt Not Commit Adultery*; *Below:* *Thou Shalt Not Bear False Witness*: Episode 8 of Mulloy's brilliant *The Ten Commandments*** (courtesy Phil Mulloy).

After enduring a good old beating by Josh, God is finally kicked straight down to Hell, where he lands on the Devil's pitchfork.

Made over a two-year period (1994–1996) in association with TV Ontario, Mulloy's warped version of *The Ten Commandments* reveals that he has little time for organized religion, and for those people who insist on having their lives dictated by a set of ludicrous rules. Adhering to this specific framework of rules, Mulloy's characters are revealed to live stifling, mundane lives. Upon choosing to step outside this framework, his characters are free to fulfill their desires, regardless of how extreme the lengths they will go to are, while under the false guise that they are living a life of normalcy. Mulloy is simply commenting on the absurd way we govern our lives around a set of rules that in today's culture have no relevance or place.

The Winds of Change

Mulloy's best work is most fully realized when the relationship between the imagery and sad and turbulent music intertwine cohesively; a good example is *The Winds of Change*. Dealing with political oppression, and based upon the reminiscences of his violinist and composer Alex Balanescu,[2] the story is the personal voyage of a young musician who tries to escape from the conformities of both the East and West.

Shot as part of the BBC2 Music Series *Sound on Film*,[3] Mulloy's movie abandons his normal stylistic traits, preferring instead to restrain the excessive imagery for a more direct and politicized narrative. Mulloy broadens his film by mixing his palette with more colors and detail, plus the inclusion of live-action footage, shot on 8mm. The irreverent humor usually associated with Mulloy's work is reined in, allowing the piece to develop into a poignantly moving tale of life growing up in an authoritarian state.

The film argues the need to remain individualistic with art, and remain expressive despite suppression from cultures that wish to stamp out artistic thought and intellect. Professor Paul Wells accurately defines *The Winds of Change*, and subsequently Mulloy's best work, around this idea in an essay for the British Film Institute:

> ... Mulloy's finest work[s] are commentaries on the necessity for art to be individualistic and expressive in the face of cultures that exhibit indifference or outright hostility to aesthetic and intellectual "difference." [His] films reject authoritarianism, materialism and conformism, and promote art, and especially music, as the conduit for liberation and individual assertion.
> —Professor Paul Wells: The Films of Phil Mulloy, British Film Institute.

The film openly acknowledges the level of suppression inflicted by the state. The authority wanted any trace of individuality stamped out, and Mulloy cleverly portrays this with the image of an iron fist stamping a succession of people on a conveyor belt. Mulloy reinforces his point by having the human heads replaced with parrots. This is to suggest that the people are being parrot-fed into conforming to the way the state deems fit. Symbols of freedom and the desire to escape are omnipresent throughout the film, yet consequently the realization of happiness fails to materialize. Arriving in America provides hope, but the competition, and the cut-throat nature of the music business, soon became apparent to Alex Balanescu; success wasn't based on musical ability but on connections. The film ends simply with the message that "there is no point in doing something very well unless you mange to express something that moves people." This statement supports the overall argument of the film: the idea that art is a source of liberation and expression and through the creativity and freedom of the artist their work has the potential to reach out and communicate to people of all cultures and nationalities.

The Sexlife of a Chair

Ever wondered what the sex life of a chair is like? Well, Phil Mulloy has enlightened us. With parallels to that of humans, it is apparent that chairs are as deviant and as willing to experiment as the rest of us, engaging in a wide range of sexual activities. Mulloy structures the film around a series of headings, before proceeding to illustrate that particular subject. The first heading is celibacy, and this is represented by a simple drawing of a chair. As the film progresses from conventional sexual practices, the behavior of the chairs descends into more extreme sexual territory, as we witness the chair indulging in a range of activities from voyeurism to anal sex, and engaging in such fetishes as sadomasochism, before culminating in more morbid and sexually perverse acts.

Mulloy is clearly commenting on the fascination today's society has for sex. The film clearly highlights, through humor, the levels to which we as a race will go to fulfill our sexual fantasies. It effectively examines the depths of sordidness to which human nature can sink, in order to reach a higher plateau of sexual experience. As funny as it may be, in reality there are those individuals that participate in such vile acts like bestiality, pedophilia and necrophilia, and harvest a great deal of enjoyment out of it. Within his films, Mulloy's portrayal of the aforementioned is darkly comic: When representing pedophilia, we witness the sight of a chair wanking (don't ask), with a smaller chair positioned on its seat (read as lap). Unquestionably there is nothing funny about pedophilia, yet there is something funny in viewing a pedophilic chair up to no good.

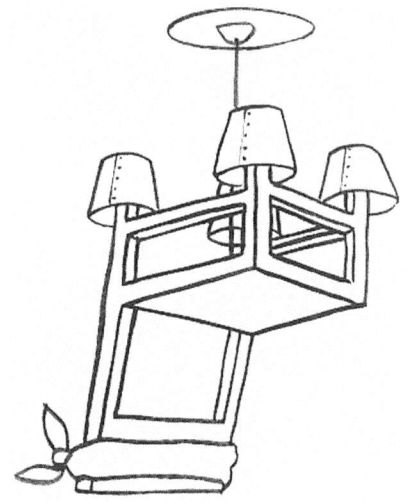

The perverse sexual fantasies of chairs is uncovered in Mulloy's hilarious *The Sexlife of a Chair* (courtesy Phil Mulloy).

Albeit controversial, the film nonetheless works as the viewer acknowledges that although you are watching the supposed behavioral traits of chairs, in reality Mulloy is parodying sexual acts perpetrated by mankind. The way Mulloy presents each episode is both amusing and inventive, and he incorporates a minimal amount of detail and movement when animating each segment. Some critics have been quick to criticize the film by implying that Mulloy is simply looking for cheap gags from an obvious and unoriginal source, an argument that remains both harsh and misguided. In a society that is driven by and revolving around sex, Mulloy is simply presenting the absurd and freaky extremes we will go, in order to satisfy our insatiable sexual desire.

Intolerance

Intolerance, parts I and II,[4] is perhaps Phil Mulloy's most widely known piece of work. *Intolerance* is intended partly as a parable of science fiction films and the prejudice we hold against different races, but equally a study of sexual behavior and social identity. When cleaning up space debris in the outer regions of the universe, astronauts discover a strange alien object, with cryptic symbols etched upon its surface. Taking it back to Earth, scientists puzzle

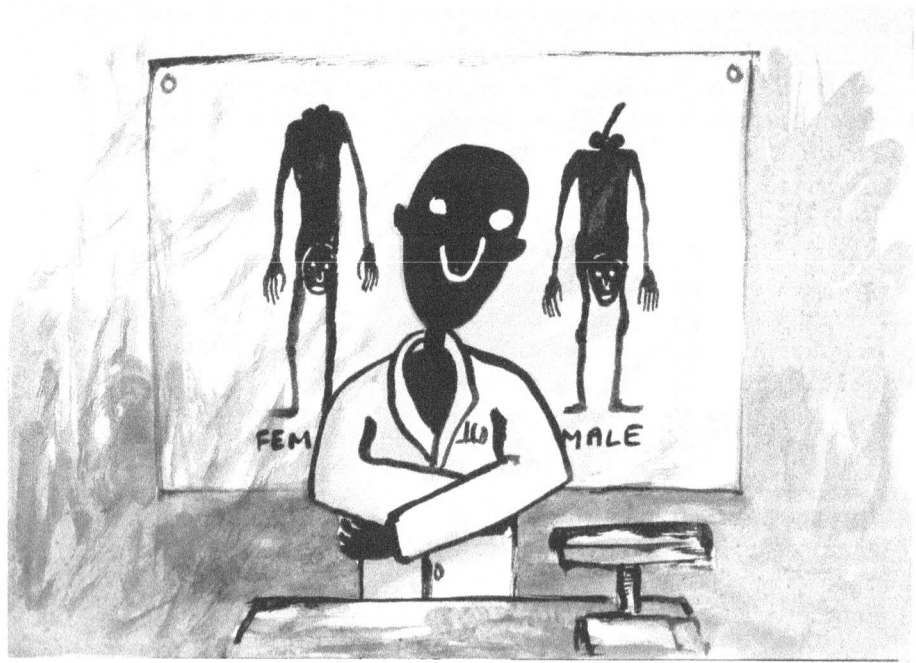

Our first encounter with the dreaded Zogs! The Zogs visually resemble human beings; however, their sexual organs and heads are the "wrong way around." Cue interstellar war between humans and these despicable aliens in the thrilling first part of Mulloy's *Intolerance* trilogy! (courtesy Phil Mulloy).

8. The Animation of Phil Mulloy (Matthew Edwards)

over its meaning and use. By accident the purpose of the object is revealed to be a roll of film from the planet Zog (this occurs when a professor is plucking his nose hairs in a mirror and he happens to catch the reflection of the object).

The film depicts the strange abnormal accustoms and habits of this alien life form. Visually resembling human beings, the creatures are different in one crucial aspect—their sexual organs and heads are, as the film accurately describes, "the wrong way around." The male has an erect penis for a head, with their brain situated within their testicles. This gives freedom for Mulloy to pursue a variety of interesting set pieces when the Zogs casually meet each other and go about their daily business. This is depicted by the act of kissing. For the Zogs, the act of kissing is what sexual intercourse is to humans. Unsurprisingly then, when presenting the film to the general public, they are outraged and shocked by what they see. Perceiving these creatures to be both perverse and depraved, they declare interstellar war on them! The film ends with the inhabitants of Earth setting off to hunt down the planet Zog intent on annihilating its people.

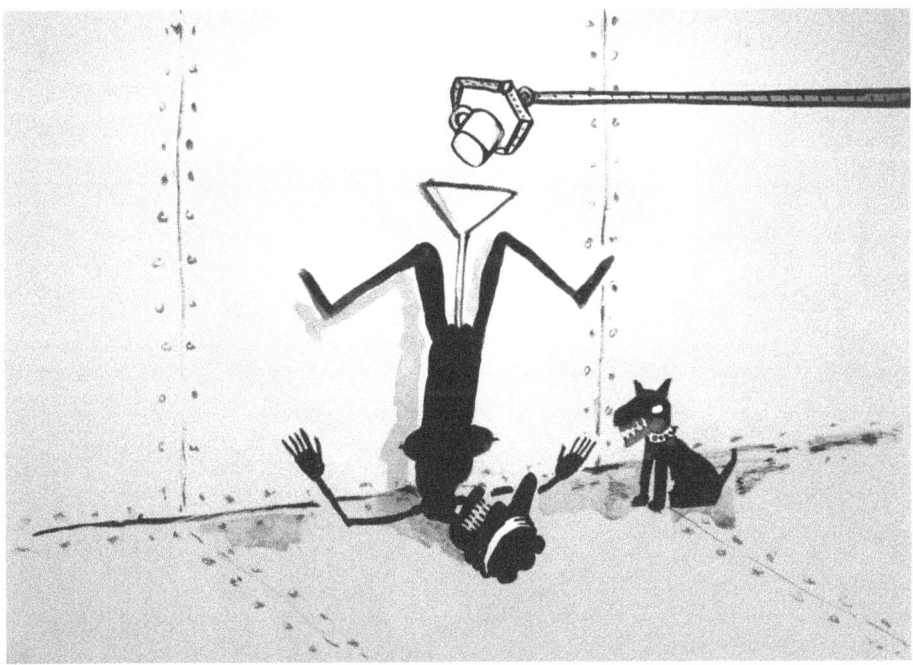

In *Intolerance II*, Dwight Hokum starts a one-man crusade against the Zogs, and founds his own religion. However, his religion states that his wife must remain a virgin! Therefore, Dwight goes to torturous lengths to get his wife pregnant! (courtesy Phil Mulloy).

This raises the important question of our inability to understand and tolerate cultures different from our own. Mulloy explicitly illustrates this idea by depicting the other race as aliens, therefore a species and society far removed from our own. The failure to comprehend their way of living provokes widespread condemnation and eventually hostility. Putting this into a wider context, Mulloy is questioning the way in which different cultures perceive one another and our ignorance as to their traditions and rituals, to the extent that we dismiss them with little regard or appreciation.

Intolerance II: The Invasion continues the saga where the first film left off, but decides to focus the plot more on the Zogs landing on Earth and infiltrating themselves into our society. Thirty years later Dwight Hokum, a local nobody, unwittingly discovers that Earth has become invaded with aliens, and sets upon a righteous crusade to eradicate these intruders. Preaching his message to the masses, or to anyone who will listen, beset with paranoia, Dwight Hokum turns to religion, but this eventually leads to his downfall when he murders his entire family on the understanding that they too are Zogs. The twist ending is unexpected as Dwight learns that he too is one of the dreaded aliens.

More seedy goings-on in Mulloy's *Intolerance II* as Dwight trains a dog to bite his wife's nose, in order to make sex as grueling and miserable as possible! (courtesy Phil Mulloy).

8. The Animation of Phil Mulloy (Matthew Edwards)

What is transparent about the *Intolerance* films is Mulloy's desire to return to ideas and themes that have generally preoccupied most of his previous work. Sexual behavior, social identity, conformism and religion all feature predominantly. Herein, Mulloy also tackles such sexual taboos as anal and oral sex, accompanied, of course, with graphic imagery.

Intolerance II is of particular interest due to Mulloy's embracing of color and computer technology, in order to fully realize his film. Resultantly, the film is given extra scope and depth; combined with Mulloy's traditional methods of animating, it becomes wholly unique. Whether this implies that Mulloy is looking to experiment more with digital technology or CGI remains to be seen, though the evidence suggests that Mulloy may continue to marry his distinctive style into more modern approaches to animation.

Notes

1. Professor Paul Wells. *The Films of Phil Mulloy*, British Film Institute.
2. Romanian born Alexander Balanescu is best known internationally as a virtuoso violinist and composer. He has worked as a composer/musician on many films, including Peter Greenaway's *A Zed and Two Noughts* and Neil Jordan's *The End of the Affair*.
3. *The Winds of Change* was first transmitted on March 29, 1997, on BBC2, as part of BBC's Sound on Film series.
4. In 2004, Phil Mulloy completed the third part of his "Intolerance Trilogy," *Intolerance III–The Final Solution*.

9

Between the Frames: An Interview with Phil Mulloy

MATTHEW EDWARDS

MATTHEW EDWARDS: *What is your background in art and what led you into making animated features?*
PHIL MULLOY: I studied painting at Ravensbourne College of Art. While there I shot a short animated film, and on the strength of it I got into Film and TV at the Royal College of Art. At the film school I concentrated on live action filming, and when I left I wrote and directed a number of live action films. I began making animated films again in 1989, and since then I have produced about thirty shorts.

Although you're recognized primarily through your work as an animator, you have previously worked as a freelance writer-director on live-action films.

During the late seventies and throughout the eighties I made a number of live-action films. I'm most probably one of a very small number of animators that actually progressed (if that's the right word) from live-action to animation. In 1988 while waiting for the money to be put in place for a film, later called *The Return*, I began making a series of drawings. This was something I hadn't done for years, since leaving Ravensbourne in fact. In the end I had so many drawings that I began thinking that they could be organized into a film. The result was a short film called *The Eye of the Storm*. I suppose the making of this film transformed my life. I realized what I had missed—the simple childish pleasures derived from manipulating paint, ink—real physical things. Playing around with images re-awoke the love I had for this. I began to really enjoy myself again. Here was a way of doing anything I wanted on screen, saying anything I wanted to say. A lot of my time during the eighties had been spent raising money for films. I was always waiting for someone to come up with the funds for something or other. The way I was now making animation, I didn't need anywhere near the amount of funding necessary

9. Interview with Phil Mulloy (Matthew Edwards) 87

for a live-action drama. In fact, it would be almost possible for me to finance it myself. At the same time, I had moved with my family to a remote part of West Wales, out in the middle of sheep-filled fields, one and a half miles from the nearest village. It was from there, in a barely converted cowshed, that I decided I would begin a visual assault on the cozy world of animation.

You have a very distinct style to your animation, in that it's been described as minimalist, almost crude to an extent. This sits perfectly with the witty and satirical tales that feature in your films. Is this deliberate?

I must say that I have never considered myself as an animator in a classical sense. I began by just wanting to make things move. The movement itself wasn't something I wasn't going to get too hung up about. It was simply a means to an end. I was primarily trying to make the images as quickly as possible, and to some degree as spontaneously as possible. The labor-intensive aspect of animation never appealed to me. I suppose I associated it with the mass of underpaid workers in the Far East doing all those mind-numbingly boring jobs to conjure up some director's grand vision. It's that sense of boredom that so much animation manages to carry with it into the cinema that puts me off watching most animated films. But anyway, that unhappy state of affairs wasn't open to me. I was working with a rostrum camera that didn't

Mulloy's *The Sound of Music* (courtesy Phil Mulloy).

really work properly. It was an old 35mm camera that one of the London colleges was throwing out. I decided I could get it working again. I sort of did, but so many things kept going wrong with it that it gave a certain look to the animation. This combined with my own limited animation abilities gave the films a very rough feel. Of course this was perfect for the type of films I was making. It gave them an identity of their own—one in which the physicality of the marks (black ink on paper) and the film material itself were foregrounded.

There was another aspect to this of which I was conscious, one that gave me a great deal of pleasure. It was to do with the idea of transformation; the idea that something relatively insignificant could almost become significant through the transforming capabilities of the projector beam. There was something wonderful about using marks that were almost throw-away and giving them an importance that perhaps they didn't deserve. It was a kind of liberating idea. Using this method of working to explore the star-studded terrain mapped out by Hollywood opened up many possibilities for me.

A lot of your films deal with contemporary themes and issues, but in an outlandish and grotesque way. Do you deliberately set out to be provocative, or to a certain degree is it a reaction against mainstream animation?

A lot of the animated films I have made are about five or six minutes long. That means I don't have a great deal of time to tell my story and get what it is I want to get across to the audience. My way of doing this is to be direct as possible. An example of what I mean would be that if two of my characters were going to have sex with one another, I would tend to cut out the getting-to-know you bit and go straight to the sex. Some people would say that this can dehumanize my characters to just carrying out bodily functions, but in the world I create, fucking is very similar to eating or just walking along the street. It's this attitude to it that can be revealing about some of the ways in which we behave, and of course this can produce humor. For instance, trying to eat dinner and have sexual congress at the same time could produce some amusing scenes. It would be an interesting take on both table manners and bedroom etiquette.

Whereas most films look at people through a telescope the right way round, at the details, etc., of human existence, I tend to turn the instrument round and look through it the other way. It's a bit like looking at the organization of an ants' nest. The ants all rush around busy with some unknown task. Quite what's going on though, other than the necessities for their survival, is shrouded in mystery. As to being provocative, I suppose it's not a bad way of getting noticed, if in turn that provocation can encourage an audience to think about things in a slightly different way.

More prudish viewers will be outraged by your work, somewhat like the audience members in your film Intolerance. *Although your films contain scenes of explicit violence*

9. Interview with Phil Mulloy (Matthew Edwards)

Double trouble! The explosive finale of Mulloy's *Intolerance* series (courtesy Phil Mulloy).

Sony Sex Box. The final part of Mulloy's *Intolerance* trilogy (courtesy Phil Mulloy).

and sex, the portrayal of it is presented in such a manner as not to slip into exploitation. That said, there are still members of the Moral Majority who will be calling for your head and demanding the censoring of your work. What is your take on censorship of animation-cartoons in the UK?

So far I have shown about 99 percent of my work on British television, including BBC, Channel 4, and MTV. The only image I have censored was of an office block being blown up. It may seem ridiculous that a drawing of an explosion should be censored, but it was due to be screened on Channel 4 just after 9/11 and I seem to remember decisions being made at the channel were getting somewhat ridiculous.

There is, however, a much more subtle form of censorship in operation today: the censorship of the market [TV audience figures], a method whereby those films that don't fit into the commissioners' idea of what people want to see simply don't get made. This tendency to exclude all but an increasingly narrow range of predictable programs and films has led the TV commissioners into abandoning not only the short animated film but also any films whose formal language could be considered "problematic." In this way innovation is discouraged in favor of the tried and tested. These days innovation is purely

Uncouth table manners in Mulloy's *The Sound of Music* (courtesy Phil Mulloy).

for the art galleries. There it can ghettoized, separated off from normal life, and rendered harmless.

There has been an upsurge in adult animation over the years, yet many consider it a medium aimed solely for children and teenagers. It's not ridiculous to think that animation can be considered a form of adult entertainment?

Yes, and I am probably not a great fan of animation for this reason. There are exceptions—The Simpsons, South Park—but that is mainly to do with the quality of the writing. The shame is that their imagery is not up to the same standard.

Are you trying to take the medium into a new radical direction, away from the cute and kitsch style of animation?

I don't think of myself in terms of taking anything in a radical new direction, I just work in a way that suits me, and with the issues I want to deal with. If other people see something in that, then that's great. The idea of sitting down and trying to think of how to work in a new direction is rather scary. It could become a purely intellectual process. I tend to work intuitively and do the rationalizing later.

A lot of animation is cute and kitschy because adults think that is what children want to see. Maybe some kids do, but I don't think I ever did. I would like to believe that most kids hate it. That would make me normal.

Has your style evolved in any way over the years? Do you strive to change the way you animate?

Evolution in style is not something I'm terribly interested in. Some animators try to change their style for each film they make. That's not my way of working. Over the years I have tried to create a vocabulary for myself. One that can create a coherent universe that has points of contact with the one in which I live. I have also tried to create a way of working where I am able to consider the act of drawing pretty much in the same way as I would my handwriting, i.e., something I don't have to think about too much when doing it. I find that because I have to do so many drawings it's impossible to become too precious about any single one of them. When I was painting I found the idea of producing just one image overwhelming. It became too important, and in the end it stopped me working. Now the real action lies between the frames and not in them, and that suits me.

Has a Catholic background had any direct influence on your films? A lot of your work features religious connotations, most explicitly the infamous Ten Commandments *films.*

All that blood-soaked imagery of torture and redemption, how could it not? Perhaps I realized that all those stations of the cross were just storyboards waiting to be animated. There were a few reasons why I chose to make *The*

A soldier takes aim at a helpless child: one of the many horrifying images taken from Mulloy's *The Chain* (courtesy Phil Mulloy).

Ten Commandments. The first was because Hollywood had made a film version. The fact that Hollywood had already used the title is always a good reason for me to use it as well. And of course *The Ten Commandments* was an epic. The idea of remaking an epic (if only in name) out of bits of paper and ink appealed to me. *The Ten Commandments* also gave me a structure—a series of ten shorts based on each of the commandments. It was a framework that most people in the Christian world were familiar with. This meant that the audiences would already have a point of reference similar to my own, and so wherever I took the film this shared knowledge would act as a communal base. The fact that it was about religion of course was important, but only in as much as it was a set of rules that God had supposedly decreed for Man to follow. You don't get much bigger than God. Again it was the whole idea of scale that appealed to me, and of course there was a chance of me creating some humor at His expense.

How easy is it to obtain funding for short animation films here in the UK? Are there many avenues open to filmmakers like yourself, or do you have to seek foreign investment?

I have two strategies to continue making my films. The first is to get fund-

9. Interview with Phil Mulloy (Matthew Edwards) 93

ing anywhere I can, and the second is to fund them myself. Why I continue to make animation films and not go back to live action is because I am able to continue making my films even when I don't have funding. Right now it's really quite difficult to get any sort of backing in Britain. I have just completed the third part of a trilogy called *Intolerance*, and to finance that I had to raise the money in Germany. It was impossible to get even co-production money in this country. But this is not just a problem that I am confronted with. It is the same for every animator that is interested in making short films, and extends out to all those filmmakers that don't fit neatly into the Film Council idea of what good filmmaking is.

I personally think it is a disgrace that the Film Council isn't prepared to support short animated films. During the nineties the UK won five Oscars for short animation, and had a fantastic reputation throughout the world. Then two years ago Channel 4 closed down its animation department and the Arts Council of England Lottery Department was transformed into the Film Council. Previously the Film Lottery Department had, through the use of a panel of people from a broad range of approaches to filmmaking, made decisions about which projects would be funded. The films made during this

The History of the World, as seen through the surreal palette of Mulloy (courtesy Phil Mulloy).

period reflected the diversity of opinion in the make-up of the panel, and consequently were healthily diverse in approach themselves. The situation as it stands now is that one or two people make the decisions, and the films that are made reflect their rather limited tastes.

How important are film festivals to you? Is it a way of getting your films shown?

Festivals are very important. As well as serving as an alternative distribution network, they give the audiences and myself the opportunity of meeting other filmmakers. There seem to be new festivals springing up all the time, which proves there are audiences out there for films that won't be seen at the local Odeon or on TV. Also the knowledge that your work will travel around the world and get seen from Taiwan to Brazil helps give you the creative strength to carry on.

It's a rare feat for a collection of British Animation to be released on home video and DVD. How did the BFI deal come about? Did they sense there was enough interest in your work to release the collection?

It was quite simple really. I seem to remember that one day someone from the BFI phoned me up and asked me if I'd like them to make and distribute a DVD of my work. I of course said yes. How they came to the decision in the first place remains a mystery to me, but I suspect they thought that it would be a marketable product.

Do you have any plans to make a full-length feature film, and what projects are on the horizon?

I am working on a few projects at the moment, one of which is a feature-length animation.* I'm writing and sketching out ideas for it, and wandering the streets hoping ideas will just materialize in my head.

Finally, what is your problem with horses? If they're not being buggered by a randy cowboy, then they're having their legs cut off!

I hate horses. Why? Because they've got two more legs than us, tails and pointy ears. They deserve all they get.

---

*Mulloy has just completed his first full-length animated feature, entitled The Christies (2006).

10

Writing Argento

Maitland McDonagh

Broken Mirrors/Broken Minds changed my life. Almost fifteen years after it was first published, I still receive e-mails from strangers praising it and I see used copies offered online for staggering sums of money. A co-worker once picked up a book reserved in my name at a cooler-than-thou shop and found himself shadowed through the aisles by a clerk who finally said reverentially, "You know Maitland McDonagh?" At a friend's wedding a fellow guest did a deep bow and declared, "I am not worthy!" while behind my shoulder I could hear a baffled voice asking my husband, "Is she famous or something?" That clearly depends on what you mean by famous: *Broken Mirrors/Broken Minds* did not make me rich or turn me into a brand name, the holy grail of savvy self-promoters. But it secured my niche in a small but intense community.

When I began writing my master's thesis in 1985 it seemed destined to go no farther than a shelf somewhere at Columbia University, where no one would ever find it. I'd been in the graduate film program for two years and I had no idea where theses went to die. I also had no inkling what a task I set myself by deciding that all I wanted in a thesis topic was not to get backed into writing about some trendy tripe like the dialectics of gender or forced to waste hundreds of thousands of words unpacking a shred of celluloid minutia that successive waves of scholars and film students had failed to pick off some classic film's bones. I wanted to write an auteur study that included close textual analysis through a variety of critical methodologies—variety is the spice—and I really wanted to write about a filmmaker whose movies I actually liked but who hadn't already been written to death by other students and academics. No candidate came to mind.

Enter my friend Gary from New Line, then a scruffier, more marginal place than it is now but newly flush with the success of *A Nightmare on Elm Street* (1984). New Line had just picked up US distribution rights to *Phenomena*. They were already casting about for a new title, guided by the wisdom that the kind of people who went to horror movies didn't go to anything whose title they couldn't pronounce. Hence *Creepers*. "What about Dario Argento?" Gary asked. I had seen only two Argento movies, and had been underwhelmed by *The Bird with the Crystal Plumage* (1970), which surfaced briefly in Times Square in 1980 as *The Phantom of Terror*. But I had vivid memories of *Deep Red* (1975), which I saw at the Victoria, a cavernous theater on Broadway and 46th Street—part of the greater Times Square area, though not on the notorious Deuce—that was later converted into a faux-delicatessen tourist trap called the Roxy. I had kept the cardboard mask, pink with black hypnovison-esque swirls, that was handed out at the ticket booth with instructions to cover my eyes with it if I became too scared to watch! Ten years later, images from *Deep Red* still festered somewhere deep in my memory, as did fragments of *Goblin*'s infernally catchy score. Prints of *Phenomena* would be coming into the New Line offices, Gary said, and he knew bootleggers who had copies of Argento's other films. That was the deal breaker, because those were the frontier days of home video. I had just bought my first VCR—shockingly expensive, nearly ten times the price of a new DVD player. It was a top loader with a wired remote—"wired," as in the remote had a long, skinny cable that plugged into the back of the VCR and coiled treacherously on the floor, biding its time until you forgot it was there and tripped. Movies you wanted to see and movies you could find on tape were two very different things, and the Internet was no help. It was still the Arpanet, domain of science wonks, not an international souk. Gary's connections made an Argento study feasible and, best of all, Argento was so far under the radar of the academic film studies community that I had him all to myself. And so it began.

Of course, what looks like chance is rooted in predisposition; I believe I was born to darkness at the end of America's baby boom, a child of the turbulent sixties who came of age just as the flower-child optimism curdled into paranoia, cynicism and self-destruction. People a few years older remember where they were when they heard President Kennedy had been shot, the moment when their memories split into before and after. I remember where I was when I heard about the murders at 10050 Cielo Drive; my memories divide into before the Manson Family and after. I grew up in New York, the greatest city in the United States and one of the greatest in the world. When my father was a child, people left the doors to their flats open and slept in public parks on unbearable hot nights. I grew up in fear city, where everything seemed to get worse every year—crime, public services, atmosphere—as New York spiraled towards its 20th-century nadir. People were strangers and when my sisters and I played in the local park we found used hypodermic needles and chicken feet tied together with bits of colored yarn strung with beads, evidence of what junkies and Santerians had been up to in the dark. My New York was strangling on the tatters of a misguided vision of shining future cities where gleaming ribbons of expressways soared above the city streets and connected urban hubs to the suburbs, exurbs and rural communities. The subsequent construction bulldozed through poor but viable neighborhoods, dispersing families and neighbors and leaving fields of rubble where violence and despair flourished. My New York burned and choked; it was financially strapped and crumbling, besieged by a climbing murder rate, strikes by rubbish collectors and policemen, widespread corruption, racial strife, angel dust and crack cocaine and abandonment by the federal government. When New York went bankrupt in 1975, no aid was forthcoming. Spike Lee's *Summer of Sam* is a brilliant evocation of my New York: Dirty, dangerous—did I mention sleazy?— and apparently headed straight down the toilet at a dizzying speed. I don't want to romanticize my New York, because it was scary. But it was also a dark dream that nurtured morbid turns of mind and rewarded them regularly. No wonder the dark dreams of Dario Argento felt like home.

I came to horror movies relatively late, excepting a traumatic experience at a very early age with *Not of This Earth* (1957) on TV. Nightmares for months about the umbrella creature. Just reading Roger Ebert's review of *Night of the Living Dead* (1968) set off a new round, and to this day when I have nightmares my unconscious always vomits up a plague of zombies. But I discovered horror literature early: Edgar Allan Poe, Arthur Machen and H.P. Lovecraft, Algernon Blackwood, Saki and Pan horror collections with wrinkled, lurid covers that I bought at second-hand shops—I still remember the image of a forlorn eyeball in a pot of strawberry jam. I found a copy of *In Cold Blood* at my grandmother's apartment and discovered the dark allure of true crime stories. I bought *True Detective* and *Official Detective* magazines at the stationery store and collected paperback accounts of sensational crimes. I watched *Dark Shadows* (1966–1971) with my mother every weekday afternoon when I got home from school; the travails of the 19th-century Collins family would have bored me to tears had producer Dan Curtis not listened when, in 1967, a lunatic voice squeaked in his ear that his gothic soap opera needed a touch of the macabre. He added brooding cousin Barnabas (Jonathan Frid), a vampire, and handsome cousin Quentin the werewolf (David Selby, who graduated to primetime soap success in the '80s on the glossy *Falcon Crest*). The baroque supernatural complications their conditions added to the usual love triangles and plots to secure the family inheritance also insured the show's place in pop culture history. My mother liked Quentin, I loved Barnabas. And ironically, it was the innocuous *Dark Shadows* that led me to the underworld of Times Square grindhouses. A newspaper ad for a movie starring Frid lured me to the Selwyn, a rundown theater whose ornate ceiling and grimy luxe carpeting gave off a whiff of faded glamour that wafted through the marijuana fumes. It was located on the north side of 42nd Street, whose raunchy reputation as a 24-hour carnival of vice barely did it justice. There, in 1974, I saw Oliver Stone's *Seizure* on a double bill with *The Beast Must Die*.

Once the Deuce was a vibrant hub of cheap, déclassé entertainment. Hubert's flea circus, peep shows, amusement arcades, adult bookstores, cheap hot dog stands and magic supply shops ... I arrived too late for most of that, and wasn't interested in live sex shows featuring chicks with dicks. But 42nd Street was a thriving bazaar of movies that never played more upscale houses and often didn't even bother to advertise. The way to find out what was playing was to stroll up one side of the street and down the other, drinking in the ever-shifting mix of exploitation, sexploitation, drugsploitation, blaxploitation, gore, mondo and martial arts movies. You paid your money—not much, considering it bought a double or even triple program—and took your chances on haphazard start times, indifferent projection, unannounced substitutions and treacherous seats. A friend and I once leaned back and discovered, as the entire row tipped over backwards, that they were no longer bolted to the floor. Entrepreneurial drug dealers walked up and down the aisles peddling their wares from makeshift trays fashioned from cardboard box lids and string, while other patrons unpacked meals or settled in for a nap. I don't know why I didn't see more Argento. European genre pictures played cheek to jowl with homegrown horrors; I saw plenty of giallo, *Night Porter* knock-offs and Euro-zombie flesh feasts.

I was primed to appreciate the Argento tapes that came trickling in, and began to see in Argento what separated contemporary European genre filmmakers from their American counterparts. There were great technicians in both traditions, attuned to free-floating cultural anxieties, steeped in horror comics and the flickering history of fright films. But the Europeans were rooted in richer soil. In America you had to find a museum to discover, for example, the baroque iconography of pain and ecstasy that colored centuries of religious painting and statuary; in Italy any little church might contain a statue of a martyrized saint with disarticulated limbs, anatomically correct right to the bloody shoulder stumps. Americans learned their gothic tropes at a remove, filtered through late night television and the sensibilities of Europeans who fled to Hollywood between the world wars, trailing Expressionist shadows. Argento's films were a graduate student's dream, their penny-dreadful narratives so intertwined with a rich tapestry of echoes and allusions that they fairly begged to be dissected and examined through a variety of critical systems. Just as I had hoped.

The Bird with the Crystal Plumage allowed me to introduce the giallo—a term unfamiliar in those dark days to most fans and scholars—and its relationship to the traditional mystery, as well as Argento's precursors, especially Mario Bava. Those themes were developed in the chapter on *Cat O' Nine Tails* (1971) and *Four Flies on Grey Velvet* (1972), which proved the most elusive of Argento's films—even *Le Cinque Giornate* (1973) was easier, although the tape was unsubtitled and I had to enlist the aid of my younger sister's Italian tutor,

Aldo, to make sense of it. Aldo also pitched in when I obtained the European cut of *Deep Red* in un-subtitled Italian, complaining all the way through that Americans are interested in the stupidest things. Why would you write about a filmmaker like this, this Dario Argento (insert appropriately dramatic hand gestures here) when you could write about Antonioni or Fellini? How remarkable, I thought, to find myself on the wrong side of the "the French and Jerry Lewis—perverse or just ridiculous?" debate. *Four Flies* was like a phantom: No one had it on tape, commercial or bootleg. No one seemed to have bought it for television broadcast, which is how I found *Screaming Mimi* (1958); a local station had a print in its Long Island City warehouse and a friend persuaded someone to screen it for me. I thought my troubles were over when *Four Flies* was scheduled to be shown at a Fangoria convention, and didn't lose heart even when I found it was being screened in a side room hardly larger than a peep show booth, with the projector clacking away directly behind the last row of seats. But when it started, the image was squished; skinny stars Michael Brandon and Mimsy Farmer so grotesquely elongated that they looked like moving pipe-cleaner people. The print was widescreen. The projectionist didn't have an anamorphic 16mm lens and couldn't scare one up; he refused to show the rest and frankly, it was unwatchable. So I turned to the Library of Congress in Washington DC, where a print of every film released in the United States is deposited for the purposes of copyright protection. (At least, every film released by a distributor who cares—you won't unearth any Andy Milligan rarities there.) The Library of Congress grants scholars access if they meet the appropriate criteria, so I gathered up my academic bona fides, filled out applications and was eventually told that I could come to Washington and watch *Four Flies* on a flatbed Moviola as many times as I could manage in one eight-hour day. Thank God for undergraduate film production classes, because they cut down the Moviola learning curve—especially since all the knobs were labeled in German—and probably kept me from destroying the library's print.

Suspiria (1977) and *Inferno* (1980), with their surreal, repetitive imagery and looping narratives, were perfect for dream analysis, while the shadowy convolutions of *Tenebrae* (1982) cried out to be examined through the prism of sexual anxiety and gender confusion—I almost wound up writing about the dread dialectics of gender after all. And so it went; each film yielded unexpected rewards. Any concerns I might have harbored about not finding enough about which to write vanished in the fear that there was so much to say I'd never meet my academic deadline. All the while, I was collecting Argento material, not just the articles and essays I needed for my research but stills and ad mats, posters, lobby cards, pressbooks ... anything I could find. In retrospect I couldn't say why, since I wasn't writing a book and wasn't expected to illustrate my thesis. But the films had cast a spell and I needed to surround myself with tangible artifacts. I was possessed. I hardly remember actually writing my

thesis. I had a fulltime job that paid my rent and a substantial chunk of my tuition, squeezing in classes and writing in the hours I had left. But in the end it got done; I turned it in, received my passing grade and thought my intense relationship with Argento was done until the phone call from *Film Quarterly*, a well-thought-of academic film journal that wanted to publish a chapter.

The publication of that piece led directly to a letter from a polite English fellow who worked for a periodicals indexing company, saying how much he enjoyed the piece and enclosing photocopies of some additional articles about Argento that he thought I might not have seen. That fellow, Anthony Blampied, eventually confided that he hoped to start a small publishing company and would love to make my thesis his first project. Yes, yes, I said, flattered but less than convinced that this was anything I should be taking seriously. That would be very nice, I said. Call me when you're a little further along in this project.

And the rest is history, in the small "h" sense of the word; Anthony pulled his resources together and in 1991 published a revised version of my master's thesis as *Broken Mirrors/Broken Minds: The Dark Dreams of Dario Argento*. My thesis was the last thing I ever wrote on a typewriter—a Brother with a two-sentence LED display, the hippest, coolest thing in new technology at the time—and I vividly remember scrambling to get the text scanned so I could revise it using the newest wrinkle in word processing: The Kaypro, a clunky, "portable" home computer (portable for no reason other than that it had a handle) that looked like a bayou fishing shack and ran off 5½-inch floppy disks that could store an awesome 30 pages of written material. I went through my original text, purging the academic defensiveness where I could, relegating particularly argumentative passages to footnotes, streamlining the prose and generally trying to make it as readable as possible.

The first time I saw *Broken Mirrors/Broken Minds*, when I visited London on a combined vacation and promotional visit, it became suddenly, vividly real to me. My thesis was a book, with a handsome cover by Andre Klimovsky—longtime collaborator with the Quay brothers—and my words invested with an authority that felt to me as though someone else had written them. A successful magazine editor I had known for years once told me that nothing improves a manuscript like time and typesetting, and as I held my book in my hands I realized how right she was. My thesis had taken on an unimaginable

Opposite: Original Japanese poster of Dario Argento's seminal Italian horror classic *Suspiria*. Regarded by many critics as Argento's best film, *Suspiria* is in fact the first film of Argento's *Three Mothers* trilogy. The second part was the equally surreal and brilliant *Inferno* (1980). Argento is currently filming part three, *La Terza Madre* (*The Third Mother*).

authority, transformed from a stack of typed pages to a sleekly bound volume illustrated with the stills, posters and ad mats I had so carefully collected. And that book changed my life, which is where we came in.

I'm not sure what the moral of this story is. That chance can take you places you never imagined, what seems like wool gathering can open doors you didn't know existed, that you should never say no when you can say sure, maybe, let me have a look? Or perhaps that monsters and marvels both lurk in the dark.

11

Requiems for Abandoned Souls: The New Wave of Spanish Mystery Thrillers

Marcus Stiglegger

The world is full of spirits—there is a world beyond our imagination. Who knows what lives between heaven and earth—between life and death? Who knows where souls go when death finally arrives. All animistic cultures believe in the soul and in spirits. Japan has its Shinto religion which builds a perfect spiritual background for the traditional and the new ghost stories—a culture in its own right. But we do not have to turn to the Far East. At the end of the Nineties we witnessed the rise of another cinematic new wave: the New Wave of Spanish Mystery Thrillers. These films—among them *The Others*, *The Nameless* and *The Devil's Backbone*—create a special *vision du monde*, influenced by catholic ideas of guilt and sacrifice, occult rituals, and ancient myths. This chapter will try to shed some light on this phenomenon and present the key elements of a special kind of European suspense cinema that is slowly but steadily acquiring a cult following.

Abandoned Souls

A mother, Grace (Nicole Kidman), and her two children (Alakina Mann and James Bentley) are living at a lonely country estate. It is the year 1944, briefly before the end of World War II. Walls of fog are covering the English countryside in autumn. Grace's father and her husband are missing in action, and the housekeepers have mysteriously disappeared. Out of the blue, a trio of caretakers appears at the estate: a friendly old lady, Mrs. Mills (Fionnula Flanagan), a mute girl (Elaine Cassidy), and a grumpy old butler, Mr. Tuttle (Eric Sykes). They could not have been aware that Grace was looking for servants, but as they are in the right place at the right time, they are hired...

This is the beginning of Alejandro Amenabar's film *The Others* (2001), a gothic dream-play inspired by Henry James' classic novella of psychological horror "The Turn of the Screw." This is at least what it seems ...

But the young mother has more severe problems: Her children both have a deadly allergy to light. They have to live in darkness by day, the curtains must be closed all the time. In their isolation the children seem to have developed a disturbing obsession: They report strange noises, curtains are opening and closing by themselves, piano music is playing ... A family of ghosts seems to visit them from time to time. As the film lingers through the gothic twilight of the foggy surroundings, Grace tries to unveil the secret. One day her husband returns home, but his behavior is as strange as everything in the house. He is apathetic, like a living dead person. And finally the housekeepers are threatening the children.

The last sequence presents one final twist to the almost classical storyline: The point of view changes to neutral observation and it turns out that we have spent one and a half hours with a family of ghosts. All the obsessions and neuroses find their explanation in the fact that the "ghost" haunting the mansion are the real people living in the house, who are not aware of their neighbors in another dimension. "The Others" is not a real terror-movie but a highly stylized drama about the loneliness of abandoned souls, living in a half-world between our world and the beyond. Amenabar created a sterile surrounding, often missing any atmospheric sound, totally reduced to elementary sounds. The visuals are dominated by brownish and golden colors, often washed out, monochromatic, sometimes covered by rising mist. *The Others* live in a world between the boundaries: a world of fog and darkness. But they still have the urge to preserve their essential family values. Grace desperately tries to save the family. She is blind to the fact that everyone around her is devoid of life and vitality. Amenabar's film breaks the rules of "reliable narration" that genre-film normally depends on. But at the same time his film does not lie. He simply demonstrates the subjectivity of cognition and narration. *The Others* is not a film about death—it is in fact a film identifying with the dead, a bleak portrait of useless longing for life.

Even in his earlier cinematic efforts, Amenabar concentrated on the darkest aspects of existence: *Tesis* (1996) is a tense thriller about snuff films produced at a film school. As a female student realizes that a teacher and other students are involved in this macabre project she finally has to fear for her life. *Open Your Eyes* (1999)—which was remade in the USA as *Vanilla Sky* (2002)—tells the baffling story of a successful womanizer (Eduardo Noriega) trapped between two different women, one of whom tries to kill him in a car crash. But he survives and is forced to wear a mask to hide his horribly damaged face. More and more, reality levels seem to shift. His consciousness begins to jump between past and present. The mystery is finally solved in the science-fiction context: He is struggling with implanted memories while his body is frozen to wait for better medical care in the future. Even here the ambitious director brings to life a cold and stylized *film noir* world, the artificial dreamstate of a haunted and disturbed character—perfectly executed in the first sequence in which Noriega's Cesar (named after the somnambulist of Robert Wiene's *Cabinet of Dr. Caligari*) wakes up in the morning, gets up and drives downtown—only to realize that he is the only living person in this world. Then the bell rings again ... But where does imagination end and reality begin? Cesar can be seen as one of those twilight creatures, an abandoned soul lost between memories of the past and an imaginative present.

Another dark ghost story, *The Devil's Backbone* (2001) by Guillermo del Toro, offers its audience a gothic-horror variation of Agustí Villaronga's intense TBC-asylum-drama *El Mar* (1998), which also takes place in the time of World War II. Del Toro's film is paradigmatic for this New Wave of Spanish Mystery Thrillers, especially for its monologue, which is spoken by an old male voice over images of an abnormal embryo with a comb-like spine: "What is a ghost? An emotion, a terrible moment condemned to repeat itself over and over? An instant of pain perhaps? ... A sentiment suspended in time? ... like a blurry photograph ... like an insect trapped in amber?" The ghost as a phenomenon questions the nature of life and death, of reality and imagination. It transcends the physicality of the human body and signifies the existence of a soul...

The world of *The Devil's Backbone* (a reference to the embryo of the title sequence) is very complex, and there are several possibilities of defining its ghost-like nature. In an impressive top shot we follow a huge black bomb falling down to earth and crashing into the inner yard of an isolated mission estate in the desert. The year is 1939, the Spanish Civil War. Ten-year-old Carlos, whose father was killed in battle, is brought to the mission, which now has the function of an orphanage. There he discovers the secrets of this estate: The unexploded bomb in the yard is a constant threat to the people; in the basement below the kitchen, the ghost of Santi, a boy who was drowned there and finds no peace, seems to live; and there is Jacinto, an angry young man who spent his whole youth in the mission and now tries to rob the gold that Carmen, the headmistress, and her elderly husband Casares guard for the rebels. Carlos soon realizes that Santi was killed by Jacinto for he had discovered the young man's secret longing for the gold treasure. Now he speaks to Carlos to warn him: Something terrible is going to happen. As Jacinto violently tries to get his hands on the gold, a huge explosion kills many of the boys and Carmen. The survivors are locked away to be killed later. But the boys manage to drown Jacinto in the fountain where he had killed Santi. Casares unlocks the door and the boys escape.

The film reaches its turning point right in the last frame where the old man Casares stands in the shadow. In the background we see the boys run away. Casares repeats his introducing monologue, closing with the insight that he himself is a ghost, having been killed in the explosion long before he could have freed the orphans. *The Devil's Backbone* can be seen as classic gothic fiction, like *The Others* very similar to Henry James' "The Turn of the Screw." For a long time the film shifts between psychological and metaphysical levels of reception. It is never made clear whether we see Carlos' subjective visions or an objective incident (dealing with the supernatural). It also appears very strange that the film starts with an old man reflecting the key phenomenon and then switches to a young boy. We could easily take the old man's voice as the adult voice of Carlos, but the turn in the end changes the perspective radically: With the shadowy ghost of Casares, the film finally enters the world of fantasy. Del Toro's best film to date is therefore closely connected to the "unreliable" narration of *The Sixth Sense* and *The Others* which are also told from the viewpoint of the dead. And yes—a "ghost" is probably everything that Casares mentions: a terrible moment condemned to repeat itself over and over—like an insect trapped in amber ... But what happens if the dead envy the living?

They're Watching Us (2002) by Norberto López Amado in a way refers to Robert Harmon's horror thriller *They* (2002) about living shadows behind the mirror terrorizing and kidnapping the unhappy chosen few who are able to be aware of "them." Amado's dark film tells the story of police inspector Juan (Carmelo Gómez) whose sister disappeared in a mysterious manner during a school play. In the present, Juan has a family of his own with two children. But a new case will knock his life out of balance: During his research on the disappearance of a wealthy businessman three years before, he discovers that during the past decades thousands of people have disappeared without a trace. The final proof of the disappeared man's life is a videotape—filmed via a mirror—on which Juan discovers strange shadowy creatures who seems to exist in a twilight world between life and death. Even in the city and on the subway he begins to see those shadows, appearing in reflecting surfaces. He discovers that these are abandoned souls who never totally passed away into the realm of death. Now they envy the living and therefore terrorize them. Juan realizes that his children, especially his daughter, see them as well. Even in his past the shadows were there and pulled his little sister over to their side. To save his young daughter the policeman sacrifices himself: He enters the real "night-train" into the abyss. In the last sequence we witness that he is still present for his daughter—who is the next of the chosen ones, but with a shadowy guardian angel on her side...

Amado's film creates a very dark and brooding atmosphere via stylistic means that we know from Jaume Balaguero's films *The Nameless* and *Darkness*: monochromatic, mainly brown and green color-schemes, a low frequency drone on the soundtrack, high-contrast chiaroscuro lightning, and finally the discovery of occult symbolism (within a dream sequence). Juan is yet another haunted soul (as in *Darkness*), a dark father figure that becomes a threat to his family (especially when he shoots at his children in panic). He is the original source of evil within the family—although that is not his fault, for he is a victim of the twilight world himself. The only way to save himself, and his kin, is to sacrifice himself for the benefit of a (fleeting) peace. In the end it is clear that he has passed the curse over to his daughter. The idea of self-sacrifice to restore the order is clearly a very conservative element in most of these Spanish films. On the surface, a skepticism concerning supernatural and spiritual elements seems to dominate, but slowly passes away. Without being explicitly Christian or Catholic in their attitude, these films nevertheless glorify conservative Old Testament ideas of martyrdom and redemption.

Pain and Sacrifice

Deeply connected with Spanish mysticism is the myth of pain, sacrifice and martyrdom. It comes therefore as no surprise that the New Wave of Spanish Mystery Thrillers often contain connections of physical pain, spiritual suffering and redemption.

The Nameless (1999) by Jaume Balaguero, the most complex key film in this context, goes far beyond any moral ideas: Here we come to know the leader of a sect that glorifies pain and agony and longs for the total destruction of individuality. The believers are called the Nameless for they lose everything except the ability to give and receive—pain and agony. Their guru had once been the victim in a Nazi concentration camp, but the conclusions he drew from his painful experiences are not the fight against inhumanity but the celebration of pure and total agony. This is a truly radical model, and the film deals quite consistently with it: The female protagonist—the mother who seeks for her daughter—will finally realize that her ex-husband belongs to the cult and uses their daughter as a means to provide her with the greatest pain of all: She will lose her beloved a second time. The adolescent girl shoots herself in front of her mother (and that's the end of the film!). From this point of view everything that happened throughout the film has been in vain: The reporter dies in vain, the mother's hopes are destroyed. Her future is bleak. In Balaguero's film we are confronted with total nihilism. The world as he sees it is built on guilt and latent evil that can break through the walls at any time. It comes as no surprise that his follow-up circles around "darkness" itself ... the end of everything. Total nothingness.

In *Killing Words* (2002) by Laura Maná, the attractive psychiatrist Laura (Dario Grandinetti) is in a desperate condition: Bound to a chair by a kidnapper, she is forced to watch videos that show him as a vicious serial killer. At the same time he shows her his list of victims—and her name is already at the end. The killer begins to play a cruel game with her: If she wins, she will be free, but if she loses, he will extract one of her eyes. And so forth. This kind of sadistic cruelty seems essential to Catholic societies. It reminds us of the great success Mel Gibson's idea of *The Passion of the Christ* had in Latin America, Italy and Spain. Catholic-dominated culture seems obsessed with violent sacrifice, passionate suffering and redemption through violence. And the New Wave of Spanish Mystery Thrillers perfectly mirrors this moralistic excess.

Impulse (2002) by Miguel Alcantud shows some similarities to *Killing Words* but appears to be more of a psychological drama than a thriller. Here a young suicidal woman, Sara (Ana Risueno), witnesses an act of murder by a passionate serial killer, Jaime (Daniel Feire), an elementary teacher in his everyday life. The attractive and cultivated man pushes someone in front of an underground train. What appears to be an accident is actually part of a killing spree. Jaime has this impulse to kill people spontaneously, sometimes in a row, sometimes within several weeks. Later he collects the newspaper articles on his victims from the Internet. Supposedly out of her latent death wish, Sara starts to blackmail the killer by saying that she has filmed the murder. Between the two disturbed characters, a strange relationship begins to grow, one that circles around the fatal "impulse" to take lives. Secretly Sara hopes that Jaime will finally help her to find—death. This could have been a suspenseful thriller filled with sadomasochistic subtexts, etc., but turns out to be a very tame psychological drama about a lonely woman in trouble. Music (very jazzy), advanced photography, and eccentric editing contribute to an existential seriousness that finally damages the sensual and metaphorical impact of the idea. In the last frame Sara finally sits in the bathtub with the blade in her hand to slit her wrists while Jaime is filming her with a video-camera—but she refuses. This strange love between two people obsessed by death gave her power to live—a macabre ending in its own right.

Father, Son, Unholy Spirit

A dark male figure slowly walks through a dimly lit hallway toward us. Photographed from a low angle central perspective, such shots remind us of classical gothic horror films. They are also a key framing device in the Spanish mystery thriller, mainly focusing on one of the most important protagonists: the evil father. We see such shots in Jaume Balagero's *Darkness* (2002) and *The Nameless*, as these films build up the whole drama around the haunted, possessed and threatening father who is unable to protect his family.

Also based on a novel of British writer Ramsey Campbell (the author of *Nameless*) is *Second Name* (2001) by Paco Plaze, a dark psychological thriller that appears to be a kind of prototype of this New Wave along with *The Nameless*.

11. Spanish Mystery Thrillers (Marcus Stiglegger)

This time the plot is told from the perspective of young Daniella (Erica Prior), who used to have a very close relationship with her caring father. Right at the beginning of the movie this man commits suicide—seemingly out of the blue. Daniella is shocked—and even more so when his grave is discovered empty some days later. Since the police do not care too much about the vanished corpse, she decides to take the investigation into her own hands. Soon her father's body is found at an old cemetery, mutilated and bound with barbed wire to a piece of wood. Her research leads her to a strange professional hitman who collects photos of her, and to a religious sect called the Abrahamites. They believe that Biblical Abraham did in fact kill his first-born child, and that the Bible is interpreted erroneously. To gain success in life, the Abrahamites ritually kill their first-born children. And that's the key to both the evil-father theme and the solution of Daniella's father's suicide. The woman soon realizes that a lot of people are involved in the death cult, even her father who tried to run away from his "ritual duty." Like *The Nameless*, this film has a downbeat shock ending that seems to affirm the continuity of the Abrahamitic cult.

Paco Plaza, here making his feature film debut, does not have the stylistic strength of Balaguero, but *Second Name* succeeds in several aspects: It has a very bleak piano score, spiced up with gothic chorals; it makes effective use of makeup and violent special effects, and it features some impressive camera angles. Nevertheless the theme of the evil father is not very elaborate because it is split up into different characters. Nonetheless, *Second Name* presents a whole society based on the concept of a destructive patriarchy. From this perspective the female point of view makes absolute sense. Unfortunately, it is not Plaze's talent to build up tension as effectively as *The Nameless* or the supernatural examples mentioned above. The highlight may be Daniella's discovery of a dead child buried under a tree in the garden of her close relatives. At that point there seems no way out of this destructive system.

Jaume Balaguero's *Darkness* also culminates in a ritual executed by a possessed father getting deeper and deeper into a fatal system. But the genre context is completely different: The film simply works on the basis of elements taken out of *The Shining* (1980) by Stanley Kubrick and *The Amityville Horror* (1979) by Stuart Rosenberg. A family with two children moves into a Spanish country house where something seems wrong. The mentally unstable father drifts more and more into the obsessive idea that there is *something* in the past of the house, while the adolescent daughter Regina (Anna Paquin) discovers bruises on her younger brother's (Stephan Enquist) face and body. She tells her very passive and ignorant mother (Lena Olin) that she suspects her father of violating the boy. Annoyed by an aggressive father and an ignorant mother, Regina escapes to her Spanish boyfriend Carlos (Fele Martínez) to help her. As the film offers up some genre-quotes, director Balaguero is finally in his element: Connected with a scientist, a friend of the family (Giancarlo Giannini), the disturbing truth about the house is revealed. It was once owned by three strange women who used to perform human sacrifices in praise of the World Serpent (Uroboros). Beneath the living room floor is a ritual place where a number of young boys were sacrificed. When the last blood is spilled, darkness will cover the Earth. The father-turned-abuser in this case seems to be the last chosen high priest to close the circle. But things are not as they seem: We learn that it is not his son that has to die but he himself. The father is finally killed by his family when he becomes a threat to their lives. Unfortunately this preventive killing closes the circle, and finally darkness is raised. Rarely has a film bathed in such apocalyptic ideas: In the end, light simply disappears out of the frame. Total *Darkness* is raised. The cult of the evil father has succeeded. The supposed "bringer of life" is really the destroyer of everything.

At another place: Santiago de Compostela 2002. Jacobo (Juan Diego Botto), a young sculptor of twenty years, returns to his hometown after a long absence. His mother is mentally ill and lives in an asylum. Jacobo wants to care for her and visits her. In the asylum he meets some figures from his doomed past whom he would have preferred to forget. They remind him of strange incidents from which he has tried to escape his whole life: Xavier Villaverde's *When the Bell Chimed 13* (2002) finally turns out to be the ultimate evil-father drama. In the first sequence we see him as a young boy trying to copy the art of his father. When the father arrives he is dissatisfied with his son's work. Actually it is the night when he wants to leave his wife together with his son—"to protect him from the mentally unstable mother," as he says. But right at midnight, when the bell chimes, the mother seems to shoot her unfaithful husband. As Jacobo remembers, just at that time the bell chimed once more: 13 times. All his life he has secretly believed that this incident had been of supernatural origin. This belief is linked to his mother's obsession that her husband never really died and is haunting her with his "eyes in the walls" around her.

Jacobo soon meets the ghost of his father in an old cathedral where the sculptor was supposed to build a marble statue. The evil ancestor wants to force his son to fulfill the unfinished work. Jacobo—who is not as talented as his father—agrees. In a strange supernatural act their hands melt together within a clay sculpture. The young man is now obsessed by the ghost of his aggressive father. Not quite himself any more, he tries to rape the woman his father once loved. His mother dies of a heart attack, and the woman is killed by accident. Every act of resistance against the will of his father results in another catastrophe. But with the skill of his father's hands, Jacobo finally manages to finish the statue.

The film makes it increasingly clear that this is only one side of events:

Jacobo's point of view. A young girl who loves him tries to solve the mystery surrounding Jacobo and realizes with the help of a befriended psychiatrist that our antihero suffers from schizophrenia—like his mother. His father seems to live within him. Villaverde's direction shifts between supernatural horror and sophisticated psychological thriller. In the film's finale within the cathedral, we reach the level of latent guilt again: The bell did not actually chime 13 times. Between 12 and 1 there is one hour lost in Jacobo's memories. And the viewer can guess what really happened: The little boy killed his father himself—trying to stop the man from beating up his mother. When this truth is revealed, Jacobo is freed of his haunting visions. Or so it seems—for the final sequence shows him in his father's working place now threatening his own little son. But he again manages to keep control.

When the Bell Chimed 13 may not be as strong as its cinematic predecessors but this film works perfectly within the father-son-unholy spirit context: The conflict is being passed on from one generation to the next like a virus. Villaverde makes prominent use of sacral locations, especially the cathedral, where father and son create a huge crucifixion scene in white marble. Even the showdown takes place in the tower of the cathedral. The sacred place cannot protect the victims of destructive patriarchy.

The "Rightful Path"

As we have seen, the New Wave of Spanish Mystery Thrillers celebrates, in a very stylish and at the same time strikingly conservative way, the battle of occult versus Christian powers. They show a world of permanent temptation—the latent seduction to take the "wrong path" willingly. Even if they show characters with a connotation of "innocence"—e.g., the children—the seed of evil is already present. The innocent become guilty simply by being the tool of evil—as shown to great effect in the end of *The Nameless*. The only way to be granted redemption is through self-sacrifice, a totally violent act to purify the "stained" world.

Most of these Spanish thrillers avoid admitting that they are constructed within a system of Catholic guilt complexes. They focus on the stated opposite: the occult world, the shadow world, the twilight zone. In these destructive circles of fate, the protagonists get punished for their involvement in occult rituals and practices. On the visual level of the films, this is represented by a conflict of ancient symbolism and the icons of Christian belief. In this context, it is also quite very fascinating that, despite being mainstream films, the films discussed also avoid happy endings. In the end there is either the destruction of the protagonist's soul, ultimately his death, or—as in *Darkness*—apocalypse itself. Through the back door, a restrictive moral, a kind of reactionary "medieval" Christian *vision du monde*, sneaks in. And this is *truly* frightening.

12

The New Throwback: The Films of Dante Tomaselli

MATTHEW EDWARDS

Horror cinema once had the courage to provoke. The bulk of material currently produced, especially from Hollywood, simply retreads familiar ground. They replicate the successful formula of the slasher genre, except the level of violence is toned down. The new generation of horror films tend to have a polished MTV-style sheen, making it a much more marketable package for the 21st century cinemagoer. The films do not give rise to wider social or political issues (the original *Dawn of the Dead* is at its heart a critique on consumerism), or possess the fundamental desire to disturb the viewer. Worryingly, the new trend has seen horror cinema become more comedy-based. Horror cinema by its very nature is designed to unsettle. There are exceptions (*Evil Dead*), but those executives and producers who wield the power insist the two genres must unite—a delusional ideology. Horror cinema reduced to vox-pop entertainment. Non-conformity is the key reaction. The central idea for these new renegade filmmakers is to remain fiercely independent; to avoid being sucked into this whirlpool; to remain true to their vision.

Fighting against the corporations is Dante Tomaselli. His films are packed with disturbing and haunting imagery. By not complying with the mainstream, Tomaselli is forced to work on a restrictive budget. This does not deter him. This he turns into a positive. It gives him greater license to fulfill his vision. His imagination is allowed to flourish, his ideas explored without studio interference. Tomaselli has won many admirers, both on a critical and fan-based level, through his simple desire to get American horror cinema back on its limping feet.

Tomaselli's arrival on the horror scene has had an immediate impact. Representing a refreshing change of pace, his features *Desecration* and *Horror* offer an alternative viewing experience to the jaded horror fan. Distrustful of modern approaches towards horror filmmaking, Tomaselli influences have stemmed from a fascination with seventies and eighties horror movies and through nightmares that plagued him throughout childhood. Recognizing the need to return to horror's roots, Tomaselli's films are drenched in atmosphere and suspense—his method of creating tension and horror. He is a self-confessed surrealist, and the non-linear approach his films employ allows Tomaselli to take the material into any direction he wishes. Not reined in by the constraints of a linear narrative, Tomaselli is free to explore territories of horror cinema that have been rarely tackled since the giddy horror boom of the seventies and early eighties.

For all the praise heaped onto Tomaselli, many critics are quick to point out that his films are reminiscent of the work of Italian horror director Dario Argento, with his expressionistic style and the use of vibrant and fluorescent visuals. Establishing a correlation is possible, yet such comparisons of Tomaselli and Argento are slightly misjudged. As Tomaselli pointed out to me, he was becoming tired of the comparisons made between himself and Italian horror icons Argento, Bava and Fulci, considering he wasn't even exposed to their work until his early twenties. In understanding Tomaselli's work it becomes more apparent that he has taken on board the key areas of horror cinema and woven them into a set of deeply personal nightmares, in an attempt to replicate them on screen. His style therefore is instinctual. Tomaselli is a throwback in the sense he has pulled out the strands that made seventies and eighties horror cinema so infamous, but ingrained this with a fresh new perspective.

Born in Paterson, New Jersey, on October 29, 1969, Tomaselli mostly spent his childhood years watching horror movies. Feeding his love, Tomaselli's mother would regularly take him to local theaters to check out the new releases. This experience taught him which concepts worked in horror cinema, eventually weaving them into his own personal style. Another factor that helped lead Tomaselli into filmmaking, giving him the belief and drive that he could achieve his ambition: His cousin Alfred Sole had directed the genre classic *Alice Sweet Alice*. Having studied filmmaking at Pratt Institute in Brooklyn, Tomaselli directed the short film *Desecration*, before expanding the original idea into his debut feature.

Tomaselli's work can be broken down into a number of key components that associate him more firmly with seventies and eighties ideas towards horror filmmaking. By dissecting Tomaselli's method of portraying horror, his visual style, his interpretation of nightmares and his use of music, we can consider more fully the argument that Tomaselli is an important emergence in American horror cinema who has taken the ethics used by past filmmakers and brought forth a new breed of horror film.

The trap many filmmakers fall into is the mistaken belief that gross-out special effects and/or outrageously grotesque violence is the only way to create cinematic horror. Realism in the portrayal of violence has been an effective method for filmmakers when depicting the horrors of crime and brutality. Equally, too much reliance has been placed on subjecting the viewer to disconcerting images, as a means of provoking a reaction—usually one of disgust, instead of the intended idea of instilling fear into the audience. Tomaselli opts for a differing cinematic experience, conjuring up horror and a brooding menace from the most unlikely of sources.

When considering the genre classics of horror cinema, taking *Halloween*, *The Shining* and *The Texas Chain Saw Massacre* as examples, the violence is mostly implied instead of being explicitly shown. In fact, the splatter quota is relatively low in these films, thus signifying that to have achieved their status as recognized classics of both their genres and as cinematic entries, then they have derived their impact from other, and more successful, sources. By incorporating a number of less obvious elements, to strategically accentuate the horror, this has acted as a better tool for filmmakers working within this field.

Studying the features *Desecration* and *Horror*, similarities can be pulled from Tomaselli's work displaying an understanding of how *classic* horror films are constructed. As we have previously acknowledged, less is more. Leaving the viewer to fill in the gaps or slightly altercating reality and our perception, as a way of violating our senses, is the mark of a good horror filmmaker. Having established a formula, it is important therefore to evidence the connections between the format employed in classic horror films, and Tomaselli's work.

This relationship between Tomaselli's work and classic horror films can be determined in Tomaselli's skill at conjuring sudden pangs of horror derived from less obvious sources, turning what can be deemed as normal practices or objects into artifacts with the capacity of possessing a sinister and twisted edge. Tobe Hooper's *Poltergeist* illustrates this point. During the poltergeist's first real manifestation, Hooper effectively ups the ante through the simple use of a clown-like doll. It is a standard item in many children's toy boxes, yet it holds the unnerving qualities that can easily de-stabilize the audience. Slumped on a chair in a corner of the room, and despite its manic expression, the toy offers little threat, or is deemed un-noteworthy in relation to the other toys. The mood changes sharply when the young child is alone in his darkened room. Against the backdrop of a raging storm, the clown suddenly assumes qualities that distort our perception of the object. As light momentarily dances across the doll, the clown's fixed eyes and inscrutable grin hint towards the pending horror that is ready to ignite.

The idea that through the playful manipulation of our senses, by means of transporting objects that on the surface pose little significance into something that has the ability to bore into our psyche and disturb, can be considered a much better method of getting under the spectators' skin. After watching *Poltergeist*, how many people would feel comfortable keeping a doll of a clown in their room? In both *Desecration* and *Horror*, Tomaselli likewise uses familiar objects, or childhood toys, as a means of driving conflicting emotions from his viewers. When we should be seeing items that bring pleasure or fondness, instead they are presented in a manner that conveys the exact opposite; for example in *Horror* Tomaselli's use of Halloween lanterns and paintings is used to startling effect.

In *Desecration* this is revealed in a scene where we see our young protagonist Bobby locked in a cage (draped in a diaper), inside a room filled with over-exaggerated childhood objects, making it seem like he has been trapped within a psychedelic funhouse. Giant toy blocks, balloons and dolls parade throughout the room, while an over-sized Jack in the Box springs maniacally up and down in a corner. The eerie nature of this scene is further accentuated when Bobby's mother enters the room, holding two balloons and a milk bottle. Yet, this is no ordinary feeding time as the mother kneels next to the cage and begins to spray her child with the milk, reveling in the torture she is administering. The central idea of the mother tending to her child, feeding her newborn within the child's nursery, has been turned on its head. Instead we are treated to this freaky act and immediately caught off guard. She does not offer her son protection or love, our perception of her is violated, and we view her as a threat.

This brings forward an interesting point. In the great traditions of horror cinema, the best films have always held a physical threat, whether implied or more explicitly revealed. *Halloween* and *The Shining* are fine examples of this idea. What is more important to consider, is that in both these cases the threat comes from within the nuclear family.

This same idea is explored by Tomaselli in both *Desecration* and *Horror*. Whereas the conventional idea that the family is symbolic of security, comfort, and love, this notion has been turned upside down, to the extent where the family is perceived as mistrustful and suspicious, with the potential to inflict pain on their loved ones. In *Desecration* Tomaselli explores the relationship between a young adolescent boy and his long-dead mother, culminating in a trip into Hell to confront her. In *Horror* our young protagonist Grace is enslaved by her parents through a combination of drug addiction and psychic brainwashing. Her only savior seems to be her grandfather, who reveals the true nature of her parents' warped pastimes. However Grace is ultimately betrayed when his true identity is revealed: He too is a sadist who tortures Grace with the same joy as her parents.

Commenting on both films, we can clearly establish that their protagonists are not part of a stable family unit, but a family unit that is broken and at conflict. Through this instability Tomaselli is able to manipulate certain family traditions and practices, presenting them in a weirdly creepy and offbeat fashion. In one instance in *Horror* we witness Grace in hospital, receiving a visit from her father. Clearly not distressed, and lacking any emotion, the father leans over his daughter and whispers, "I am going to stay here with you tonight," before administering an incestuous kiss. Grace's parents are painted as sadistic and abusive, ready to violate her at any point. This immediately identifies the family as a severe threat, demonstrated further in *Horror* when we witness both parents entering Grace's room and drugging her. What makes this an ordeal is that both the parents gleefully enjoy this ritual, culminating in the father licking the syringe he has just used to administer drugs into his daughter.

Tomaselli's exploration of this theme, the threat coming from within the family base, connects with his own personal experiences as Tomaselli has asserted in many interviews that he was constantly in conflict with his father. This may account for the reoccurrence of this theme in Tomaselli's work, as the family is not portrayed with any unique bond, but a base with a simmering undercurrent that is ready to boil. Whether this theme is deliberate or subconscious, what we can ascertain is that Tomaselli's films partly concern the breakdown of the family unit, and the psychological effects that this can have. As the family base disintegrates, paranoia and fear invade, where the final climax inevitability turns into violence and destruction.

A characteristic trait that occupies the work of Dante Tomaselli is his artistic visuals and use of atmosphere. This directorial style has been influential in the disturbing and shocking imagery within his films. Tomaselli's aesthetic approach differs greatly from his contemporaries. Whereas a masked murderer slicing through victims is about as scary as Ed Wood's awful classic *Plan 9 from Outer Space*, in contrast the image in *Desecration* of a faceless nun in the mist most definitely is scary. Both *Desecration* and *Horror* contain numerous visually stylized set-pieces that reinforce the notion that horror cinema is at its most effective when combining these elements cohesively, instead of resulting to cliché through poorly executed cinematic offerings that offer little more than half-naked women being stalked and butchered. American horror cinema is still under the misguided belief that churning out horror films of this type is the best practice, when in reality they are setting themselves up for ridicule. The stalk and slasher genre had its glory days back in the seventies and eighties, but now the whole idea seems contrived and lame. The *Scream* films merely parodied the genre, mocking the narrative devices these films used—and inadvertently kickstarted a whole string of films destined to go no further than the bargain bin of numerous rental outlets.

Through close scrutiny of Tomaselli's work we can identify specific examples that rightfully distinguish Tomaselli as a director with flair, when stylizing sequences that are both visually arresting and heavy on atmosphere. Certain examples immediately spring to mind, and can be deemed genuinely

12. The Films of Dante Tomaselli (Matthew Edwards) 117

The sadists are loose in Satan's playground. Actress Felissa Rose, of *Sleepaway Camp* fame, in a tight spot in Dante Tomaselli's gothic nightmare *Satan's Playground* (courtesy Dante Tomaselli).

frightening moments. In one *Horror* scene we see Grace being chased by her mother. Fleeing down a flight of stairs, Grace rushes towards the front door, only to find it locked. Tomaselli has edited this scene in a manner that incorporates interesting shots that heighten its weird and horrifying nature. The first establishing shot sees the camera static as we witness Grace charging down a flight of spiraling stairs, closely followed by her mother. The next shot sees the camera positioned at the foot of the staircase, where the chase is seamlessly continued. Fairly standard so far, yet interestingly Tomaselli now adopts a combination of point of view shots that elevates the sequence into more terrifying realms. The first shot implies that we are looking through the mother's eyes as she is racing towards her daughter, while the shot that immediately follows indicates we are seeing this from Grace's perspective. Therefore we clearly see the reactions of both the prey and the predator. The terrified expression of Grace is juxtaposed with the eerie sight of her mother's twisted smile and dead eyes. Furthermore, there is an unearthly and supernatural quality that is present. Tomaselli's camera glides effortlessly down the hall, giving off an aura that the mother is floating, therefore adding to the nightmarish effect of this scene.

It is fair to comment that both *Desecration* and *Horror* rely exclusively on their visuals, incorporating gothic tendencies fused with the surreal use of pop-art colors. Tomaselli mainly utilizes icy blue tones and fluorescent reds in his work, drenching the landscape with an expressionist sense of the macabre. A swirling mist is everpresent, cutting up the landscape, allowing for unknown forces to lurk within the shadows. This is best represented in a *Horror* scene where we witness a woman running out into a snowswept forest, frantically trying to flag down a passing car. A solitary tree stands in the middle of the frame, from which a hooded figure emerges, clutching a spade. This unexpected moment is decidedly creepy, offset even more by the strange atmosphere. The pure white snow has been replaced with a cold blue glaze, while the tree resembles a black monolith, devoid of character. The faceless killer emerges nonchalantly, ready for the kill.

Part of the genetic make-up of Tomaselli's films stems from nightmares from his boyhood and adolescent years. These nightmares have impacted greatly on Tomaselli's work to the point that he has looked to interpret them within the framework of his own movies. *Desecration* and *Horror* are punctuated with numerous dream sequences, indicating justifiably that Tomaselli has set about to replicate the feel of these experiences. In many respects we could argue that Tomaselli's films are essentially his way of capturing and painting these experiences onto celluloid. On many occasions Tomaselli has referred to these nightmares as being very vivid and real, and left a clear imprint within his psyche. We can argue that the nightmares we see in both *Desecration* and *Horror* are effectively his visual interpretation of the traumatic dreams he frequently encountered as a youngster. Considering that Tomaselli layers and constructs his film around these dreams and nightmares is suggestive of their key importance within the context of his films. Instead of using them for purely a narrative function, Tomaselli essentially propels his films into motion by their inclusion. Their function is to add a surrealist element into the proceedings, and to make the viewer wonder, "Is this real or not." Such is the structure of Tomaselli films that we begin to question whether what we are witnessing is real or the psychological nightmares of our particular protagonist. This leads to multiple interpretations, giving the viewer greater license to absorb and reflect on the film, instead of having to endure a horror film that offers little in thought and follows the well-trodden path so many other films have followed.

Tomaselli's nightmares were both nasty and disturbing in content, so it seems quite apt that they represent some of the most unnerving and frightening aspects of his work. Both *Desecration* and *Horror* contain some truly weird and frightening dream sequences. In particular, *Desecration* reveals one memorable nightmarish dream where we witness a nun being ravaged by two freaky circus clowns. Situated behind an iron gate, and surrounded in a thick pink mist, the nun frantically clutches onto the railings attempting to pry them open. The clowns descend onto her like starved vultures; her habit stained with blood. The macabre final shot sees the clowns slowly opening the iron gate for her, but her lifeless eyes and ghastly demeanor reveal she is no longer of this world—she is undead.

Another important feature in the films of Dante Tomaselli is his use of music as a means of increasing their haunting nature. As a general rule, music can lend itself superbly to horror pictures, creating the right mood and atmosphere when used correctly. In Hollywood's horror cinema their manifesto towards music reveals that its design is to specifically dictate how you should feel. During quiet and romantic interludes the music suitably fits the mood. Likewise, during moments intended to provide shocks, this is aptly represented with quick short-fire bursts of music. In contrast, influential soundtracks like *Halloween*, *The Exorcist* (through the use of Mike Oldfield's *Tubular Bells*) and *Suspiria* all feature a particular signature song that sets the tone for the movie. What defines *Suspiria* as one of the scariest movies of all time is Goblin's legendary soundtrack, both deafening and brimming with a suitably eerie texture, making it sometimes sound like a perverse nursery song. Tomaselli has recognized the importance of the soundtrack, realizing that both the marriage of visuals and music is fundamental in horror cinema. His dedication to ensuring that both merge together seamlessly is a testimony to his commitment. Composing and designing his own soundtracks, through layering synth tones and samples, has helped his films take on a more trancelike feel, further accentuating the horror.

Operating outside the commercial mainstream has undeniably allowed Tomaselli to compose films that utilize the basic rudimentary principles of classical horror filmmaking. This is where Tomaselli has excelled. By incorporating this retro stance into his directorial and narrative style, he has conjured moments that get beneath the skin of the viewer, consequently leaving a lasting impression. Painting the frames with haunting images that strike a powerful chord with the spectator, reflects a filmmaker more concerned with the mechanics of horror cinema, as opposed to an onslaught of visceral imagery.

Tomaselli's latest offering *Satan's Playground* indicates that Tomaselli's creative vision is pulling together more with each passing picture. On one level *Satan's Playground*'s premise seems to be a nod to *The Texas Chain Saw Massacre* and *Evil Dead*, yet the wave after wave of gloomy and macabre imagery is suggestive that *Satan's Playground* has the potential to be much more than a lame rehash of horror cinema's most established films. *Satan's Playground* is certainly Tomaselli's most stylized work. We witness the camera methodically creeping through New Jersey's Pine Forest, or eerily gliding down half-lit corridors, that hint towards an unknown presence, lurking, waiting to attack. This idea, as we have already discussed, generates far more horror, by the simple means of signaling a perceived threat, but *not* to illustrate or reveal the true nature until the climax.

Demonic daughter! Actress Christie Sanford as the evil daughter in *Satan's Playground*. Sanford has appeared in Dante Tomaselli's two previous features, *Horror* and *Desecration* (courtesy Dante Tomaselli).

Satan's Playground is very much retro in style and execution, as the film is representative of many elements that can be associated with classics of horror cinema. We can establish similar tracking shots and point-of-view shots that have been inspired by *Evil Dead*, but Tomaselli has injected a fresh perspective onto a widely copied shot, culminating in an inventive variation. Although the film displays *Evil Dead*-esque moments, in that we witness a character being chased through the woods by an unknown force, Tomaselli expands on this style of filmmaking by having his camera sweeping down from the pine trees, attacking the victims. *Satan's Playground* does reveal a scene straight out of *The Shining*, where our protagonist is locked in a small room and an axe comes crashing through the door. You kind of expect to see Jack Nicholson peer through the gaping hole. This is not implying that plagiarism is at hand. It merely serves to point out that we have gone full circle, by means that the new generation has reinterpreted styles and concepts, as a means of creating original work. All artists learn from others—it's an essential component that feeds and inspires our own creativity.

Dante Tomaselli is an interesting anomaly in American horror cinema: He understands the basic principles of horror filmmaking as a means of extracting the correct emotions from his audience, without pandering to more conventional tactics of spraying the screen with graphically ripe images. Splatter

12. The Films of Dante Tomaselli (Matthew Edwards) 121

films rightfully have a place in cinema, as demonstrated by successful filmmakers like Herschell Gordon Lewis, primarily because they have recognized the need for their work to not be taken too seriously. It has been unsurprising then that critics have cast their critical eyes upon Tomaselli's films with some authority. Tomaselli's work has its cinematic roots more closely associated with the horror cinema of yesteryear, as opposed to the current breed of offerings that pour out from the American market. Tomaselli's work is retro in style and structure, taking what was successful during horror cinema's glory days and simply transporting it into contemporary filmmaking.

Tomaselli's penetration into the horror community has been more noticeable by his love of the genre, and his clear manifesto—to create a body of work that sets out to embed a sense of dread and fear into the spectator. Both *Horror* and *Desecration* display the key elements required to create a successful horror picture—suspense, shocks, gore and, to some degree, a sense of realism. *Desecration* and *Horror* prove that Tomaselli is an exciting discovery. The promising nature of his work suggests that if Tomaselli can remain true to his artistic sensibilities, it will only be a matter of time before he delivers a film on a par with the retro horror classics he so treasures.

Tomaselli regular Danny Lopez with the late Irma St. Paule in *Satan's Playground*. Irma St. Paule also appeared in Dante Tomaselli's debut feature *Desecration*. She sadly passed away on 6th January 2007 (courtesy Dante Tomaselli).

An Interview with Dante Tomaselli

MATTHEW EDWARDS: *Do you feel like you're part of a new vanguard of filmmakers that are reacting against the current trend of "horror movies"?*

DANTE TOMASELLI: At this point, yes I do. But then again, I'm a surrealist first ... a filmmaker second. So I march to the beat of my own drummer anyway. But yeah, I hate most modern horror films; they're not even real horror films anyway, in my opinion. All the good ones stopped around the mid- to late eighties. *Hellraiser* was the last great one. I do feel part of this new wave of horror filmmakers. I want to try to help bring back true horror.

Your three films have been strictly independent features, but interestingly they have all gained widespread acclaim and interest. How have you managed to provoke interest in your work?

I think maybe because I am sticking to my guns and making the movies I want to make. And maybe there's a connective style that some people appreciate, if you're into dreamlike movies. I don't know. I definitely only want to make horror films. That's where my passion is. There's really so much to explore. I'm so fascinated by the supernatural! I would like to investigate ghosts, haunted houses as an alternative career. Parapsychology is very interesting. All my films are explorations into the supernatural and the paranormal. You can always be sure that I'll be trying to make each film scarier than the last. I think I am a unique director in the sense that—that is my goal, aside from translating my nightmares. I want each film to be more frightening. It's like each film is a funhouse ride for me. Of course I want each new one to be more effective.

How much of a struggle is it for you to compete against glossy high-budgeted horror films like the Scream *franchise and* Jeepers Creepers? *Do you even care whether you do or not?*

Oh, I don't think about other films at all. I'm completely in the mindset of the movie I want to make. I don't feel any sense of competition, especially since those films you mentioned cost many millions. I like being different; I want my films to be an alternative to what's out there in the horror world. I don't pay attention to trends. I know what I like. I'm stuck in the seventies, early eighties.

I do get a sense that your films are trying to connect back with seventies and eighties horror cinema, with their strong emphasis on atmosphere, tension and visuals as shock tactics—instead of the tried-and-tested formula of blood and guts. This I believe has made you one of the most interesting new filmmakers to have emerged out of American independent cinema. Are you aware of your importance as a filmmaker, especially to the horror community?

Thanks. Ummm ... yes and no ... I feel I am not really embraced by magazines like *Fangoria*. Yeah, I'll get a one-page article here and there when the DVD is released by Image or Elite but ... well ... I get e-mails a lot from people wondering why I'm not in there more. And I don't know how to answer them. So I feel there is this club that I am not a part of. I mean ... I never get mentioned when [*Fangoria* editor Tony] Timpone talks about the "new wave of horror filmmakers." You know the names ... I don't even have to tell you. I'm always left out. Maybe he's waiting for me to make a hit, then things will be different ... hmm. *Rue Morgue* shows their support. And of course, *Deep Red* magazine ... Chas Balun was one of the earliest supporters of my work. And I am really grateful, because I always loved reading his bombastic articles in *Gorezone* magazine growing up. For as many good reviews that I get, there are lots of critics who hate me and my films with a passion. I seem to polarize audiences. So I guess the answer is that I feel a mixture of insecurity and, I guess, to some degree, a sense of confidence about my status in the horror community. I'm an outsider. I always will be. Astrologically, I'm a Scorpio with my Sun in the First House.

Talk us through the filming process of your latest film Satan's Playground. *Did working on a tight budget hinder the production at all?*

Actually *Satan's Playground* had my highest budget of all so far ... somewhere around $500,000. But of course, in the scheme of things, $500,000 is

Actress Ellen Sandweiss, star of *Evil Dead*, in Dante Tomaselli's brilliant horror shocker *Satan's Playground* (courtesy Dante Tomaselli).

nothing compared to how much most features cost. I think, with horror films, working on a relatively low budget is a good thing. Think of all the classics ... *Night of the Living Dead, Halloween, Phantasm, Texas Chain Saw Massacre* ... I can go on. But you get the point ... all low-budget and all quality scary movies. But if you want to make a really classy movie, something ultra-polished like *The Shining, The Changeling, The Exorcist, The Omen* ... you'll need a few million at least.

The filming process? Basically I start off with a script that I'm passionate about, something I feel I need to make. Then I go and find the appropriate actors, because you need a package—something to show to the executive producer or investors. Finally, hopefully things gel into me actually making the movie—through the sheer force of my will! I start hunting for locations. That's the fun part. For *Desecration*, I explored places from my childhood, like Paterson, New Jersey. With *Horror*, I got to explore a very gothic area of upstate New York, called Warwick ... very Salem Witch Trial–like ... lots of rolling hills and infinite horizons. And for *Satan's Playground*, I got to explore the creepy area known as the Pine Barrens in New Jersey. A huge stretch of woods, with the legend of the Jersey Devil alive and thriving. So, once I lock down on locations, I start making presentations to an executive producer, telling them I'm basically ready to go. Once it's given the green light, I work with the cinematographer and we storyboard for about a month. All the while I'm having rehearsals with the actors and attending auditions for roles that haven't been filled. I work with the art department and special effects supervisor and try to tell them my vision ... what I am seeing. Finally, the shoot date looms closer and it's usually pushed back a bit, sometimes a month or two or more. It feels very organic ... and comes alive when it wants to. So many elements have to be set in place. After principal photography, I start to get to know the footage inside and out. I become obsessed with it. At the same time, I'm planning the soundtrack, working with different composers and designing soundscapes. Finally, when picture edit is locked, I start the sound mix, which is my favorite part, actually.

You work with a close-knit group of people on your films. Is this an essential component for any independent filmmaker?

I'm not sure. But it works for me. I'm very loyal too. I do expect the same back. It's a synergy that has to exist, or it won't work at all. I especially enjoy working with my script supervisor, the art department, the cinematographer, the effects supervisor, assistant director and on set with the actors. Once it's shot, "in the can" as they say, I love the period of working with my editor. But like I said, hands down, my favorite part of the whole filmmaking process is working on the sound mix. I love designing the soundtrack.

Your next proposed project is a sequel to your cousin's film Alice Sweet Alice.

Is there a sense of pressure on you to deliver a film on a par with what has been regarded as a masterpiece of horror cinema?

I really can't speak for that film yet, because I am finishing off *Satan's Playground*. And, mainly because I've decided that I want my next film to be *The Ocean*, a supernatural horror film set on an island. There will be demonic possessions, riptides, nature running amok and, at the core, a haunting brought on by grief and guilt.

How easy is it for you now to get your films funded? Are there many avenues open to horror filmmakers?

Hopefully, it'll get easier. I will pursue it relentlessly! I have a feeling I'll always somehow get the money I need to make the movies I want. The horror movies I want. As long as I keep them relatively low-budget.

Do you intend to keep working within the confines of independent cinema, or is the lure of Hollywood too tempting?

Independent cinema. I need a degree of creative control. I'm more impressed by Felissa Rose or Ellen Sandweiss than Meryl Streep.

13

Godspeed You! Black Emperor and the Japanese Underground Biker Phenomenon

Matthew Edwards

During the 1950s, at the height of the Hell's Angels craze in the United States, Japanese society witnessed the rise in a new underground phenomenon that spread its way across the country's major metropolises. Groups of biker gangs suddenly surfaced in major cities like Tokyo and Kyoto, yet they were unlike their American counterparts, from whom their inspiration derived. In the United States, American bikers saw riding as a lifestyle; a way of life. Japanese gangs represented more of a meeting ground for disaffected youths and the unemployed. Known as Boso-zoku gangs in Japan, their longevity has seen them slowly evolve from petty crooks and a public nuisance towards affiliations with the Yakuza and violent crime. By the early 21st century a number of high-profile incidents saw a national crackdown on the Boso-zoku biker gangs. The larger cities introduced new laws to combat biker gatherings, effectively banning them. Fines were imposed, and in some extreme cases (in cities like Hiroshima which had introduced zero tolerance measures), six-month jail sentences were handed out.

They were originally viewed as nothing more than night-time rebels, but this view has been radically reassessed as violent crime has soared. Murder amongst rival biker gangs has become a common occurrence. In Tokyo a teenager was beaten to death after he was mistakenly identified as a gang member, while in Nagano, eight bikers were imprisoned for battering a rival to death. This blazing trail of violence and murder reached boiling point in November 2002, when motorist Eiju Cho made the mistake of confronting a biker gang named the Dragons after they had deliberately clogged up traffic. Surrounded, he was pushed to the ground and beaten and stabbed to death by 30 members of the gang. Such was the climate; a crackdown was inevitable.

Yet, when placing the biker phenomenon in a wider historical context, such extreme levels of violence seem absent from past generations, indicating that this is more a contemporary problem that is infecting Japanese society (or certainly an issue that has been sensationalized by the Japanese media). Fistfights have now been replaced with a whole array of weaponry such as baseball bats, steel pipes and knives.

Aside from the book *Boso-zoku* by photographer Masayuka Yoshinaga, very little has been documented on their day-to-day activities, especially outside of their homeland. Through seminal Japanese films such as *Burst City*, Sogo Ishii's *Crazy Thunder Road* and Katsuhiro Otomo's *Akira*, some insight was given into the nature of the riders and their gangs, their street fights and the general havoc they create on Japan's streets; these films by their very nature are intended to focus more on the exploitative elements of the biker gangs. The seventies also saw the arrival of Teruo Ishii's successful series *Detonation* (Bakuhatsu!) based on the biker gangs. Yet the best representation of the biker culture comes from an obscure and decidedly rare 1976 Japanese documentary by Mitsuo Yanagimachi, fabulously entitled *Godspeed You! Black Emperor* (*Baraku Emperoru*).

The name *Godspeed You! Black Emperor* is widely recognized, primarily through the legendary instrumental band from Montreal, Canada. Taking their name from Yanagimachi's film, the band was championed by such publications as the *NME* when they released their classic debut album *f# a# ∞*, a beautiful sound score of aching violins and raging guitars. Subsequent albums *Lift yr skinny fists, like antennas to heaven!* and *Yanqui u.x.o* further cemented their position as one of the most influential bands to have emerged during the last decade. Their songs resemble beautifully lost soundtracks for abandoned films, their songs slowly building before a crashing crescendo. Their prominence was further enhanced when Danny Boyle used the segment *The Sad Mafioso*, from the track *East Hastings*, during his apocalyptic zombie film *28 Days Later*. Because they lifted their name from Yanagimachi's documentary film it has become a highly sought-after item, yet any firm reviews or film criticism on *Godspeed You! Black Emperor* remains non-existent.

Shot in black and white on grainy 16mm film, *Godspeed You! Black Emperor* charts the exploits of the Japanese biker gang The Black Emperors, documenting their existence from the make-up of the group, its hierarchy, and their run-ins with the law. Yanagimachi was given free rein to film just about every aspect of the gang. Therefore his documentary manages to escape from the confines of the biker gang itself, giving us access to, and shedding valuable light on, certain gang members' personal lives. Yanagimachi also treats us to interviews with family members, who give their perspective on their children's activities. Through this more candid approach, Yanagimachi allows the audience to understand what drives adolescents to join biker gangs, invariably an outlet to escape their personal and family problems.

The opening frames of *Godspeed You! Black Emperor* are extremely chaotic. Yanagimachi's camera roams freely as The Black Emperors clash with police, who attempt to put a stop to their illegal gathering. As the police act to disperse the group, The Black Emperors become more confrontational, goading the police with taunts: "You wanna fight?" and "I'll smash your balls." Between these jibes, Yanagimachi cuts to an officer arriving in riot gear, clutching a shield. The leader of The Black Emperors hollers in the face of an officer: "My name is none of your concern. I'm [the] leader of the riders here. You can't beat me." The gang screams and shouts childishly, before Yanagimachi cuts to an extended montage of The Black Emperors riding off in a magnificent procession.

This opening segment perfectly juxtaposes both the good and bad qualities of the biker groups. Our first introduction to The Black Emperors forces us to formulate an opinion shared with a majority of Japanese society, that these biker gangs are unruly hoods, intent on causing disruption to the general public. The opening shots portray the gang members with little grace, as they come across as aggressive, arrogant and juvenile. They lack any respect for authority or society in general. They band together within their tightly knit group: social outcasts fighting against the system. What immediately follows this is a number of shots highlighting the impressive spectacle of biker gangs on the move. With headlamps flashing directly into the lens of the camera, the bikers ride off, waving and smiling, each readily accepting their moment of fame on celluloid. The mere sight of The Black Emperors weaving through the streets is inspiring, as the hundred-strong group rides en masse, hogging the roads, no doubt to the consternation of the other motorists. There is an element of coolness, and a sense of belonging. Glimpses of The Black Emperors' uniform are caught, although most establishing shots feature a precession of faceless riders, their features hidden by the violent glare from their lights.

As the credits fade to black, the next sequence introduces us to the biker gang, this time in the more intimate surroundings of the Hanaya social club, The Black Emperors base. Here, Yanagimachi films the initiation of a new gang member. At only seventeen, the young man looks shy and nervous standing in front of the established members of the group. After his introduction, the gang's most prominent members introduce themselves. First we meet Decko, who proudly proclaims that he is jobless and lives in a tunnel. Next we meet Takahashi, Kanehara and Pants, a nickname given to this rider due to his love of pornography. They are unemployed and live in Shinjuku. All members seem to have a fascination for Nazi iconography, either by painting swastikas on their bikes or on their heads, or through Hitler impersonations.

Within the context of the film, this scene is highly crucial in demonstrating the lifestyle and the togetherness of the biker gangs. All share the common trait of being jobless, stuck in a rut that seems to be everlasting. The audience is struck by the close bond the key members have with one another. They joke and feel at ease in each other's company, always hanging out together. The Black Emperors are seemingly a family unit, looking out for one another, warning their riders of rival gangs and to ignore the police.

Yanagimachi then cleverly contrasts this togetherness by focusing the next segment purely on Decko. Contrary to his claim of living in a tunnel, Decko is seen to be living with his parents. His demeanor is in stark difference to that at the Hanaya. He now seems a pale character compared to our first glimpses of him. He stares vacantly at the television screen, taking the occasional drag on his cigarette. We learn that he was busted by the police for gathering with weapons, and has been served a notice of judgment. He stands accused of destroying a taxi, but denies any involvement. Yanagimachi asks whether he is concerned that he may well be sent to reform school or, even worse, prison. Unfazed by the entire incident, Decko seems confident that the worst that will happen is that he will be tailed by a probation officer.

During this conversation, what comes to light is the lack of love and support Decko feels he receives from his parents. He claims his mother doesn't care and that his father is out to make sure he goes down. He labels them as bad parents who are unconcerned with his welfare. We see Decko at conflict with his mother, over the issue of her attending his court judgment with him. In a further interview with Decko he actually looks agitated, believing that his father told officers to keep him in jail the night of his original bust. Decko informs us that he could have killed his father for that.

It would have been easy for Yanagimachi to accept Decko's perception of events, and comment that the biker gangs largely come from dysfunctional families, hence their decline into petty crime and violence: But he opts for clarity, as there are two sides to every tale. Trying to remain objective, Yanagimachi interviews Decko's parents, allowing them the opportunity to defend themselves against Decko's allegations. Both give their version of events, with the father stating he quizzed the officers as to why his son was arrested. Challenging their decision for arresting him for "merely hanging with hoods," he states that he asked the police to release his son immediately. Refusing also to apologize for his son's actions, the father points out that he criticized the police, and says that Decko heard him do so. Decko's father continues that, although he recognizes his son is a bad boy, he must protect him from the police.

What is evident is that there seems to be little dialogue between the two parties. Decko feels his father has let him down, yet in contrast, his father believes that he beat the police, and that Decko is aware of this. This confusion and lack of harmony within the family base is revealing as to why so many disillusioned youths join such gangs. Regardless of what party is giving us the most truthful account, the upshot of this is that Decko lacks the encouragement and guidance his parents should be offering him. His trip to Tokyo District Court ends merely in a ticking off, and a driving ban, which Decko dismissively shrugs off. Greeted outside the court by a fellow gang member, it seems Decko has learned nothing from this episode.

Yanagimachi cuts directly to a Black Emperor meeting; some members of the group seem concerned by the lack of commitment by other members. The spokesperson says that The Black Emperors seem to be split into two parties, those who come daily and those who turn up sporadically. The spokesman continues that the group must deepen their friendship, as they have a duty not to let their seniors down and to keep the group running. Suddenly a quick cut sends us back out into the dead of night, as The Black Emperors prepare for another gathering. The trend of the group being stopped and searched by the police continues, with certain members yelling "He's touching my balls" as they are frisked. As the riders move on, Yanagimachi continues with his unique brand of guerrilla filmmaking, as his cameraman rides with The Black Emperors, giving viewers the sense that they too are part of the group, as they weave in and out of the busy Tokyo traffic. Incorporating this technique into the film, Yanagimachi is conveying the thrill the riders experience, allowing the viewer to understand the attraction of being a part of this club. The riders sound their horns with glee; the occasional dart of light illuminates various riders, their faces making it clear they are reveling in the moment.

On this occasion the gang stops for a group huddle. There is the distinct possibility of a gang fight. Some members listen tentatively; others mill around, barely paying attention. Geared up for a fight, the group members once again mount their motorcycles. As the camera glides past the riders, all the motorcyclists sport bandanas. Somewhat confusingly, Yanagimachi switches to another group huddle. We are unsure whether this is the same night or not. This time the group is advised to avoid trouble with the cops: "We fight sometimes, but we aren't gangsters." This speech raises an interesting point: Although the biker gangs did get involved in a few scrapes, the riders themselves did not set out to become involved in major crime. While they were disruptive, they seemed conscious that there is a fine line between what is deemed acceptable and what is deemed not. This is what sets the previous generations of biker gangs apart from their contemporaries. Worryingly, today's biker gangs have become more obsessed with violence, as the spate of inter-gang killings has risen to alarming levels. If the Japanese media are to be believed, the 21st century biker members have ties with major crime syndicates, with many progressing from bikers into full Yakuza members.

The second half of the film is filled at first with various fodder footage, before we convene with The Black Emperors within a small diner. Trouble is at hand. One Black Emperor is accused of collecting money from other members and using the funds for himself. The gang leader confronts him with an onslaught of questions. The accused sits, head bowed, in silence. No answers, no apologies, simply no response. Infuriated, the leader strikes out, landing a forceful punch on the jaw of the accused, before declaring that he is selfish and that he must repay the money. This tirade is followed by three sharp kicks straight into the man's head. After another beating, the accused is instructed to repay the money by the following morning. In a close unit like The Black Emperors, this kind of behavior is intolerable and detestable. The beating the accused receives is seen as justifiable. In the gang's eyes, the accused has not only let himself down but he has let the group down. Therefore some form of punishment or retribution is warranted.

What is disconcerting about this scene is that the leader is at one point talking in a calm and controlled manner, the next he is lashing out with malice. We see the accused receiving these thumping blows, his head jerking forward on impact of the leader's foot or fist. There is no voyeuristic element when watching the beating, and thankfully the footage is relatively tame. What we do learn is that the leader of The Black Emperors feels he is well within his rights to beat members who have seemingly betrayed him. We never know if the allegations presented are true. What is more interesting is that the accused just remains seated, incapable of defending himself. His silence may signal his guilt, but it is still peculiar to see an individual willingly submit to a beating without putting up some kind of defensive struggle.

From here on, Yanagimachi focuses less on images of The Black Emperors charging around Tokyo's suburbs, instead concentrating on the hierarchy that binds the group together. We see the trials of various gang members, who have been accused of lying and being dishonest to their seniors. The most prominent members of the gang are present, and to them this is a serious matter. You have two choices, abide by The Black Emperors' rules or quit; you submit your resignation. We quickly recognize that as in any club, attendance is important. Yanagimachi makes us realize that the group functions on far more levels than most people think. The conception that the biker gangs merely gather for the thrill of riding is fundamentally incorrect. They adhere to strict guidelines and a biker code that all members must follow. To break this code results in punishment. Being part of the group generates a high degree of pride and respect. We see that those involved in The Black Emperors are very serious about their gang and their responsibilities.

Typically, in *Godspeed You! Black Emperor's* finale we see the riders at loggerheads with the fuzz. The police attempt to break up their rally. The Black Emperors are defiant; nothing will stop them. The final frames feature Yanagimachi again riding with The Black Emperors to the deafening soundtrack of revved-up motorcycles. We race one last time with The Black Emperors, full throttle into the night, before the credits roll.

In order to make *Godspeed You! Black Emperor*, director Yanagimachi set up his own production company called Gunro Films, utilizing the limited resources he had at his disposal. The lack of proper financing does show: The sound is at times muffled, and the film at points suffers glaringly from under- or over-exposure. Distinguishing one character from the next is difficult, as certain gang members' features are sometimes obscured by the poor quality in film stock and the lack of light. When Yanagimachi films on location with the bikers, certain scenes are drowned in brilliant white. This mainly occurs when Yanagimachi films the bikers riding towards his camera, their powerful headlamps blocking out the bikers in an explosive haze. In certain instances, all that the viewer can make out is a sea of light racing towards the camera. Some viewers may find this annoying; however, the style and quality lends itself to the documentary in an endearing manner. Yanagimachi is clearly not interested in delivering a polished and sleek documentary, as his inspiration has derived from the new wave documentary filmmakers of the sixties, who radically re-evaluated the whole concept of documentary filmmaking with their *Cinema Vérité* films.

Stylistically, *Godspeed You! Black Emperor* is closely associated with the ideals connected with *Cinema Vérité*, by way that it deliberately eschews conventional methods of documentary filmmaking. This can be demonstrated in the film's absence of a straightforward narrative, commentary, or proper story for that matter. Like pioneering *Cinema Vérité* filmmaker Robert Drew, Yanagimachi relies on portable cameras and sound equipment with the aim of putting the viewer closer to the action. The film is cobbled together with footage accumulated by Yanagimachi during the autumn of 1974 and the summer of 1975. Despite the documentary lacking fluidity, because of the way that the narrative is decidedly fragmented, *Godspeed You! Black Emperor* refuses to pass judgment, remaining objective at all times. By denying the audience of a narration, and therefore a particular view or opinion on the biker gang, Yanagimachi has subtly allowed the viewer to make up their own minds about The Black Emperors. Such an approach is likely to alienate many viewers, who will be perplexed, or indeed bored, by the documentary's refusal to be even remotely accessible. Yanagimachi documents the gang as they speak for themselves. *Godspeed You! Black Emperor* does not answer, resolve or comment on any issues pertaining to the biker phenomenon. There are no messages, no conclusions. Its agenda is relatively simplistic, for its concern is to paint an accurate portrayal of the life and community of the biker gangs.

Tracking down a copy of *Godspeed You! Black Emperor* remains difficult, as the documentary is currently only available in Japan in an un-subtitled edition. Luckily, a bootleg DVD has been making the rounds in the US, through www.5minutestolive.com, enabling the curious to seek out and lay their hands on this cinematic rarity. This release seems for now the only way Mitsuo Yanagimachi's landmark documentary will reach a wider audience, whether this comes from fans of the band or fans of Japanese cinema in general. Perhaps what is more troubling is how documentary filmmakers find it increasingly hard to release their work through the retail market, both at home and abroad—unless a prominent filmmaker is attached to the project, or if the documentary has a marketable gimmick.

Recent evidence would indicate that there is a market for documentaries, as proved by high-profile films like *Super Size Me*, *Fahrenheit 9/11* and by Anchor Bay Entertainment's decision to release Werner Herzog's *My Best Fiend*, *Little Dieter Needs to Fly*, *Fata Morgana* and *Lessons of Darkness* in their intended cuts. A courageous move for an independent distributor and a decision that seems to have paid off as Anchor Bay's releases have provoked much interest, primarily from supporters of Herzog's incredible body of work. While only a small fraction of Herzog's documentary films have managed to escape the television schedules, winding up on DVD (the recent critical acclaim of Herzog's *Grizzly Man* and *The Wild Blue Yonder*, has seen further titles emerge on DVD, notably *Wheel of Time* and *The White Diamond*), it is still a privilege very few film directors enjoy. Herzog's status as one of world cinema's most remarkable filmmakers, as well as one of the craziest directors to have ever graced the medium, has helped his documentary work find an audience that may not have had an interest in documentary film otherwise, or were his name was not attached to the project. Unfortunately for filmmakers like Mitsuo Yanagimachi, who remains an enigma in his homeland, the likelihood of *Godspeed You! Black Emperor* receiving a widespread DVD release in the foreseeable future remains slim. The nature of the industry dictates what is deemed a sellable product, and sadly, *Godspeed You! Black Emperor* will only be perceived as a cult oddity of negligible interest.

Yanagimachi is a name not readily associated with followers of Japanese Cinema. With a relatively slim filmography (only seven efforts), it is understandable that Yanagimachi has slipped under the radar of some viewers. After *Godspeed You! Black Emperor* came two more independent features, *A 19 Year Old's Map (Jukyusai No Chisu*, 1979) and *Farewell to the Land (Saraba Itoshiki Daichi*, 1982). Although both were critically acclaimed on the festival circuit, neither was a commanding success. It was his next feature *Fire Festival (Himatsuri*, 1984) that brought Yanagimachi to a wider audience; it is widely perceived as his most mature and best work. The film deals with a typical Yanagimachi theme and motive: the conflict between society and nature. After *Fire Festival*, Yanagimachi embarked on a trilogy of films connected with Chinese culture. This fascination was first started with the John (*The Last Emperor*) Lone vehicle *Shadow of China* and was followed by the independent feature *About Love Tokyo (Ai ni Tsuite, Tokyo)*, the story of a Chinese student who works in a Tokyo slaughterhouse. Yanagimachi's most recent cinematic effort is the 1995 documentary *The Wandering Peddlers (Tabisuru Pao-Jiang-Hu)*, for which he and his crew went to Taiwan to film a number of medicine peddlers who traversed the country selling their wares and entertaining small audiences.

For now, mass commercial success has eluded Yanagimachi. To Western audiences his films are like the Japanese biker gangs, an underground phenomenon known only by the critics and cinephiles who have waded past the glut of gangster, horror and sex films of the Japanese film industry. Luckily, *Shadow of China* and *Fire Festival* have received limited releases in the US, allowing the curious the opportunity to sample some of Yanagimachi's exquisite work. In the case of Yanagimachi's debut film *Godspeed You! Black Emperor*, if it were not for the band of the same name, then the documentary would have tumbled further and further into obscurity, becoming nothing more than a footnote on Yanagimachi's filmography.

Cosmetically, *Godspeed You! Black Emperor*'s footage is extremely poor and will infuriate any viewer with the inability to handle films not presented in digitally re-mastered and widescreen prints, offset with DTS surround sound. If the latest Hollywood blockbuster is the pinnacle of current technological advances in picture and audio quality, then *Godspeed You! Black Emperor* is the polar opposite, a film seemingly stuck in the dark ages of cinema. *Godspeed You! Black Emperor* is a difficult film, and will potentially appeal to those viewers who are sympathetic towards the *Cinema Vérité* films of the sixties or those purveyors of Japanese Cinema who have sought to escape from the more commercialized films on offer, opting to delve into the realms of Japanese alternative and experimental cinema instead. Those who can escape from the minor quibbles in visual quality will be rewarded with a deeply subtle film that tries to objectively capture the true nature of these biker gangs, revealing them to be more than a bunch of misfits intent on causing destruction and mayhem. The documentary observes that while they can be a nuisance, and a thorn in the side of the police, once together, they act as a family unit—the family unit they could be missing from their own families. Behind all the macho talk and pandering, the members are seen as deeply caring towards one another. Today's biker gangs are galaxies apart from The Black Emperors, making the documentary a more interesting item, as we can assess how the biker gangs have slowly evolved over the last thirty years. The final word goes to Mitsuo Yanagimachi for constructing a documentary that does not set out to stamp its own viewpoint all over the film, or attempt to swamp the viewer with a preaching message so the viewer is tricked into siding with the filmmaker. In this rare little film, the viewer is left to decide whether to enjoy the ride with The Black Emperors or simply dismount and walk away.

14

A Permanent State of War: A Short History of North Korean Cinema

Johannes Schönherr

> Like the leading article in the Party paper, the cinema should have mass appeal and should keep ahead of new developments, thus playing a mobilizing role in each stage of the revolutionary struggle.
> —Kim Il Sung[1]

The Pyongyang Film Festival

The 7th Pyongyang Film Festival of Non-Aligned and Other Developing Countries was September 2000. The female brass band of the Korean People's Army played snappy military marches, moving their legs in exact sync while proceeding ahead of the slightly bewildered, motley crowd of international delegates. Thousands of girls in traditional Korean garb lined the concrete slabs leading towards the Pyongyang International Cinema House, a huge structure on Yanggak Islet in the River Taedong, performing dances, waving artfully with colored cloths, or drumming old-style Korean changgos. The forty or so delegates fired at them round after round of photo film while their minders had a hard time reminding them that "this is an official function and not a tourist trip." But the international guests did feel like being kind of trippy—they were TV directors from Russia and China, indie filmmakers from Malaysia and Iran, documentary filmmakers from Egypt, festival curators from Finland, and movie house programmers from Germany—and none of them could ever expect an even remotely similar welcome back home.

A small army of North Korean newsmen shot back with all the "firepower" they had available—from new Sony video cameras to vintage 16mm hand-cranks from the sixties. This was headline news after all—the arrival of the international guests for the opening ceremony of North Korea's film festival "that draws great attention of the public at home and abroad as it is opened at a time when there is a bright prospect for national reunification and the DPRK enjoys ever growing international prestige in the wake of the historic north-south summit talks and the publication of the north-south joint declaration in June last under the experienced and tested guidance of the great leader Kim Jong-il," as North Korean Minister of Culture Kang Nung-su claimed in his speech at the pompous ceremony inside the Cinema House,[2] using the official title of North Korea, Democratic People's Republic of Korea (DPRK).

A documentary screened at the ceremony, depicting the international delegates marching into the event center at the last Pyongyang Film Festival (1998), immediately belied any special importance of this first film festival after the summit meeting between South Korean president Kim Dae-jung and North Korean leader Kim Jong-il in June 2000. About 100 international delegates could be seen cheered at two years before; this year, the number of foreign attendees was less than half. And despite all the unification talk of the post–summit meeting days, not one South Korean film director was in sight.

After lengthy speeches by people holding titles like "vice-president of the presidium of the Supreme People's Assembly of the DPRK," Iranian director Afshin Sadeghi took to the stage. He read a "greeting from the international film community" to the North Korean hosts from some sheet of paper, his voice uneasy and his hands shaking noticeably even from the distance of a viewer sitting in the tenth row. As he would later tell in private, he had been singled out to read that speech—written entirely by the North Korean organizers—and he had been asked to "not make any mistakes in reading it."

Since its inception in 1987, the Pyongyang Film

Johannes Schönherr's ID at the Pyongyang Film Festival 2000 (courtesy Johannes Schönherr).

14. North Korean Cinema (Johannes Schönherr)   137

Top—Opening of Pyongyang Film Festival 2000: The female brass band of the Korean People's Army shows their knees at the festival opening; bottom—girls lining the way to the festival venue (courtesy Johannes Schönherr).

Festival is one of the few international events with which the Pyongyang regime tries to reach out to the outside world. Since 1990, the festival has been staged every two years during the autumn months. The festival organizing committee does try actively to get as many foreign films and foreign guests invited as possible. Films covering any subject under the sun are permitted—the only exceptions being sex movies and films that take a stand against North Korean society. Even American films would be welcomed and their directors could get invitations. The only problem is that the sole screening format at the festival is 35mm and hardly any adventurous independent filmmaker who might be willing to travel to Pyongyang has the money to work in that format.

However, the festival provides a rare opportunity for Pyongyang residents to see some foreign films. The only opportunity in two years, actually, to see them on the big screen. North Korean movie theaters don't show foreign fare outside the festival and only one foreign film is shown per week on North Korean TV—usually an old Eastern European film. The crowds showing up at the theaters were accordingly big; people starved of outside images would fight about tickets for pretty much anything.

For the international guests, however, it was less fun. The various delegations were split off according to their nationalities and each got separate

Young pioneers greet the guests and reporters at the entrance of the festival hall (courtesy Johannes Schönherr).

screenings in the vast confines of the Cinema House. They were subjected to what was called the "Film Market Screenings"—a feeble excuse to provide foreigners with movies without them witnessing the reactions of the local audience.

North Korean audiences tend to respond to movies very strongly (they do in the South, too) and Japanese film critic Takashi Momma was able to see a Vietnamese picture with a North Korean audience at the Pyongyang Film Festival in 1992. Vietnam, of course, is a country full of bicycles and in 1992, bicycles were still banned in Pyongyang. All the street pictures of Hanoi with thousands of bicycles in view got lots of cheers and amazed "uhhh"s and "ohhh"s from the Pyongyang audience. The organizers made sure they did not have reactions like that being reported again in the foreign press.

For anyone trying to catch up on recent developments in North Korean cinema, however, those "market screenings" are a good opportunity (although the North Koreans don't really seem to have a concept of what a new and what an old film is). At the screenings, movies from the seventies deemed important are served up alongside the most recent productions. The few catalogues available on North Korean cinema usually don't even mention the year a film was made. The delegates who had a minder who was connected to the film industry were lucky; regular tourist guides (the majority) would just shrug their shoulders and answer film-related questions with "dunno." But after viewing their first two or three North Korean films, most foreigners would go out of their way to avoid further exposure to what they largely considered dire wastes of celluloid.

Aside from the "market screenings" foisted upon the foreign guests, there was actually a designated "film market area" on the second floor of the Cinema House. Alas, it only consisted of a few posters, empty chairs and a few video booths. With some pre-arrangements, it was possible to see North Korean films at the video booths. Always without subtitles and with the respective delegation's guide haltingly translating the dialogue into English. No foreign production company had reserved any screening time there.

A rigid itinerary had been set up for the foreign guests, visiting monument after monument. That made it difficult for foreign directors to attend the screenings of their own films. Most didn't mind but a Russian director who had shot a documentary on the treatment of drug addicts at a Siberian rehab facility persisted. He was seeing performances at the Children's Palace when he asked the organizers to get real on their promise to have him introduce his own movie. "Too difficult," he was told. He made sure there was a way, pressing the minders into calling him a taxi in a country where calling a taxi is quite an alien concept—not only because of lack of taxis but also of a lack of working telephones. He made it to the show despite the taxi sign falling off the car on the way. Upon his arrival, however, he wasn't permitted to take to the stage to introduce the film.

The official booklet of North Korean feature films.

14. North Korean Cinema (Johannes Schönherr)

The cream of the crop of the North Korean film industry assembles for a publicity shot in front of a Kim Il-sung statue inside the studio (courtesy Johannes Schönherr).

Despite all the big banquets, minister's speeches and whatnot served up at the festival, it's difficult to ascertain if North Korean cinema had really something to celebrate these days. Only one (!) feature and one feature-length documentary from North Korea was premiered at that most important showcase for North Korean cinema. Low-ranking North Korean industry insiders, acting as guides for some of the delegates, hinted that the bad economic situation had hit the film business just as hard as other parts of the economy. They sounded rather gloomy and made vague mentions of only three to four features made per year now. But can those sources be counted as reliable? One of them had maintained that Kim Kil-in, one of North Korea's biggest directors, was always "too busy" for an interview this writer tried to schedule—until it turned out that Kim Kil-in had died three years before.

It's hard to come by hard facts on the actual annual output of North Korean cinema. Brian Barron of the BBC reports that "despite the hardship, North Korea still manages to produce around sixty films a year."[3] But that number seems highly unlikely and most certainly includes all short films, documentaries and all short animation ordered and paid for by foreign companies. On the other hand, North Korea continuously produces one-hour installments of long-running film series; should one count each of them as a "feature"?

North Korea's official news agency KCNA (Korean Central News Agency) reported on 18 December 2000: "Many films of high ideological and artistic value have been released in Korea this year." It gives the titles of seven features produced in 2000, though strangely, the title *Land of Love*, the film premiered at the festival, was not among them.

KCNA added: "Other feature films are of great cognitional and educational significance as they represent those who think of others more than themselves and devote themselves to society and the collective. Many other films portray young people who give a steadfast continuity to the revolution." How much is "many other films"?

Hyanjin Lee cites in her book *Contemporary Korean Cinema*, a North Korean Film Yearbook from 1986, which claims that during that year thirty-one feature films were made. Lee goes on to say that this number of productions remained stable into the early nineties. She does not provide any information about times after that.[4]

But whatever the numbers given—where are the titles that support the numbers? A booklet named *Feature Film List*, and published by the (North) Korea Film Export and Import Corporation in September 1998, gives a chronological listing of the features made up until the date of publication but it

The headquarters of North Korea's Hollywood—the Korean Film Studio (courtesy Johannes Schönherr).

14. North Korean Cinema (Johannes Schönherr) 143

doesn't give years of production. All in all, 259 films are listed as being made as of then; the multi-series films are only mentioned once, not their various installments. A few outlawed films are missing (no *Pulgasari* on that list) but judging from the years of production of films known to me, it can be roughly asserted that the eighties were the peak time of North Korean cinema with about 15–20 films per annum and that the output declined from then on. In South Korea, for comparison, 59 films were produced in 2000, including some big international successes like Park Chang-wook's *Joint Security Area* and Kim Ki-duk's *The Isle*.

North Korea has quite a number of different film studios. Feature films are made at the Korean Film Studio, the main studio, founded in 1947, and the April 25 Film Studio of the Korean People's Army (founded in 1959 and known until recently as February 8 Film Studio of the Korean People's Army), the April 26 Children Film Studio (founded in 1953) which makes movies for kids and animated pictures, a Documentary Film Studio (founded in 1946) and the Korean Educational and Scientific Film Studio which produces educational films and anime.

The animation film studios are the only ones making more than just a few bucks on the international market—they are heavily in demand for cheaply shooting labor-intensive stop-motion for cartoon companies from Spain, Italy and France. The North Koreans' own productions, carrying heavy political messages, fare less well, though.

A visit to the Korean Film Studio, the main and biggest film studio, is a customary part of the official tours given to the delegates of the Pyongyang Film Festival. Aside from outdated technology, it mainly the degree to which the country's film producers are out of step with the rest of the world.

The "old Korean Street," resembling a medieval village, seemed pretty convincing but the "South Korean Street" much less so. Maybe South Korea looked that way in the fifties—it certainly doesn't now. The "Chinese Street" resembled old postcards from Dandong than anything current Chinese, and the "Japanese Street" had simply nothing in common with any looks of Japan today anywhere. The "European Street" came a little closer to reality, though; building formations like that can still be found in a few East German small towns suffering economic mishaps. All in all, the folks creating the sets seemed very much out of touch with what the outside world looks like nowadays.

A lame simulated production of a medieval scene was staged for the delegates to show them the current state and technological level of filmmaking at the studio. The simulated shooting felt rather lame and uninspired—until the state of North Korean technology really came to the surface. One of the diesel generators providing the voltage for the floodlights overheated and burst into flames and sparks, filling the set with smoke and the stench of burned rubber. Now, that was a show!

Inspired by East Germany? European Street at the Korean Film Studio (courtesy Johannes Schönherr).

A meeting with North Korean film people including directors and performers was arranged to wrap up the studio tour. But alas, that potentially interesting meeting was kept so short that no introductions of any significance could be made.

The Early Years

Korea had been annexed by Japan in 1910 and big efforts were made to Japanize Korea. Korean language and culture were actively suppressed and supplanted with Japanese ways of living. These efforts met fierce resistance by the Koreans who staged various large-scale rebellions and riots, and had guerrilla troops in the Northern mountains battling the colonial masters. The end of Japanese rule over Korea, however, could not be achieved by these means. It needed Emperor Hirohito's unconditional surrender of Japan to the Allied forces at the end of World War II, after the nuclear destruction of Hiroshima and Nagasaki, to get the Japanese to give up on the colony and pull out. The day of Japan's surrender, 15 August 1945, is still a holiday in both North and South Korea and is celebrated as "Liberation Day."

But a "liberation" of Korea was hardly what the war's victorious powers had in mind. In an agreement drawn well before the end of the war, the U.S. and the Soviet Union had Korea split up in their respective zones of influence. The Soviet Union was to move their troops into the area north of the 38th parallel, the U.S. to the areas south of it. And both installed their "puppets" to run things for them. The Americans opted for anti-Communist Rhee Syngman as "the man" in their territory, while the Russians went for a Soviet-groomed former anti–Japanese guerrilla fighter who was born with the name Kim Sung-chu.

Kim Sung-chu had always had kind of an artistic inclination—especially in the art of self-promotion. While fighting Japanese occupation forces with little success in the cold mountains in the far North of Korea and in Manchuria in the thirties, he decided to meld his personality with that of a far more legendary and daring guerrilla warrior who had, conveniently enough, been dead for a few years by then—a man named Kim Il-sung.

Upon converting to Communism, Kim Sung-chu / Kim Il-sung went to Stalin's special training grounds to learn the art of surviving and succeeding in one of the most deadly political minefields that modern history had to offer—Stalin's Soviet Union.

He was still a minor political figure when he marched into the Soviet zone of Korea as a major of the Red Army in 1945. That was to change soon. After a lot of behind-the-scenes maneuvering, he convinced the Russians that he would be Stalin's perfect man here. At a dramatic speech to the residents of Pyongyang two months after the town's occupation by Soviet forces, the Russian commander in charge introduced him to the confused locals as the man who would have all the say from now on—this fellow here ... Kim Il-sung.

Kim Il-sung had learned his Stalin lessons well—purge the higher-ups to keep 'em in check, and barrage the common folks with propaganda till they believe you are the savior of the fatherland. And, dating back to Lenin, there was the expression "Cinema is the most important of all arts." Film historians are still trying to discern if Lenin actually said that (most of them doubt it) but the legend of him saying it has persevered for a long time—and Kim Il-sung certainly believed in this message.

He had the first North Korean documentary film crew set up in 1946 and founded the Korean Film Studio outside of Hyonjesan District on the outskirts of Pyongyang a year later. Their first film was released in 1949.

My Home Village, directed by Kang Hong-sik, was Kim Il-sung's first cinematic foray into the build-up of a myth that would from now on be state doctrine: It was not the Allied victory in WWII that liberated the Koreans from the Japanese and it was not the Soviet Red Army either. The task of throwing the Japanese out of Korea was accomplished by only one force: Kim Il-sung's "Korean People's Revolutionary Army." They, and nobody else battled the Japanese out from the holy soil of Korea; along with the Japanese, their

Farmer Gwan-pil battles the evil Japanese in *My Home Village*.

main allies within the country, the reactionary class of Korean landowners and feudal lords, those damnable traitors of the nation, were also eliminated. Nobody but Kim Il-sung, the "Great Leader," could have achieved all that.

The North Korean propagandists hammer this point home in their description of the film: "This was the first feature film to be produced after the country's liberation. It gives a picture of the boundless joy and emotion of the Korean people who are now liberated from the colonial yoke of Japanese imperialism thanks to the glorious anti-Japanese armed struggle organized and led by the great leader Comrade Kim Il Sung" (*Korean Film Art*).

The film starts with a shot of a rather unconvincing model of Mount Paektu, the water-filled dead volcano on the Korean-Chinese border that the Koreans consider the holy mountain of the nation. According to legend, 5000 years ago a god named Hwanung had his residence up there. One day, a bear and a tiger approached Hwanung and asked to be transformed to human beings. Hwanung gave both of them 20 pieces of garlic and told them to eat all of it and to avoid the sunlight for one hundred days. Only the bear followed the instructions and was turned into a woman after 37 days. Hwanung married the woman and they had a son, King Tangun, who became the ancestor of all Koreans and who founded the first capital of a Korean kingdom, Asadal—the city which is now Pyongyang. All things purely Korean started from Mount Paektu—and so of course also the liberation of the country by Kim Il-sung. It was on the slopes of that mountain that he had fought, according to North Korean propaganda, his most important battles against the Japanese oppressor troops. From there, with Mount Paektu as a base, he liberated the rest of the country. So, it was quite logical to start the first North Korean movie with a picture of that holy place; that it was only a tacky model must be attributed to the limited resources of the film studio at the time. Indeed, the film's production values jump upwards quite a bit after that introductory image with good photography and fairly good acting.

The film cuts to a farmer named Gwan-pil who rents his land from a vicious feudal lord. Not able to endure the daily insults by the landlord any more, he vents his rage by beating the landlord up. Of course, after that he loses his land and ends up in a Japanese-run prison. There, he meets Hak-jun, an operative of Kim Il-sung's Korean People's Revolutionary Army, who introduces him to Kim Il-sung's nationalist-communist ideology. Together, the two guys start a prison riot and manage to escape in the ensuing confusion. Hak-jun heads with Gwan-pil towards the guerrilla fighters in the mountains, near Mount Paektu of course. Right before they reach them, the police catch up with them, opening fire. Hak-jun is killed. Right at that moment the guerrilla fighters appear from behind the bushes, firing at the police. They wipe out nearly the whole police squad, only a few of them running away in a manner that clearly depicts them as cowards. Gwan-pil joins the guerrillas and we see him being trained as a fighter and then, together with his guerrilla friends, ambushing Japanese army units and blowing up bridges. Eventually, he takes part in the liberation of his home village where the feudal landlord and his son receive a cruel punishment by the hands of the farmers. After the victory, he is celebrated by his mother and the villagers. Together with his girlfriend, he starts to work on the creation of the new, Kim Il-sung–run North Korean society.

There was one problem with the Kim Il-sung–led "liberation of Korea" glorified in *My Home Village*: The power of Kim Il-sung ended to the South at the 38th parallel. According to Northern propaganda, that part of Korea was now under the colonial rule of a new power—the United States. Soon, Kim Il-sung would do something about that and liberate those poor brethren down south too...

The Korean War

Kim Il-sung had bugged Stalin for quite some while about conquering the Southern half of Korea. But the great dictator was reluctant. In 1950, he finally gave in and told Kim Il-sung to go ahead—but he made clear that the Soviet Union would officially stay out of that war and that all support delivered would have to remain on the quiet side. In June 1950, Kim Il-sung's troops attacked. The Northerners made an advance, overrunning most of the South except for a small pocket around Pusan. Then, the U.N.-backed, American-led invasion at Inchon changed the fortunes and Kim Il-sung's troops were pushed way up north towards the Chinese border. Mao Tse-tung, the "Great Helmsman" of China, sent in hundreds of thousands of his soldiers as "volunteers," pushing back the U.N. forces. The result of that? Trench-fighting roughly along the same lines which were the border between the Southern and Northern zones before the war. A treaty drawn up between all parties involved (except Rhee Syng-man, who refused to sign) at the border village of Panmunchon ended the war in 1953 with a truce.

Pyongyang had been reduced to rubble by American bombing during the war and the North Korean film studio had also been turned into a heap of ashes. Film production however did not stop. Aside from making war newsreels, the studio started a new genre in North Korean film—the war film, for now dealing with current events. In 1951, *Boy Partisans* was made, in 1952

Female fighters to the front! Yun Ryong-gu's *Orang River*.

14. North Korean Cinema (Johannes Schönherr) 149

Battle scene set in the Korean War. *The Defenders of Height 1211*.

Again to the Front. In 1953 came the premiere of *Scouts* by Chon Dong-min. The latter film describes the advance of a reconnoitering squad into the rear of the Southern enemy in the early stages of the war—when the North was advancing fast. The squad of not very credible heroes attacks a Southern headquarters and snatches the enemy's military operation plan away from the U.S. military adviser in a rather unlikely daytime battle. On their way back North, they discover a Southern artillery installation. Of course, the bold heroes obliterate that installation in another superhuman gunfight.

As far removed as the heroic action in the film was from the dirty daily shoot-outs in the trenches, its formula of invincible might and greatness of the Northern army must have worked well with the audience—or rather the agitation officials keen on upholding the spirits of the fighters on the front and in the bombed-out towns in the hinterland.

The end of the war didn't bring an end of the war film genre. On the contrary, on the movie screens the war had just begun. In battle epics like *Orang River* (by Yun Ryong-gyu), *The Defenders of Height 1211* (by Li Gi-song), and *Namgang Village Women* (by Pak Dae-sik and Ham Un-bong), Northern

Victory is secured in Li Gi-song's *The Defenders of Height 1211*.

superheroes and their equally heroic and determined civilian supporters went on slaughtering cartoonish-evil Southern soldiers—to "serve as a powerful means of ideological education instrumental to arming our people with the anti-imperialist revolutionary thought and high class consciousness and to infusing them with a correct view of war," as the hacks at Korea Film Export & Import Corp. put it (*Korean Film Art*).

The Establishment of Juche

The war, although not producing the desired results, namely the unification of Korea under Kim Il-sung's rule, did provide some benefits for Kim. First of all, Kim Il-sung could start to feel safe. He could be sure that his protective powers China and the Soviet Union would not agree to some democratic unification of Korea with the United Nations as politically neutral but capitalistic entity the way it happened in Austria after the Russians pulled out of their section of occupied Vienna. The lines were clearly drawn in Cold War fashion. Kim Il-sung got a perfectly sealed border towards the South and, with the stepped-up presence of the American military in the South, a perfectly evil enemy to exploit for his own ends.

Stalin had put him in power, Mao had saved his ass in the war but Kim was not inclined to become a serving vassal for either of them. Just like Marshall

14. North Korean Cinema (Johannes Schönherr)

Tito in Yugoslavia, or Enver Hoxha in Albania, he wanted to run things his way, creating a nationalist version of Communism which truly made him the boss of the country instead of a proxy of Moscow or Beijing.

In 1955, Kim Il-sung introduced the concept of *Juche*. From now on, *Juche* was to be the new ideology of the country and it was to be propagated by all means and obeyed by everyone within the North Korean borders. *Juche* means self-reliance and proclaims a special, North Korean way of achieving Communism and national independence, based on Korean specifics of national character and development, with Kim Il-sung being the undisputed leader. The one and only goal of all arts, and that includes cinema, is to strive for a most perfect propaganda of *Juche* and to glorify the "Great Leader" Kim Il-sung.

Although the film industry had (since *My Home Village*) already worked along the lines of what now became called *Juche*, adjustments to the post-war situation of the country had to be made.

Right after the end of the war, in 1953, the Pyongyang University of Dramatic and Cinematic Arts was founded to groom future talent. This school (reorganized as Pyongyang Film University in 1972) became the central film teaching institution of the country; almost all North Korean movie directors learned their craft there.

On the North Korean cinema screens the war went on. Battle after battle against the evil Southerners and Americans was won. But now, a new genre

Proud working-class heroes of the new Korea. O Byong-Cho's *The Spinner*.

was needed to deal with the situation of reconstruction and building up *Juche* Korea, a genre that became labeled "Feature films on the theme of the socialist reality."

Within this genre, current problems could be dealt with—namely the adjustment of North Korean society to the principles of Kim Il-sung's leadership. Thinking along old feudal lines was severely denounced here, as was any pro-Western thoughts.

It took a few years for this new genre to mature—it didn't happen until the early sixties actually—but from then on "socialist reality" films were produced seriously. One was O Byong-Cho's *The Spinner* (1963) for which the hacks at Korea Film Export & Import produced a great description, as they do so often: "The film begins with a scene showing the spinner Ok Rim being

Really, North Koreans are the happiest people in the world! *We Are the Happiest.*

maltreated and humiliated at a spinning mill before liberation. After the country is liberated, she becomes a worthy master of the country, an initiator of the multi-spindle, a Chollima-rider[5] making innovations in production, a Labor Hero, a Deputy to the Supreme People's Assembly and the director of a factory" (*Korean Film Art*). From problem-ridden the focus soon shifted to the sheer glory of the new North Korea. A film aptly titled *We Are the Happiest* was advertised this way: "Through the images of the central characters, the film shows in great style the life of our people who are the happiest in the world under the care of the Party and the shining achievements of the *Juche* art which is in full blossom in the era of the Worker's Party" (*Korean Film Art*). *The Girl Barber* finally tried to get the point across "that under our socialist system there is neither 'noble' nor 'mean' job as any place is for the good of the people" (*Korean Film Art*). Certainly a politically correct statement in North Korea—but who would voluntarily want to watch a film like that?

Kim Jong-il giving "on-the-spot guidance" at the film studio in 1979.

Kim Jong-il Enters the Scene

If those latter movies sound stupid, unconvincing and of rather dubious artistic value to you, you are in good company. A young Kim Jong-il thought the same way.

Kim Jong-il was the son of Great Leader Kim Il-sung, and according to Western sources born in a village near Khabarovsk in Siberia in 1941. North Korea gives a different account: He was born in a guerrilla fighter camp near Mount Paektu, the holy mountain of Korea. Somewhere down the line, they changed his year of birth, too, making him a year younger. Kim Il-sung liked even numbers better.

Kim Jong-il had been a movie nut from early on—and as the son of the Great Leader his power was tremendous even while he was a kid. This according to a booklet titled *Great Man and Cinema* which was distributed to the foreign guests at the Seventh Pyongyang Film Festival. According to that booklet, Kim Jong-il attended a preview screening of *My Home Village* in 1949 and this is the "anecdote" *Great Man and Cinema* has to report from that screening:

> Comrade Kim Jong-il has been very fond of the cinema since his childhood. After Korean liberation he often accompanied the great leader Comrade Kim Il-sung and his mother Kim Jong-suk, anti–Japanese women general, to a film studio. One spring day in 1949 when he was seven years old he went there and joined in previewing the working film *My Home Village*, the first of its kind in Korea.
> The film showed the winter scenes of the falling snow. At this sight Comrade Kim Jong-il shook his head dubiously and told an official of the film studio that he wondered why no snow was found on the heads and shoulders of the characters while it came down copiously.
> The official blushed with shame in spite of himself because Comrade Kim Jong-il was right. He noticed that a bad job was made of trick shots.
> Comrade Kim Jong-il again remarked that the snow was not lifelike, and asked the official if it was bits of cotton wool.
> It was true. Bits of white cotton wool were sprinkled to make them look like snowflakes, but they were too crude to produce the intended effect.
> Afterwards, these scenes were re-photographed.[6]

Later "anecdotes" in the booklet sound a little more convincing but they are all from the late sixties onwards, when Kim Jong-il started to make his "guidance" visits to the Korean Film Studio almost daily affairs. Want to hear another one? Here we go:

> This happened when the interior of a room was shot.
> Comrade Kim Jong-il came to the studio. He examined the installations and props one by one. He saw a towel on a wall and asked why it hung there.
> "Because the wall looks empty, we..." replied an official, failing to complete his sentence. He had done so without any creative purpose.
> Comrade Kim Jong-il asked again why a foreign-made towel was hung.
> The officials and creators could not answer him because they had not paid much attention to the props.

14. North Korean Cinema (Johannes Schönherr) 155

Comrade Kim Jong-il told them that even a towel on the wall should mirror the times and tally with the circumstances in a film, and that there should be sufficient justification for it.[7]

Kim Jong-il had the power of a big Hollywood studio head of the thirties and he wanted to put them to a more creative use than complaining about prop details. He wanted to produce films. Not any films—he wouldn't make anything less than "Immortal Classics" [8]

Kim Jong-il kept a "low profile" while working on the "immortal classics" by not being mentioned in the film's credits—and all North Korean info maintains that he only gave "guidance" but never acknowledge Kim Jong-il being anything like a "producer." A huge painting covering a whole wall in the entrance hall of the Korea Film Studio, however, contradicts those statements.

The first "immortal classic" Kim Jong-il was involved with—of course, that being the first "immortal classic" in North Korean cinema history at all—was an anti–Japanese guerrilla movie named *Sea of Blood*, made in 1968, depicting the filming of a battle scene; Kim Jong-il standing on a hill, with his arms crossed over his chest, looking down at the filmed mayhem in the pose of a Roman emperor in a 19th century battle painting, overlooking, say, the destruction of Carthage. A big display board in the same room lists more than 10,000

The first of the "immortal classics"—Choe Ik-gyu's *Sea of Blood*.

visits to the studio by Kim Jong-il until 1993. Sounds like quite a number but that is what the tour guide–translator said.

Kim Jong-il's input may have helped produce some of North Korea's better films but they were also limiting the operation of the film studio to quite an extent as a rather bizarre exhibition on Kim Jong-il's visits to the studio proves. A female guide speaking in that typically North Korean exhortative manner of excited official announcement—sounding like a cross between an over-excited sports commentator and a chanting priest—explained the main items in the collection to the foreign film festival visitors: chairs Kim Jong-il sat on during one of his visits, desks he used to write a note on, lenses he peered through, cameras he touched. Everything that could possibly carry his fingerprints was immediately removed from the shooting locations and put into that exhibition. The film directors saw some of their best equipment gone after a visit by the Leader; once he touched it, it became a holy artifact, removed from its mundane use and placed under glass. The museum spans quite a number of rooms and, after completing the visit, the visitors came away with the impression that North Korea could have produced twice as many films as it did if the moviemakers only would have had access to the material stored there.

The village is massacred by the Japanese *Sea of Blood*.

Desperate children during the village massacre *Sea of Blood*.

The immortal classics

The first of the "immortal classics," *Sea of Blood* (1968, directed by Choe Ik-gyu) was based on a stage play by the same name, supposedly written by Great Leader Kim Il-sung himself at the time when he was an anti–Japanese guerrilla fighter. The movie tells the story of a mother who experiences 1930s Japanese oppression the worst way: Japanese collective punishment against villagers who support the anti-Japanese guerrilla. Her children join Kim Il-sung's "Korean People's Revolutionary Army" (KPRA) while the mother, after meeting

158   Film Out of Bounds

Top: The mother kills the guards and opens the gate of the town in *Sea of Blood*. *Bottom:* Guerrilla fighters on their way in *Sea of Blood*.

14. North Korean Cinema (Johannes Schönherr)

5 Guerilla Brothers: The five brothers are "ready to lay down their lives to defend and safeguard the great leader."

The Flower Girl. Ain't she cute?

one of Kim Il-sung's propagandists, becomes both a Communist women organizer in her town and a smuggler of explosives to the KPRA rebels deep in the forest. The Korean authorities acting on Japanese command catch and torture her but she won't budge. The guerrillas lay siege to the walled town she's held at. The mother kills the guards and opens the gate of the town...

It's great drama and very violent. *Great Man and Cinema* describes the shooting this way: "When ... actors balked at piercing old people with their bayonets and throwing children into the fire, [Kim Jong-il] told them that they should act boldly to lend realism to the film."[9] The writer of the booklet obviously got carried away a little when praising the efforts of the Dear Leader as Kim Jong-il was known then...

By telling its story of liberation by the forces of Kim Il-sung's guerrilla army, *Sea of Blood* harks back to *My Home Village*, propagating the same myth of Kim Il-sung as the sole liberator of Korea from the Japanese occupation forces. But this time on a much grander scale than the humble predecessor. In fact, promoting his father as a god-like founding father of the *Juche* nation became one of the trademarks of Kim Jong-il.

In the same year, 1968, Kim Jong-il oversaw the production of the three-part *Five Guerilla Brothers*, directed again by Choe Ik-gyu. This film did not become recognized as an "immortal classic" but did become a "People's Prize Winner," an award handed out only to the best productions. This film is

The flower girl takes revenge on the landlord couple, throwing boiling soup into their evil mugs.

another reinforcement of the Kim Il-sung legend—an anti-Japanese guerrilla movie very much along the lines of *My Home Village*. It's five brothers this time who "under the wise guidance and amid the warm love of the great leader Comrade Kim Il Sung ... join the revolutionary struggle and grow up in the course of the revolution to be revolutionaries of a *Juche* type who are ready to lay down their lives to defend and safeguard the great leader politically and ideologically" (*Korean Film Art*).

Intrigued by the apparent domestic success of *Sea of Blood*, Kim Jong-il headed for his next "immortal classic" project. It would be released in 1972 under the title *Flower Girl*, directed again by Kim Jong-il's favorite Choe Ik-gyu. He did however not direct the whole movie. The project was taken over by another director who already had a rather large number of pictures under his belt, Pak Hak. What happened to Choe Ik-gyu? Did he die during shooting? Did he suddenly fall out of favor? The information that could be gleaned on him only indicates that he never made another movie. His name still being printed in North Korean film literature, however, leads to the assumption that he was in "good standing" till the end of his career[10]

With *Flower Girl* Kim Jong-il got finally to do what he had always wanted to do: make a great, moving film of epic proportions. It's in color and set in the late twenties or early thirties, and based on a play supposedly written by Kim Il-sung. Ostensibly about the effects of "Japanese imperialism," it's actually more about life in feudal Korea and the class conflicts playing out there.

A poor mother and her children work at the house of an evil landlord and landlady. They are so mean, the son of the poor mother finally lashes out at them. He goes to jail. The mother continues to be humiliated by the feudal landowners while, on the streets, the older daughter sells flowers that she has picked in the mountains. Her little sister (blinded by the landowners when they threw a pot of hot water at her) joins the flower girl once, singing in the street. That makes a lot more money than selling flowers but the mother severely reprimands her: Singing and begging is even worse than working hard and being humiliated. Singing on the street—that is like prostitution! The flower girl starts a long walk across the country to see her brother in jail, only to be told that he has died. Being left alone, the blind little sister goes crazy and disappears. There is no hope for our flower girl who is on the verge of dying, starving on the road ... until the last 10 minutes of the film when everything is solved. The son has not died but has escaped from prison. Joining Kim Il-sung's "army," he rescues the blind kid, and he also rescues the flower girl who in revenge burns the faces of the oppressive landowner couple by throwing boiling food at their evil mugs.

The last ten minutes are standard propaganda but up to then, it's a great and very moving anti-feudal drama. The main focus here is on class relations under feudalism, as the Japanese occupiers play only a marginal role in this film.

In general, the Japanese occupation forces play two main roles in the films promoting the legend as Kim Il-sung as liberator. On the one hand they are the foreign invaders that must be driven out of the country; on the other hand, they are the power that keeps the feudal lords of Korea in charge. Here the emphasis is on the latter.

The artistic qualities of *Flower Girl* did finally bring an international breakthrough for North Korean cinema: It won a "Prix Special," coming with a medal and an ornamental flower pot, at the 1972 Karlovy Vary Film Festival in Czechoslovakia. The big Eastern bloc film festivals in Karlovy Vary, Moscow and Sochi (Russia) had shown North Korean films before more out of political than artistic considerations. But with *Flower Girl*, even jaded Czech intellectuals (well, some of the few still residing in the country after the Soviets quelled the Czech attempt at democracy in 1968) gave a thumbs-up for the Kim Jong-il production.

Emboldened by his newfound international reputation, Kim went for his next historical epic: *An Jung-gun Shoots Ito Hirobumi*. If *Flower Girl* left doubts as

The assassination scene in *An Jung-gun Shoots Ito Hirobumi*.

to the extent to which the film is about Japanese involvement in the unfolding story, *An Jung-gun Shoots Ito Hirobumi* is a straight anti-Japanese story. It purports to be as historically correct as possible, detailing the moves made by Japanese special emissary Hirobumi Ito to annex Korea to Japan. The "success story" of evil Ito is counterpointed by the actions of a group of Korean nationalists. It goes into a lot of finer historical details, like the "debt-paying movement" in the early 1900s when a lot of wealthy and not so wealthy Koreans parted with their valuables to pay the national debts the country owed to Japan. All that failed in the end and Japan annexed Korea in 1910—thanks to clever mastermind Ito. Ito was not going to live and see the fruits of his dealings: In 1909, young Korean nationalist An Jung-gun shot Ito at the train station in Harbin, China.

For anybody interested in the history of Korea, it might be interesting to follow that dramatic event. No Kim Il-sung in sight and no communist propaganda here—the film is strictly nationalist—and the film does indeed provide a rather accurate depiction of events back then.

Unfortunately, it's all told in a heavy-handed, dull way. Released in 1979 and directed by Om Gil Son, *An Jung-gun Shoots Ito Hirobumi* was clearly inferior to *Flower Girl*. The jury of the Karlovy Vary Film Festival thought the same and didn't hand out any special flowerpot this time.

On the Art of Cinema

Kim Jong-il did not only produce films and give his "on-the-spot" guidances to film crews at work; he also had aspirations as a film scholar. In 1973, he published his book *On the Art of the Cinema,* outlining his views of how to create films. The book became the new bible of North Korean filmmaking. All directors, actors, technicians, etc., have been working along the precious principles laid down in the book ever since. So they claim.

But in actuality, the book had few new thoughts to offer to the

KIM JONG IL

ON THE ART OF THE CINEMA

PYONGYANG, KOREA
1989

Upon the publication of Kim Jong-il's On the Art of the Cinema, film students and filmmakers across the globe went running to their nearest bookstore to purchase a copy.

North Korean film world. What it does elaborate on is previous Kim Il-sung statements on the importance of film as a means of propaganda and its central status in the arts. It also drew on Kim Jong-il's experiences in the film industry, where he apparently encountered a lot of sloppiness and thoughtlessness, and urged workers to be more focused.

Kim writes in the preface: "The cinema is now one of the main objects on which efforts should be concentrated to conduct the revolution in art and literature. The cinema occupies an important place in the overall development of art and literature."[11]

By "revolution in art and literature" he means of course that the *Juche* ideology must be put into the center of all artistic production. Films must be realistic, he says, and film workers should actually have lived with the popular masses to know about their problems, hopes and sentiments and thus be able to connect to the audience. But the realism he talks about here is not the gritty realism of, say, the Italian Neo-realism. He means the "realism" of *Juche*. A "realism" that endlessly glorifies Great Leader Kim Il-sung, paints a picture of a single-minded *Juche* nation striving to achieve *Juche* paradise and otherwise condemns all Western thinking foreign to the *Juche* ideology like Western ideas and feudal remnants. He wants pictures which press the right buttons with the audience while successfully preaching the gospels of *Juche*.

He says that North Korean films have to be made with the special needs of the North Korean situation always in the mind of everyone involved in the filmmaking process and that incorporating Korean traditions is necessary in order to reach the hearts, minds and sentiments of the prospective audience. But, he continues, the traditional Korean arts cannot be fully trusted. They have to be used—but in a modified way, a way which promotes the current ideological lines and purges any "feudal ideologies" which may still be contained in much valued traditional Korean legends and tales.

His advice on how to achieve this is hardly surprising. He demands that the process of making a film must start from a strong, convincing idea of what to tell (the "seed" as he calls it), that the right ideological content always has to be the main focus of the work and that the aesthetics and the storytelling always has to be strongly put to work to emphasize the ideological message.

This, of course, had been done before by propaganda film directors of all persuasions all over the world. In practical terms, the book tends to deal with the obvious. Kim Jong-il's experiences at the film studio must have been far from satisfying if he had to tell these things to the industry insiders the book was aimed at: "The director is the commander of the creative group," "In creative work one must aim high," "The quality of directing depends on the director," "The secret of directing lies in editing," "The actor is the face of the film," "A screen portrayal demands first-class filming techniques," "Make-Up is a noble art," "Custom and hand props should conform to the period and the character," "The sets should reflect the times," "Musical arrangement is creative work."

If one reads the anecdotes about Kim Jong-il on the film sets in *Great Man and Cinema*, one gets the impression that the Dear Leader was surrounded there by fearful and uncreative dimwits. Reading in *On the Art of the Cinema* Kim Jong-il telling his film workers the absolute basics of filmmaking is a sign that Kim did not hold the professionalism of his film people in high regard.

The movies that he does praise as successful examples of *Juche* filmmaking are logically the ones he produced himself, like *Sea of Blood* and *Flower Girl*. These movies are quoted throughout the book as examples of how to make a good and successful movie. They are dealt with as the high standard to which all other North Korean productions should rise ... which, unfortunately, very few had upon publication of the book.

Watching North Korean movies from before and after the publication of the book, one can discern that it made very little impact. The North Korean film productions, while of course (before and after the book came out) always emphasizing their political messages, were much more influenced by actual political and economical situations than by the teachings of this book—which is still enshrined as the holy text on North Korean filmmaking.

Shin Sang-ok

By the late seventies, even while producing the boring historical accounts of *An Jung-gun Shoots Ito Hirobumi*, Kim Jong-il had his eyes already on some new ideas. Sensing perhaps that his domestically groomed directors from the Pyongyang University of Dramatic and Cinematic Arts lacked a bit in terms of international standards, Kim Jong-il clearly needed fresh blood flowing into the inbred North Korean movie scene. A really good and famous South Korean director would be perfect, one with a sharp eye towards social conflicts...

Shin Sang-ok proved to be the perfect choice. He was one of South Korea's biggest and most controversial directors well into the seventies, running his own studio, producing social-realist masterpieces like *A Flower in Hell* (1958) as well as genre films like the 1961 historical drama *Yeongsangun*. In the sixties his Shin Film Studio was the biggest in South Korea. By the mid-seventies however, his luck had run out. His films lost money, and his pretty open depiction of sexuality (well, "open" by Korean standards of the time) got him into trouble with the censorship office of dictator Park Chung-hee. In November 1975, his inclusion of two censored scenes in *Rose and Wild Dog*, as well as his announcement of a movie about the kidnapping of dissident (and later president) Kim Dae-jung by Park Chung-hee's secret service from exile in Japan, caused the South Korean government to revoke Shin Film's certificate.

Shin Sang-ok began to make movies in Hong Kong, including the 1978 women-in-prison sexploiter *Revenge in the Tiger Cage* about a female concentration camp in the Japanese-created state of Manchukoku in Manchuria in the thirties.

According to Shin, at that time Kim Jong-il had already sensed Shin's desperation—and Kim, unbeknownst to Shin, began financing Shin's Hong Kong films through North Korea–affiliated investors. A sly preparation of what was to come? Was Kim testing what Shin was able to do with North Korean money?

In January 1978, Choi Eun-hee, legendary South Korean actress and Shin Sang-ok's estranged wife, suddenly disappeared from Hong Kong. In July of the same year, Shin also disappeared.

We will not know the exact details of what happened till the North Korean secret police archives are open to the public—which might take a while. If we believe Shin Sang-ok, as he talks about the events now (after having defected from North Korea in 1986), they were both kidnapped by the North Koreans and taken to Pyongyang. "As soon as the car door shut, someone suddenly put a sack over my head, and I couldn't see anything or even breathe properly," Shin told BBC World Service's The World Today program.[12] "Then they sprayed something inside the sack, and I started to lose consciousness. A short while later I was being loaded onto a big ship, having been wrapped in some kind of plastic sheeting." According to Shin, in December 1978 he tried to escape from North Korea but got arrested. Upon being released by a special amnesty in early 1979, he tried to flee again. This netted him a stay in a concentration camp for the next four years, during which time he was tortured. Upon his release in 1983, Shin feigned a conversion to the Northern ideology and was allowed to reunite with Choi Eun-hee and to re-establish Shin Film in North Korea.

But should we believe Shin? Japanese film critic and early friend of Shin Sang-ok, Tetsuo Nishida, tells us not to in his book *Fictional Image*.[13] There, he says that Shin Sang-ok told him various times before disappearing from Hong Kong that he had gotten an offer from North Korea to make movies there freely—and that he considered going there voluntarily. Given that he was severely at odds with the South Korean government and couldn't work in the South any more, it certainly made sense for him to consider such an opportunity...

In any case, with Shin's appearance in Pyongyang, Kim Jong-il had gotten a powerful new force into his film industry. *An Emissary of No Return* (1984) was the first film Shin made in the North, under the "wise guidance" of Kim Jong-il, of course. Shin avoided overt North Korean propaganda and opted for a historical theme from the beginning of the 20th century, centering on the Korean nationalist feelings at the time when Japan took over the peninsula.

He was playing it safe: The film was based on a stageplay called *Bloody Conference*, allegedly written by Great Leader Kim Il-sung himself.

The film fictionalizes the true story of Ri Jun, one of three Korean emissaries at the "Second The Hague International Peace Conference" in 1907, when three emissaries of the Korean emperor tried to convince the international community to help reverse the Ito Hirobumi–drawn Japanese-Korean Protective Treaty of 1905 which essentially subjugated Korea under Japanese leadership. The two others were not successful nor was Ri Jun, who delivered a longish speech at the conference (featured in full in the film) and finally, frustrated, disemboweled himself in front of the watching diplomats. The conference ended after that gory incident.

That film could easily have been just as boring a lecture as *An Jung-gun Shoots Ito Hirobumi*, and yes, partly it is, but Shin Sang-ok managed to introduce some groundbreaking changes in the North Korean film industry with this work. First of all, this was the first North Korean film that had shooting locations abroad. Not in Holland, of course, Shin couldn't get that far and use a Western location, but in Communist Czechoslovakia. The Czech Barrandov Film Studio provided plenty of Western extras—giving the film a much more realistic feel than *Ahn Jung-gun Shoots Ito Hirobumi* for example, where all the Russian envoys are played by Koreans with blond-dyed hair. The experienced folks at the Barrandov studios could also provide European-looking sets way beyond the capability of the Korean Film Studio's "European Street."[14] Though of course, The Hague seen in the movie is still a far cry from the real The Hague.

The film's beginning is also quite unusual: A North Korean shipwright arrives in The Hague in the 1980s, the first since World War II. He visits the grave of Ri Jun and meets a Dutch lady who is the daughter of the landlord who owned the house where the three emissaries stayed. Her reminiscences provide the starting point of Ri Jun's story in the movie.

Shin Sang-ok cared about his cast and crew: this was the first film to include every crew member's name in the final credits. Previously, final credits were not used—only a few "big name" actors in the front credits and an END sign when the movie was over.

Shin was not quite happy with the film and thought he could have done better. But the Karlovy Vary Film Festival thought differently and awarded Shin the Special Jury Prize as Best Director. Subsequently, the film was released not only in the countries of the Eastern Bloc but also in Japan.

The 1984 Karlovy Vary Film Festival also had another, quite different impact. It was here that Shin Sang-ok announced that he went voluntarily to North Korea, alongside Choi Eun-hee, and that the South Korean sources who had previously announced that he had been kidnapped were lying.

Kim Jong-il must have been delighted: Shin went with the program 100 percent and earned him and North Korea great international reputations. Shin Sang-ok now got a lot more leeway. In addition to directing, he would now also supervise the making of plenty of other films. Suddenly, North Korean cinema became the cinema of Shin Film.

The next film Shin made was *Runaway* and he still considers it the best film he made in North Korea. It's a historical drama again, from the 1920s this time and based on a story by pre–World War II leftist writer Choi Suh-hae. Young man Park (played by Choe Sang-soo) and his wife (Choi Eun-hee, Shin Sang-ok's wife) live in the Japanese-controlled Gando area of Manchuria in poverty and under feudal oppression. They try to survive by being tenant farmers, writing letters for the illiterate peasants and selling self-made tofu but nothing works out. Bad as this is, the Japanese prove to be even worse: The evil, greedy Japanese pharmacy owner doesn't provide medicine to save Park's mother from dying because Park is broke as always. Park smashes the pharmacy, gets arrested and is put on a train to be transferred to jail. Kim Il-sung's revolutionary army attacks the train, frees the prisoners and our hero Park eventually becomes a member of Kim Il-sung's underground army, fighting for the homeland. Sounds familiar and is along the lines of *Flower Girl*— where Socialism also comes in only at the very end of the picture, tagged on as a happy ending after the audience has already been led to believe that everyone on screen has ended up either mad or dead.

Shin Sang-ok followed *Runaway* with *Salt* (1985). Having re-established his marital relation with Choi Eun-hee, who plays the lead role, the film is about illegal salt transport in the 1930s in a region where the Japanese colonial masters had forbidden the import of salt to quell Korean independence insurgents. The film won Choi Eun-hee a Best Actress award at the Moscow International Film Festival and it was the first North Korean film to feature local dialect (official North Korean language is always supposed to be Pyongyang speech). Shin being an old sexploiter, there was even a rape scene.

The year 1985 also saw Shin direct *Pulgasari*, the film he is most well-known for internationally. Inspired by the on going Japanese kaiju (monster movie) series *Gojira* (*Godzilla*), Shin, with the full support of *Godzilla*-loving Kim Jong-il, went out to make the first North Korean monster movie.

Based on an old Korean legend, *Pulgasari* tells the story of a farmers' uprising in the days of the Koryo dynasty (935 A.D. to 1395). The governor's soldiers confiscate all iron from the farmers—their tools, pots and pans. The farmers are unable to make a living without those things. An old blacksmith gets arrested for rebellious activities: He refused the governor's order to forge the confiscated metal into swords. Held prisoner in a wooden hut, he sculpts a little figure—a dragon-style toy with horns on the head. The blacksmith dies in prison and his daughter Ami (played by beautiful Jang Son-hui) inherits the figure. While sewing, she cuts her finger and blood drops onto the figure and it comes alive as a little critter. Cute in the beginning, it eats all iron available—and grows quickly. Soon it has become a huge monster, now named Pulgasari, and it's as strong as all monsters are and it's invincible of course. Pulgasari fights alongside the farmers against the evil authorities and is soon the farmers' wunderwaffe: nothing can stop him. He stomps the king's soldiers by the hundreds and when they trap him in a cage and try to burn him, he just heats up (he's made of metal after all), glows red and jumps into the nearest river, fatally boiling the soldiers who fled there. They fire rockets at him (yes, the Chinese and Koreans used primitive rockets 700 years ago), try to kill him any way they can, but Pulgasari remains the undying friend of the farmers—smashing even the emperor's palace to ensure victory. The farmers win the rebellion and chase the feudals off their territory. But Pulgasari, who had been eating the metal weapons of the enemies, now becomes a burden: He eats the farming tools, pots and pans of the people he used to help. To rescue her village from starvation, the blacksmith's daughter hides in a big bell. Pulgasari eats the bell and with it the girl. But he is meant to eat iron, not girls. Upon tasting the girl, he explodes into concrete-looking fragments. A tiny Pulgasari, running around the debris, is then hit by a light beam and dissolves. The blacksmith's daughter is sleeping in the midst of the rubble with a tear on her face. End.

What's the message here? The friend of the people becomes as bad as the worst enemy in the end? Any parallels to the Communist party? Maybe ... but Kim Jong-il had approved of the story after all.

Aside from this rather dubious ending, the film plays like pure entertainment in the most touching type of campy fifties monster movies—a real highlight for every fan of early *Godzilla* pictures with a sense of humor.

To get as close to the *Godzilla* original as he could get, Shin had flown in several technicians and special effects experts from the Toho Studios in Japan, where the original *Godzilla* movies are made. The actor wearing the Pulgasari rubber suit, Kenpachiro Satsuma, had destroyed Tokyo several times before, being the man acting in the Godzilla outfit. He would later write a book about this experience, *North Korea Seen Through the Eyes of Godzilla*.[15]

Kim Jong-il was quite delighted with the film and sent Shin Sang-ok and Choi Eun-hee on a mission to the West in early 1986, promoting North Korean film at the Berlin Film Festival, at the Cannes Film Festival ... and in Vienna.

Kidnapped to North Korea or not, by now both Shin and Choi were sick of living under that regime and wanted to get the hell out of there. In Vienna, they evaded the guards Kim Jong-il had sent along and made a dash to the American embassy, asking for asylum. The Americans flew them to Los Angeles and they resumed filmmaking there, producing, among other works, a straight-to-video remake of *Pulgasari* in 1996. *The Adventures of Galgameth* was the title and Shin was active as executive producer under his American pseudonym Simon Sheen while Michael Angeli re-wrote the story. The director was Sean McNamara and the movie is kiddie entertainment at its silliest. More of a box-office success, but just as silly, was "Simon Sheen's" American production of the *3 Ninjas* series.

But hey, switching almost overnight from North Korean propaganda to American teenage mall rats fodder (and making money with it)—it's quite an adaptation! Has any other North Korean film personality ever been able to do anything like that? North Korean actress Kim Hye-young, who had played in seven North Korean features, and who defected to the South in 1998, had to start her South Korean acting career in a toothpaste commercial. She is now building up a reputation as a "gagwoman" (comedienne) in TV, with people laughing about her Northern accent.

Well, in America it went well for Shin but in South Korea it didn't. In 1989, Shin and Choi moved partially back to Seoul while remaining active in the U.S. In an apparent stab at schmoozing his way back into South Korea's (now democratic) society, Shin made the 1990 movie *Mayumi*.

Mayumi was the assumed name under which North Korean terrorist Kim Hyun-hee operated. Together with an older accomplice and in the disguise of a Japanese tourist, Kim had smuggled a bomb on a flight from Baghdad to Seoul in November 1987, causing it to explode over the Indian Ocean and killing 115 people. It was Kim Jong-il's way to show his appreciation of the Olympic Games being held in Seoul the following year ... While her accomplice killed himself, Kim Hyun-hee was arrested in Bahrain and extradited to South Korea. She went to court, was sentenced to death but then forgiven and released from jail. She told her story in a bestselling book[16] and is now walking around free in South Korea.

The films starts off with three different stories: a Korean laborer who gets injured in an accident and is heading home from Baghdad; three truck drivers crossing Europe from Spain; and the North Korean spy couple acting under the cover of being father- daughter Japanese tourists. The stories intersect at Baghdad Airport when all the characters enter the plane, the spy couple leaving on the next stop. A slow-motion explosion of the plane follows, as does a depiction of Kim Hyun-hee's capture and trial. Set free in the end, she attempts suicide by jumping from a Seoul skyscraper but is unable to kill herself.

Treating a still very hot issue, the film felt too much like a superficial entertainment picture for the Southern audiences. With another South Korean airliner having been shot down over Sakhalin Island by the Soviets in 1988, nobody was primed for air terrorism as movie-house action. At the box office, *Mayumi* sunk like a stone.

Shin's next South Korean venture, *Vanished* (1994) gave a fictive depiction of the birth and death of the era of dictator Park Chung-hee (1962–79).

The film netted Shin an invitation to Cannes but in South Korea, audiences showed little interest. Shin went back to America to continue his 3 *Ninjas* series.

Shin Sang-ok's Influences on North Korean Cinema

Shin and Choi's defection must have been a real blow to Kim Jong-il; it certainly was to the North Korean film industry.

Shin had made a total of seven films in North Korea and he oversaw the production of thirteen more. Not all of them were masterpieces, his supervision of Pak Sang-bok's *The Road* for example could not prevent that film (about a hard-working female truck driver and single mother) from feeling like a very long and tedious road trip. But he also supervised one of *the* outstanding North Korean films of all time: the historical sword-fight drama *Hong Kil Dong*.

Directed by Kim Kil-in, the film recounts the old Korean legend of Hong Kil Dong, Korea's Robin Hood. Making great use of North Korea's rugged mountain landscape, the plot unfolds with Hong Kil Dong being born in the

A very long-winding road trip! Pak Sang-bok's *The Road*.

midst of a thunderstorm in the home of a servant of an influential minister at the emperor's court. He is an illegitimate child by the minister and his servant. The wife of the minister hates the offspring and plots to kill him. When Hong is about ten years old, the minister's wife arranges that Hong and his mother travel a remote mountain road (she has paid a gang of robbers to kill them both). The robbers attack but Hong and mother are saved by a flying monk who is a master of the sword. They take refuge at his mountain retreat and here young Hong learns the martial arts.

As a young man, he has a coincidental run-in with the robbers again. They fight and, by accident, Hong kills their leader. They leave a sack with booty behind; a beautiful (actually not so beautiful) girl is in the sack, the daughter of another Seoul minister, a guy always plotting behind the back of Hong's father. Hong falls in love with her and leaves for the city, returning with his mother to his father's house where he can be close to his beloved.

Ready for battle. Kim Kil-in's *Hong Kil Dong*, North Korea's version of Robin Hood.

14. North Korean Cinema (Johannes Schönherr)

Continual plots against his life by his father's wife prompt him to leave again. Wandering around the country, he learns about feudal injustices and becomes a hero of the farmers whom he helps in often hilarious ways to drive away greedy tax collectors and to punish local lords who waste their farmers' money by indulging in orgies.

But suddenly, a foreign force threatens the country: a small army of black-clad ninjas speaking Japanese under the Korean voice-over. They steal the crown jewels and kidnap scores of young girls—Hong's beloved among them. They fight with the help of black magic and the emperor's army is helpless. Only Hong Kil Dong can save the country now—and he does. He unites all Koreans, from the robbers in the woods to the emperor's army, and now the action starts to get serious. In all the movie's previous fights, Koreans were pitted against Koreans, and except for the leader of the robbers, nobody was killed in the rather humorous clashes. But now a true Hong Kong–style

The Korean hero fighting the foreign ninjas in *Hong Kil Dong*.

gorefest begins, with very elaborate martial arts and truly great evil ninjas. Of course, Hong and his men beat the ninjas in the end. But since Hong is still a low-class "bastard"—even after saving the country—he is not allowed to marry his upper-class girl. They sail away in search of "a country of justice." They sail away right into the sunset! This in a movie from North Korea where in all other movies the heroes fight it out to the last man standing. It's a very surprising ending: Leaving the country as a solution to domestic problems is not condoned by any other North Korean movie.

Made in 1985, only months before *Pulgasari*, *Hong Kil Dong* is considered to be the very first film made in North Korea solely for one purpose: entertainment. And it delivers—despite the tackling of feudal problems and the we-Koreans-against-the-evil-outsiders theme. To ensure that the martial arts were topnotch, genre masters from Hong Kong supervised the shooting.

In a 2002 survey among ex–North Koreans living in South Korea, conducted by the newspaper *Choson Ilbo*, *Hong Kil Dong* was named "best North Korean film ever."

Encouraged by Kim Jong-il's approval of this film, directors outside the direct radius of Shin Sang-ok began to take things light-heartedly as well. The war-action movie *Order No. 027* (1986) by Jung Ki-mo and Kim Eung-suk was basically a remake of the story already told in the 1953 *Scouts*, only here the Korean War becomes a pure martial arts battleground. The reconnaissance group going behind the enemy lines here is employing first-rate taek-won-do to attain their goals.[17] The martial arts scenes seem to have been more important to the filmmakers than sending political messages. It's simply good guys versus bad guys, the war just a customary backdrop for the often comedy-like fighting scenes. As the plot unfolds further, though, firearms are also introduced, the film making the transition from martial arts to big-scale gun battles and explosions—all for the sake of politically correct but hilarious entertainment.

Neither *Hong Kil Dong* nor *Order No. 027* received any festival prize but they both got wide distribution in the whole Eastern bloc.

Even propaganda flicks with heavy political messages came under the influence of the new openness. The 1985 defection drama *The Separation* by Park Chang-sun, for example. After it opens with a shot of the Eiffel Tower, the camera pans to a Paris circus hall, then cuts to posters announcing "Le Cirque de Coree" in big letters. A North Korean film team had finally made it to the West, shooting documentary footage of an actual performance of the internationally recognized North Korean State Circus. Around this footage, the fictitious part of the movie was woven.

The North Korean circus is the attraction of the season in a "foreign city"*

**Paris is not mentioned by name and we may doubt many in the North Korean audience would know where or what the Eiffel Tower is.*

14. North Korean Cinema (Johannes Schönherr)　　　175

Tae kwon do action set in the Korean War in *Order Number 027*.

and Su Ki-ho (played by Yu Won-jun), the fabulous trapeze artist, is the talk of the town. This is a fact that the evil South Korean agents notice, too. And they get hold of another fact: Su Ki-ho and her father were separated during the Korean War, haven't seen each other since then, and bingo!, that father lives in Seoul. In abject poverty, of course. The evil agents approach an old friend of the father, a fellow who now lives in the "foreign city," and tell him

The stunts are up to standard (yes, this train is moving!). Jung Ki-mo and Kim Eung-suk's *Order Number 027*.

that they would arrange a reunion of father and daughter. Well, we are in the fiction part here and that was not shot in Paris. The friend of the father and the agent meet in what is unmistakably a cafe in the old town of (then communist) Prague—standing in here as a "Korean tea house in a foreign city"! From here on, the film will jump back and forth between documentary footage from Paris and the location of the fiction plot, Prague. The Eiffel Tower and Hradshin Castle in one unified city! With the help of the teahouse-operating friend, the father (played by Park Mi-hwa) is brought over from Seoul—a city where poverty-stricken folks line up in the rain outside the employment office, U.S. military trucks and Jeeps being the only cars on the street.

The plan of the evil Southern agents is that the father shall convince his daughter in a dramatic meeting to defect and go with him to Seoul. The meeting takes place—and the daughter convinces her father that the North is better. Now, *he* wants to join *her*! But the Southern agents kidnap him, lock him up at their embassy, and finally fly him back into South Korean poverty. It's great drama and quite effectively played out. Presumably scores of girls in the North Korean audience wept and men gritted their teeth when the evil agents force the father into the plane at the end of the movie, his daughter looking on and screaming: "Father! Father!"

Heavy-duty propaganda indeed but still, the film did give its home audience some rare exposure to what the outside world looked like.

14. North Korean Cinema (Johannes Schönherr)

In Park Chang-sun's *The Separation*, Su Ki-ho (played by Yu Won-jun) cries out for her father when he gets kidnapped back into the poverty of South Korea.

Not as much as *Thaw* however. Made in the same year, it was probably the most liberal-minded movie in North Korean history. Directed by Kim Chang-bum and co-produced with the Chongryon Film Studio in Japan, the film production outlet of the pro-North Korean organization of Korean residents in Japan, this film shows clearly that a fresh breeze of freedom blew in the North Korean film world of the mid-eighties.

The film opens with a scene of men forcibly taken away from their Korean home village to serve as forced laborers during the Japanese colonial period. That is the old routine, of course, but the next scene is not: shots of the Statue of Liberty and the Manhattan skyline, cutting to a lecture room at an American university. Chol-mun, an American professor of Korean heritage, has a discussion with students. His views are pro-North and he easily manages to counter the views of the pro-South student who challenges him. His class is applauding and the student who was out-debated admits defeat. Back at his office, Chol-mun receives a letter from Tokyo, inviting him to the wedding of

The sad bride is singing the blues in *Thaw*.

the daughter of his old Korean friend Hyung-chol who now lives in Tokyo. He flies over, arriving at Haneda Airport and then staying at the spacious upper middle class house of Hyung-chol and his family. Sang-ho, a wealthy businessman from Seoul, is also invited by Hyung-chol. Big surprise—all the Tokyo scenes were really shot in Tokyo! An absolute first in any North Korean film! But what follows is even more incredible. Hyung-chol, it turns out, is a member of Mindan, the pro–South Korean organization of Koreans living in Japan. His daughter loves a Korean boy named Namsu and we see them rolling around on the floor in clearly sexual poses at the house of the boy's parents. His parents, though, belong to the rival group of Mindan, to the pro–North Korean association of Koreans in Japan, Chongryon. Once Hyun-chol finds out about that, the problems start. Because of his political opinions as pro–South guy, he suddenly changes his mind and tells his daughter that, sorry, no, she cannot marry a boy with a pro-North background. The father and daughter go to a Tokyo strip club and see a performance. In the beginning, the girls are dancing fully clothed and rather awkwardly—kind of like a North

14. North Korean Cinema (Johannes Schönherr)

The bride's father drinks it up in Kim Chang-bum's *Thaw*.

Korean might imagine a strip club. But then, after the father tells his daughter that she cannot marry her boyfriend, we see real topless girls on stage. Probably the only time ever in North Korean cinema that bare tits have been shown! (Well, admittedly, it's a rather strange idea that the father takes his daughter to a strip bar to tell her she cannot marry. Is this how North Korean script writers imagine what things are like in the "rotten" West?)

Feeling guilty about this decision, Hyung-chol gets drunk and, when he arrives home, he picks a fight with his wife. Disgusted and desperate, the daughter runs away to join her boyfriend, who is working as a volunteer at a ski resort in Hokkaido.

All through this North Korean version of *Romeo and Juliet*, we see flashbacks involving Hyung-chol as a forced laborer for the Japanese in the colonial times. He and another guy beat up a guard at a quarry, incite a riot and flee. The other guy is shot in the legs and falls into the sea. After living in the woods and almost starving, Hyung-chol is rescued by a Korean family.

Now, at the dramatic climax of the movie, it turns out that that other guy, the one who got shot in the legs, is the wheelchair-bound father of Namsu! A big reunion of the old comrades follows and of course their children are given the green light for a happy marriage. Shots of melting arctic ice-blocks crashing into the ocean conclude the movie.

America depicted as a country of free speech? A pro–South Korea family in Tokyo living in a big mansion and even having a Japanese maid? Their daughter driving her own car? Japan generally depicted as a wealthy country where it's easily possible to see topless girls and customary to drink large amounts of Hennessy cognac at any given time? A South Korean businessman wealthy enough to be part of all that? And the pro-South people as well as the Korean living in America all portrayed as thoroughly likable characters? It's all here. One character (the American professor) is even shown watching *Shaft* on TV! What happened to North Korean cinema at that point? *Thaw* looks all the way through as if North Korea would suddenly embrace reconciliation

Get out of here, son of a traitor! Jo Kyung-soon's *A Bellflower*.

with the South, Japan and even America—and slyly hint at knowing quite a bit about their cultures. A "thaw" seemed suddenly to have set in. International film festival jurors thought the same and gave the film the main prize at the Karlovy Vary film festival in 1986. To what extent the film was shown in North Korea itself, however, could not be clearly ascertained. It may well have been made mainly for export.

The End of the Thaw

Shin-Sang-ok was able to open North Korea's propagandistically very important film industry to the outside world to quite some degree and make the cinematic realization of a lot of new ideas possible in only two and a half years of active involvement in the North Korean film scene. One is left to wonder what he could have done had he stayed longer. Could he have become North Korea's Mikhail Gorbachev?

After his escape, things took a sharp turn. Not only was Shin gone (a fact that greatly embittered Kim Jong-il) but both in the Soviet Union and in China big-scale reform movements were in full swing. The new Soviet Union leader Mikhail Gorbachev preached "glasnost" and "perestroika" (openness and change), China's Deng Xiao Ping opened up the economy to capitalist ways—very threatening developments in the societies of North Korea's main allies. Kim Il-sung and Kim Jong-il had to renew their propagandistic efforts to keep any such influences out of their half-peninsula. By 1987, the time of openness was over in North Korea's movie world and now productions took a sharp turn and bitterly retreated to a fanatical "Hermit Kingdom" stance.

This development is most evident in Jo Kyung-soon's 1987 film *A Bellflower*. Here, a young man has many ideas on how to turn his remote mountain village into a modern place to live. His girlfriend (nicknamed "Bellflower") loves him for that and he also enjoys all the appreciation by her sister. Suddenly, the young man changes his mind. He wants to move to the city and take his girl with him. But she feels responsible for the people in the village and begs him not to leave. He leaves anyway, but the sister of his girlfriend stops him on a little bridge leading out of the village. She has laid out his drawings on how to improve the village in the snow and he has to stomp over his own old plans if he really wants to leave. He does. Fiercely angry, the sister makes him sign a paper that says that he is never going to be allowed back to the village.

With him gone, the two girls realize his old plans. They get electricity into the village, build a successful farm, erect a cultural center and make the place a model village. Bellflower dies a heroine's death trying to save a sheep from a landslide during a rainstorm.

Many years after his departure, the young man, now an old man, has had no success in the outside world and feels homesick. He approaches the hills near the village and sends his son down to test the waters. At first rejected, the son is eventually accepted and in the very end, even the father is forgiven—but the latter only as an act of mercy.

"Stay home!" the movie essentially screams all the way through, "work at your own place!" One can read that message on at least two distinct levels. On one level one can read the young man's departure and "betrayal of the village" as abandoning the country or the way things are done in that country. He only leaves the village and not the country in the movie, though—but why is he so unsuccessful elsewhere in the Worker's Paradise? Isn't there a place for everyone to be happy all over the DPRK? Well, only for those who remain where they belong ...

On another level the film can be read as trying to convince people not to come to Pyongyang, the glorious capital. Village life is poor and hard and Pyongyang is attractive—but only people with special permits are allowed to live there. "Don't try to come here, make *your* own place better," the film tells people who have to remain outside the Pyongyang city limits.

1987 was the year of the first Pyongyang International Film Festival. But instead of opening up the country, the festival became a showcase of a closed society. *A Bellflower* won the "Golden Torch," the biggest prize at the festival. Good-bye openness and easy-going ways!

Harking back to the super-heavy propaganda of the pre–Shin Sang-ok days was another major film made in 1987: Kim Young-ho's *My Happiness*. Here, as in *A Bellflower*, the propaganda messages feel like slabs of lead sinking onto the heads of the viewers. This despite the film being about two cute-looking girls.

Hong Su-jung (Kim Jung-hwa) and Ri Ji-eun (Kim Ock-hee) are young girls and best friends in the early days of the Korean War. Hong's boyfriend is drafted into the army and the two girls follow soon after, serving as nurses in a stretcher platoon. Hong is still a little light-hearted in the beginning, causing trouble for her unit by trying to reach her boyfriend who is fighting nearby. She learns quickly that war is a tough business—the war scenes of the film are actually pretty dirty and realistic. But soon, the picture shifts gears and moves into unabashed heroism: The girlie platoon is trying to rescue wounded soldiers when an enemy boat attacks their coastal position. There is only one way out—destroying the boat. The chief nurse does it, swimming over to the boat in the guise of a deserter and blowing herself up with the whole crew of devilish-looking Southern soldiers. She yells "Long live Kim Il-sung!" the moment before she evaporates in fire along with the boat. Now, the rest of the girls can save the wounded they were carrying.

Cut to post-war times. The two heroines continue living in the spirit of war. The country has to be rebuilt and they are on the forefront, Ri as a doctor and ambitious academic, Hong still serving in the army, also as a doctor.

14. North Korean Cinema (Johannes Schönherr)

In *My Happiness* Hong Su-jung (Kim Jung-hwa) is a nurse in the Korean War. The North Koreans surely love their girls in uniform.

Hong's boyfriend was declared missing in the war; now news arrives that he survived but without his legs. One day, he surprisingly shows up at Hong's hospital—his legs intact. Emergency battlefield doctors had saved his legs by transplanting their own flesh and bones into his legs! ("We live in a great society!" he declares.) They marry and have a kid but Hong's true happiness lies in her work. She is director of an army hospital now and also acting as head surgeon, making bricks to enlarge the hospital, raising chickens, pigs and cows to feed the patients and growing herbal medicine to heal them. Serving the country in many capacities is making her happy—hence the title of the film. She is a true heroine of the new Korea and worth taking part in that gigantic parade we see marching over Kim Il-sung Square in Pyongyang in the finale.

For her, the war has never ended—it just moved to other fronts. But the war with the "imperialists" is never quite over—her husband is killed as a ship captain in a "peace-time naval battle" by the "American imperialists" towards the end of the movie. Well, this is a pretty realistic way of dying actually; as recently as December 2001 a North Korean spy ship was sunk by the Japanese Coast Guard, with no survivors left.

While A *Bellflower* told the audiences not to look any place else and just work on where they are, *My Happiness* takes that position even further: Work as hard as you can where you are—and do it so hard as if you were in the midst of war. The liberal messages of *Thaw* were clearly out of date now.

Nation and Destiny—The World's Longest Movie Series

This new kind of hardcore propaganda soon ran out of steam, though. All the themes were just newly cooked-up 1950s propaganda, reviving outmoded ideas from even the days before Kim-Jong-il's involvement in the movies. Subsequent movies had less and less impact, turning out to be pale shadows of their predecessors. Take A *Far-Off Islet* (1992) as an example: A young female schoolteacher running a school with only two pupils on a remote island yearns for Pyongyang because there, she thinks, she could be close to the Great Leader. She heads for the city but is told to return home. There, she miraculously saves a ship from crashing into the cliffs by powering the failing lighthouse with the dynamo that runs her bicycle lamp. The Great Leader, hearing of that heroic deed and of her bravely teaching the only two kids on the island, gives her a special medal, honoring her for staying at her own place and being a heroine there. But compared to the big drama of A *Bellflower* which was centered on the same subject, A *Far-Off Islet* comes up short—tedious, powerless, uninspired. The bicycle scene is quite something but it cannot save the picture.

But Kim Jong-il is a wise man. Seeing his film industry deteriorating, he came up with a bold concept: making the most gigantic film series in cinema history. Multi-part features were nothing new to North Korean cinema; the sixties intelligence–counter-intelligence series *Unknown Heroes* was spread over twenty parts for example. But the new enterprise, *Nation and Destiny*, was destined to break every record.

On 7 January 2001, KCNA reported: "Part 5 of multi-part feature film the *Nation and Destiny* part 54 was released." KCNA went on, on 4 February 2001: "The April 25 Film Studio of the Korean People's Army recently produced part 6 (*Choe Hyon*), the multi-part film the *Nation and Destiny* part 55. The feature film deals with the historical facts that during the Fatherland Liberation War Choe Hyon's army corps followed up victories in battles behind the enemy's line in hearty response to the order of supreme commander Kim Il Sung."

Part 6 of part 54—how is that possible? The series, intended to have 100

14. North Korean Cinema (Johannes Schönherr)

Poster for *A Far-off Islet*.

Nation and Destiny: Slated to become the biggest movie series of the world. Ever.

parts altogether, deals with different subjects, each of them spanning a few installments of the multi-part picture. Therefore, "part 6 (*Choe Hyon*), the multi-part film ... part 55" translates to: It's part 55 in the whole series and the sixth installment of the series dealing with Choe Hyon.

Nation and Destiny started in 1990, when seven one-hour installments were produced. It was announced as a new "immortal classic" from the day of its inception and sure enough, part 1 and 2 of the series went on to win the "Golden Torch" main prize of the Third Pyongyang International Film Festival in 1992.

Parts 1–4 show "how the main character Choe Hyon-dok, who has followed an anti-communist path and is roaming about in an alien land like an 'international orphan' in the twilight of his life, deserted by his fellow countrymen, finds the genuine road of life, the road of rebirth in the embrace of his dear home and fatherland."[18]

Parts 11–13 deal with the heroic deeds of Ri Jong-mo, who spent 34 years

A revolutionary among the bourgeois in *Nation and Destiny*.

in a South Korean prison. Parts 17 and 18 focus on 1920s revolutionary heroine Ho Jung-sun, parts 19–24 on the story of A *Naturalized Japanese Woman* (that means here a Japanese woman who followed her Korean husband to North Korea and was naturalized there) and her daughter visiting from Japan, both of them of course realizing that North Korea is the best place to live in. Parts 25–32 (this section being named *Workers*) show "the contents that everyone is transformed on the pattern of the working class while finding himself among the workers, just as scrap metal is turned into the glowing molten iron in the electric furnace."[19] The quote means that a bunch of people from different backgrounds are interacting, overcoming personal difficulties and ending up as heroes.

With all these different stories told, ranging from the 1920s to the contemporary settings, what holds the big soap together? Not much actually: its name, of course, the studio and special unit that produces all the various installments, and the fact that many of the actors appear over and over again on screen, playing different roles. A series of smaller soaps presented under one gigantic title ... and a one-line directive by Kim Jong-il: "A multi-part feature *The Nation and Destiny* should be produced based on the song 'Best is My Country.'"[20]

Here the lyrics of that song, written by Choe Jun-gyong:

> I saw flowers blooming, too
> In the fields of an alien land.
> But none so pretty
> As the flowers of my country.
> Refrain: Vast is the world
> I looked around.
> Best is the country
> I call my own.
>
> I'd drink a cup of water
> Offered by a foreign friend.
> But never did it taste sweeter
> Than the spring water of my own home.
> Refrain ... [21]

Basing a 100-movie series on that song? Quite a task! And not accomplished yet by part 56—or did any of the films seriously explore the refrain line "Vast is the world, I looked around"? No. While the line "Best is the country I call my own" applies to virtually every single film ever made in North Korea.

Myself in the Distant Future

Spending much of its resources on the *Nation and Destiny* soap, the North Korean film industry went into further decline during the nineties, winning

14. North Korean Cinema (Johannes Schönherr)

Filthy reactionaries in rage in *Nation and Destiny*.

not even a single major prize (Gold, Silver or Bronze Torch) at their own festivals in 1994 and 1996, let alone any foreign festival.

Economic problems became pressing, too. After the fall of the Berlin Wall in 1989, the dissolving of the Soviet Union in 1991, and China's switch to a market-based economy, the former international markets of the North Korean film industry broke away. The same political developments affected the whole of North Korean society: The formerly generous economic support handed out to North Korea by its communist "brothers" stopped flowing in. The country was on the verge of bankruptcy, wide-spread starvation set in.

In addition to all of that, in 1994 Great Leader Kim Il-sung died. He remained (and still remains) "president for eternity" while his son Kim Jong-il took over the post of Great Leader. (For the first time in history a communist head of state had inherited his power dynasty-style.) The era of the so-called "Arduous March" began—an era of famines killing up to two million North Koreans during which Kim Jong-il had to consolidate his power.

But did Allied bombing of Germany's Babelsberg studios at the end of World War II cause another movie-mad dictator, Adolf Hitler, to cease film production? No! He would even withdraw soldiers from the front, dress them in Napoleon-era uniforms and have them shoot grand-style color pictures to enhance the morals of the population—like the 1944 Veit Harlan epic *Kolberg*.

A hostile general situation would not keep Kim Jong-il away from producing films, either. Quite the contrary. If he wanted to stay in power now, rice and kimchi was not what he had to feed his people with—he needed to feed them propaganda to make them stay in line. "Indeed, in the middle of a famine in 1997, North Korea is believed to have spent $780 million on propaganda," South Korean newspaper *Korea Herald* reported later.[22] The time of starvation was turned into a propaganda campaign named the "Arduous March": Bad weather conditions were blamed for the poor harvests and of course, as always, the "imperialists" were blamed for everything that went wrong. The population was whipped into building ever bigger monuments to Kim Il-sung and the Juche ideology. Of course, some of the pressing problems had to be addressed cinematically; the endless repetition of anti-Japanese guerrilla fables alone wouldn't do anymore.

The first film to tackle this task was the 1997 feature *Myself in the Distant Future*, directed by Jang In-hak. It somberly starts with lots of (cotton flake–looking) snow streaming down, the clock on Pyongyang train station showing midnight on New Year's and an abundance of North Korean flags on display—we know we are in here for something important. Celebratory music playing, we see a young man being escorted to a train by tearfully waving people. Once inside the train, the young man tells his story to a journalist in the restaurant car. He used to be a bad guy, actually ...

Flashback and now the movie really begins. Sin-jun, the young man (played by Kim Myong-mun) is fairly lazy and believes that all the honors of his labor hero–architect father will automatically be his as well. He lives in luxury in his parents' apartment in a Pyongyang skyscraper and does nothing but dream, play Nintendo games, listen to dance music (North Korean dance music but it obviously stands in here for the illegal reception of South Korean broadcasts) and argue with his father. The father is flabbergasted by what he hears from his son. In one crucial dialogue, he berates his son for taking luxury for granted and for not doing anything for the improvement of the country. He scolds the son for breaking off his education at the "Institute of Engineering" in favor of trying to secure a place at the "University for International Relations." Failing that, the rotten son is nothing more today than a driver at the Foreign Ministry. Ha! The dialogue means that the son cared only about getting out of the country—or tried to stay in close contact with foreigners. The father continues his scolding: "The whole country is in the period of the Arduous March and you don't participate in any way."

"Uhhm, the Arduous March is only a temporary campaign," the son replies. What an antisocial statement! The "Arduous March" was the main theme of North Korean propaganda throughout the nineties and this guy says it's "only a temporary campaign"? What a failure of a son this father has!

The plot continues with Sin-jun meeting beautiful Su-yang (Kim Hye-gyong), with whom he immediately falls in love. To his astonishment, she works in the Shock Brigades that build skyscrapers at super-human speed. And unbeknownst to him, his father has just met the same girl as she was a model worker on the realization of one of his architectural designs. The girl is just finishing her time as a Shock Brigade laborer and returning to her home village (in the vicinity of Korea's holy Mount Paektu, where else) to help in the farming work "the Party worries so much about these days." The Party had reason to worry about farm work indeed: 1997 was the worst year of starvation. Sin-jun volunteers at her farm for a few weeks—his only motivation being to be close to her. At the end of his stay, he confesses his love to her. She rejects him, telling him that working at her own village and making it more successful is more important to her than following him to Pyongyang.

They meet again in Pyongyang a while later when she is visiting. When he makes a new proposal to her, he has to hear her real reasons for rejecting him: She was working hard in cold winter with her hands bleeding to build the skyscraper he is living in—and he did nothing to deserve that. He is just a slacker, depending on his famous father.

Sin-jun is really moved and wants to change himself. He goes to her village a second time, to settle there and to do something good for the village and the country ... like inventing a wood-fuel tractor. With a lot of help from his mother he succeeds and proves the new tractor's worth by driving it along a wintry forest road that has to stand in as an important mountain pass, pulling a trailer loaded with potatoes, and feeding the wood-fire engine with his own shoes to get the tractor going.

Of course, that makes him a labor hero himself and nets him a medal—and the girl.

The film addresses a lot of issues. First there is an apparently rampant problem: The children of the elite don't want to play by the rules of the Great Leader anymore. They want to get jobs outside of the country—and often use their high status to break all rules. *The New York Times* interviewed a very young North Korean convict named Ahn Hyuk for an article called "Survivors Report Torture in North Korea Labor Camps" after he had managed to defect to the South:

"'It was very natural in my home for my parents to praise Kim Il-sung,' Ahn says. He grew up the spoiled son of two senior officials, enjoying every luxury available in North Korea. He even had a radio to listen to South Korean stations (which is prohibited) and occasionally looked at pornography or videotapes smuggled in from Japan. He roamed the country without the passes that are required for domestic travel, and even sneaked into China for day trips

Sin-jung (Kim Myong-mun) faces the village people after one of his many failures in *Myself in the Distant Future.*

in the company of other children of high officials. Finally, he said, the government made an example of him for his free-wheeling life and trips to China: arresting him, torturing him and imprisoning him in a concentration camp."[23]

The Sin-jun of the beginning of the movie is portrayed as a much more harmless character than the Ahn Kyu *The New York Times* presented—but he's a character destined for the same fate. It's the girl who saves him and shows him the way: "Work for your country, dude!" The real bad-ass elite youth of Pyongyang must have taken that not as a message but as a big joke, though, perhaps hooting and hollering at the screen in Pyongyang theaters. Sin-jun is quite a mother-dependent weakling after all.

Su-yang on the other hand could be straight out of *A Bellflower*. She loves nothing more than building up her own village—after helping to build up the glory of Pyongyang, that is. Sacrificing herself for her country and her own place is all she cares about, inheriting the position of Hong Su-jung in *My Happiness*.

But there is more to the film. It's not only "girl awakens lazy guy to his true calling": Sin-jun does invent a tractor that works "independently from the expensive oil imports." He works hard on that vehicle and would have never succeeded without the extensive help his mother provides. But why does he do that and not something else? Didn't these same vehicles drive around in post–World War II Germany already? Aren't they still driving around the poorer rural parts of China? And don't we see them driving in North Korea in the same movie—before Sin-jun "invents" his tractor? What's the message here? Getting people to "invent" something that has existed for more than fifty years? That can't be true! Making the country independent from imports sounds like a goal but why bring in those poorly functioning tractors when every North Korean has seen them operating there for such a long time? It's a mystery.

Just mentioned in passing in the summary above, but it's a potent subtext, too: "Eat potatoes instead of rice!" To ease the famines of the nineties, the North Korean government called for the planting and eating of potatoes as it was a plant that can survive during poor weather conditions. In the village, Sin-jun would constantly tell his visiting mother, "The girls here are especially beautiful because they eat potatoes since a long time ago!" In the happiest moments of village life, they bake potatoes over campfires and smear their faces with the ashes sticking to the potato peel—then laughing at each other's ash-smeared face ... what happiness that brings! And, of course, it's potatoes he carries over the pass in his heroic tractor drive ...

All in all, *Myself in the Distant Future* was a scattershot directed at a lot of the current problems. Did it successfully disperse much needed propaganda? Nobody ever did a market research poll asking that question at Pyongyang theaters. But the film received one official blessing—winning the Golden Torch at the 1998 Pyongyang Film Festival.

Forever in Our Memory

In *Myself in the Distant Future*, North Korea looks like a rich country with plenty of food. The characters eat all the time, carry bulging bags of apples and harvest fields of ripe wheat. But in reality, the famine went on and eventually not even the official propaganda could ignore the problem any longer or just deal with it in hints in the subtexts of films. So, why not turn the poorly managed paddy fields into new heroic battlegrounds? That's exactly what Kang Jung-mo's 1999 *Forever in Our Memory* does.

The film starts out like a war movie: Regimental commander Ri Chol-suk (Ri Ik-sung) receives the order to march with his men into a rural area and wage a war for higher agricultural output and to defend the country against droughts and typhoons. Together with the local state farm folks, they start the battle: turning swamps into paddy fields (no, nobody talks about potatoes in this movie) and planting the rice even after midnight while lighting the fields with torches. When a tractor's tires go flat, the commander has the tires of his own Jeep planted on the tractor—thus cancelling out a visit to his ill wife in the hospital.

The movie is crowded with characters, not all of them perfect heroes. There is on the one hand the female boss of the farm who pledged after a visit to the village by Kim Il-sung that she would not marry before they achieve a real bumper harvest there. But there is also the soldier (the assistant of Ri Chol-suk, actually) who steals vegetables from the private garden of an old woman. He is dealt with seriously but carefully and he becomes a hero later on to prove that he has learned from his mistake. There is a vice chief of the farm who would occasionally barter rice against needed farm supplies. He is presented as a character who still has a lot to learn about the Juche ways—though there is no mention how he could have otherwise arranged for those necessary supplies.

But the main heroes, aside from Ri Chul-suk, are the anonymous soldiers working the fields. For a good reason. Kim Jong-il's power depends mainly on the military. So, he adjusted his father's Juche ideology to install the military as the "ruling class." Classical Marxism / Leninism always placed the working class at the center of interest, and claimed that history intended them to be the rulers of the world. Kim Jong-il threw this concept out the window and called his new policy *Songun*. *Songun* means that the military is the most advanced class, that they were the center of society. That had to be reinforced via propaganda, of course. *Forever in Our Memory* is full-force advertising for the internal might of the military—and the always proclaimed "unity between military and the people" with the military being in the lead. It's up to them to save the asses of the farmers in this movie, after all.

The deed of successfully planting the crops and claiming new arable land is finally done—green paddies up to the horizon—and then a drought hits the country. Now, the brave soldiers and farmers carry water in buckets for miles to save the fragile plants. The sun burns with demonic intensity ... but suddenly that same sun, still in the midst of the drought, is eulogized by a hymn-like musical score. Cut to the farmers carrying water. A girl yells the news to them: "The Great Leader has just been here!" Shaken by religious love, they run into the village—and we see a convoy of cars disappearing on the horizon. The happy regimental commander tells the farmers that, yes, the Great Leader has just visited here and he is in good health. The farmers kneel down and touch the tire tracks the Great Leader left in the dust.

The Great Leader, the "Sun of the 21st Century" as propaganda calls him, treated as a real deity. But right when the sun was scorching the plants, that same sun announced the Great Leader. What's that going to mean? A thought-

14. North Korean Cinema (Johannes Schönherr)

less script? Or a deliberate indication that the Great Leader, the "Sun" he is, is killing the country? A hint to the audiences that the real "natural disaster" was the leadership of the country? Unlikely. The movie is so full of glorification of *Juche*, the leader, the military and the hard-working, deeply believing common folks that it is almost unavoidable that sometimes some of the hosannas cancel each other out.

When the drought is overcome, a typhoon now threatens the harvest. The following scenes one has to see to believe. The flood is introduced by fierce waves running over the dikes and easily uprooting telephone poles. And how do the soldiers and farmers keep their paddy fields dry? By a few thousands of them standing on top of the dike, their arms linked, yelling "Long live Kim Il-sung!" into the face of the angry ocean and keeping the flood away with their own bodies. No ocean wave can break this spirit of unity between the army and the people!

The harvest is saved and the heroes return to their barracks. The army and the people have just won another victory!

An incredible piece of hyperbole? Definitely. But North Korean cinema has always featured characters accomplishing unlikely feats powered by nothing other than their will, the strength of their love of the leader and of the *Juche* ideology. In fact, whenever the word "impossible" turns up in a North Korean movie, there will be a cut to a group of dedicated people fiercely accomplishing what has just been called "impossible" (a military task in a war movie, the building of a bridge, dam, highway, etc.).

Still, the dike scene in *Forever in Our Memory* is unprecedented in its suicidal loss of any connection to reality. Was that how North Korea saw itself at the time? Standing on top of a dike and defending itself by nothing than their bodies and their belief in the leader against the flood of problems hitting the country?

Small Steps Towards the Outside World

North Korea had arrived at a dead end in 1999. It was isolated, famines raged, the country was an international pariah for sending several hostile submarines to South Korea. A North Korean spy boat was sunk with fifty sailors on board by the South Korean navy. In 1998, Japan freaked out when the North Korean tested their new Taepodong missile by firing it right over Japan to crash into the Pacific Ocean. Regular Pyongyang tour guides told me on a visit that year that "the situation is so desperate—even dying in a war would be better."

But at the same time the tide turned in South Korea. Former dissident and new president Kim Dae-jung introduced his "Sunshine Policy" and handed the olive branch over to Great Leader Kim Jong-il.

In June 2000, Kim Dae-jung went to Pyongyang to meet Kim Jong-il at a summit meeting. That move seemed a great success—both parts of Korea ended the previously customary hostile propaganda against each other, vague talks about unification took place and great plans of reconciliation were made.

Now there was new hope in the North. A new period of openness was announced. Economic collaboration with the South seemed feasible. All of that had its repercussions in the film industry, too.

In 1998, Japanese film historian Edoki Jun convinced the North Koreans to sell him the Japanese rights for *Pulgasari*. Screening the film in art houses in the home country of the original *Godzilla* proved to be a great success. People just loved the campy ways the movie portrayed the heroic monster. That same year, Roland Emmerich's Hollywood adaptation of *Godzilla* appeared on Japanese screens. The Emmerich film was big budget and had slick special effects—but Shin Sang-ok's wacky film had the charm of the old and less than perfect Toho *Godzillas* of the early days.

South Korean distributors took notice and bought the film for a big chunk of cash. In the summer of 2000, *Pulgasari* was the first North Korean film ever released in South Korea. With devastating results. Only 500 people showed up in all of movie-crazy Seoul to see the film, which meant that theaters were running shows with hardly any people watching. Many theaters pulled the plug on the movie before the first week was over.

South Korean newspapers tried to explain that the low-tech, campy special effects were not attractive to South Korean youngsters who buy the bulk of the tickets. Maybe so ... but not very likely. This seems to be a better explanation: Until 1999, Japanese movies were not allowed to be imported into South Korea. Thus, no real *Godzilla* cult could develop there like the one that had Tokyo kids embracing odd-looking *Pulgasari*. The rather weird South Korean clone of *Godzilla*, Grand Evil Monster *Yonggari* (1967, by Kim Ki-duk,[24] re-made in 1999) was of no great help here. And the fact that Pulgasari originated in the North was certainly no enticement for the Southern youth, most of whom don't give a shit about anything North Korean. They are happy if they don't hear a word about their uncool cousins up North ... those guys and gals with the funny accents who aren't even able to tell the difference between Armani and Versace!

In 2001, *Pulgasari* finally received an American video release via Rubbersuit Productions, the kaiju subdivision of ADV Films. On the tape, the film is dubbed into Japanese and features English subtitles. American kaiju movie and anime critics showed it little mercy.

South Korean independent production companies jumped at the opportunities presented by a Summit meeting and tried to arrange co-productions with the North. Southern production and film-import company SN 21 Enterprise got in contact with Korea Film Export & Import Corp. in Pyongyang to collaborate on a remake of a film called *Arirang* by early Korean moviemaster Nah Wun-kyu, who had made or starred in 28 films at the time of Japanese rule. His most important film, *Arirang* is now a lost masterpiece of Korean cinema. It's considered the first nationalist Korean film. In dizzying black-and-white pictures, it tells the story of a young man who is beaten up by Japanese police during a student demonstration. He goes mad and starts to attack everyone who works for the Japanese. An agent, working for the Japanese, is harassing his sister. This makes the young man snap back to "sanity." He kills the agent and goes to jail for the rest of his life. Nah Wun-kyu wrote the script, starred in the movie and directed it. It took him from 1921 to 1936 to complete that film.

The new North-South *Arirang*, to be directed by South Korean Lee Doo-young, was supposed to feature actors from both sides of the 38th parallel, but shooting was not planned to take place in either part of Korea. For political reasons, China or Japan were eyed as possible shooting locations.

The negotiations came to naught, however, and the film premiered in 2003 as a solely South Korean product. It did get a North Korean premiere in October 2003, the first South Korean film ever shown in the North.

Meanwhile, South Korean director Kim Ho-sun was negotiating with the North to make the story of Empress Myongsung into a movie. That empress, the wife of Kim Kojong, the second to last king of the Yi Dynasty (1392–1910), was slain by a Japanese assassin in her Seoul palace in 1894. Those negotiations also failed. The project was renamed *The Last Empress*, turned into a 124-episode TV drama and produced by South Korean broadcaster KBS. As in the case of *Arirang*, however, the filmmakers wanted their work to be shown in the North even though the North was no help in realizing the project. In June 2004, the *Korea Times* reported that *The Last Empress* was donated to North Korea and that the TV drama would play on North Korea TV at some point.[25]

In November 2000, a group of South Korean cinema bigwigs made a visit to Pyongyang. Famous director Im Kwon-teak (who had just released his new film *Chunhyang*) was part of the delegation, as was the chief of the Pusan Film Festival, Kim Dong-ho, and the vice president of the Korean Film Commission, Lee Yong-kwan. The visit was planned to be nothing more than a chance to get to know the Northern side. The Southern delegates saw the film studios and realized that they would not shoot anything there soon—the technology was just too poor—and they also couldn't imagine using any Northern actors in the near future—North Korean actors totally depend on post-dubbing while productions in the South work with synch-sound.

A delegation member told me, on condition of anonymity, that the treatment they received from their North Korean minders enraged them much more than the failed business negotiations. The delegates were constantly under watch, they couldn't even walk out of the hotel for a minute unaccompanied, and they had to suffer through the whole standard tourist program every visitor to the country has to endure: monuments to honor Kim Il-sung here, monuments to Kim Jong-il there, and over there, the monuments to the glorious Worker's Party of Korea and the Northern "victory" in the Korean War. According to this author's source, the delegates hated it all—and returned to Seoul "disgusted and being absolutely against any re-unification" of South Korea with the North.

Souls Protest—*The North Korean Titanic*

Kim Dae-jung's Sunshine Policy toward the North had a big supporter— the Clinton administration in Washington. In January 2001, George W. Bush took over in the White House and called off the Washington support for several months to re-evaluate the situation on the peninsula. This severely damaged Kim Dae-jung's reconciliatory stand towards Kim Jong-il and greatly enraged the men in power in Pyongyang. Heavy clouds began to hang over the Sunshine Policy which wouldn't move away even after Washington gave its final okay that Kim Dae-jun was right in what he was doing.

The dire political situation less than a year after the greatly celebrated summit, however, didn't deter the entrepreneurial folks at Seoul's Narai Film Company and they shelled out $320,000 for the South Korean rights to the latest Northern movie extravaganza, *Souls Protest*. Quite a whopping sum to pay for the rights, especially after the disastrous failure of *Pulgasari*.

But *Souls Protest* was not a monster movie—it was the North Korean *Titanic*! And it was overtly anti-Japanese. The relations between South Korea and Japan had soured in the Spring and Summer of 2001 with the Japanese government approving of the publication of a school history book that Koreans claimed "whitewashed Japanese war crimes." Also, Japanese Prime Minister Juzohiro Koizumi visited Tokyo's Yasukuni Shrine in which all Japanese victims of World War II are honored, including convicted and executed Japanese war criminals. Demonstrations took place in Seoul to rail against Japan and Koizumi, and people seemed ready to pay money to see something anti-Japanese—like *Souls Protest*.

Made by Kim Chun-song, a Japanese-born Korean director "who had repatriated to the DPRK,"[26] the film tells a story with a strong historical background—the explosion and sinking of the Japanese vessel *Ukishima Maru* in the days following the defeat of Japan in 1945. The ship was bringing home Koreans who had been forced laborers in Japan during the wartime.

The number of victims and the reasons for the explosion are still subjects of debate up to this day. On 23 August 2001, a Japanese court ruled that 15 of the surviving Koreans would receive $375,000 in compensation altogether—although it held onto the always maintained Japanese stance that the ship hit an American mine left over from the war.

On the very next day, *Souls Protest* was up on the screen in Seoul, telling the story from the side of the Korean survivors. According to them, at least 7,000 people had been on the boat, thousands of them perished (not 500 as the Japanese court said) and Tokyo was entirely to blame for the explosion—the ship was sunk intentionally to kill potential witnesses to Japanese war crimes. This was a point of view not only held in Pyongyang but in Seoul as well.

That screening was a special event for survivors of the sinking. It took place on the 56th anniversary of the disaster.

From what could be gleaned from press articles covering the special screening, the film is North Korea's attempt to hit international markets with its own version of *Titanic*. 10,000 extras from the Koran People's Army were recruited and the director had to watch the 1997 *Titanic* more than 100 times to get the details right. The film also features a fictional love story resembling the one between Kate Winslet and Leonardi DiCaprio. It's quite entertaining with lots of special effects and it was as grand-style as possible—you guess who might be the mastermind behind such an "immortal masterpiece." Back home in the North, the film ran in theaters and on TV and was reportedly a smashing success.

The survivors in the South, though, had some quibbles with the film: "I didn't like the propaganda stuff about Kim Il-sung," said survivor Lee Chul-woo, 75.[27] Another survivor criticized the love story: "There was no time for such romance. It was hell."[28] Narai Film Company had complied with the censorship office and cut out the few minutes of hailing Great Leader Kim Il-sung for the official release, but they showed the film intact to the survivors.

Since that screening, however, the movie has not surfaced again on any South Korean screen. For some mysterious reason, Narai simply shelved it without even trying to turn a profit with it.

Shin Sang-ok Revisited

The Seoul box-office failure of *Pulgasari* did little to further damage Shin Sang-ok's already questionable reputation in South Korea. After he had disappeared into North Korea, Southern critics "forgot" to mention him in their publications; he was persona non grata. The few Korean films he made after his partial return to Seoul didn't win him much public approval either.

But high-ranking international institutions remembered his important works from the fifties and sixties. The Museum of Modern Art in New York arranged a retrospective of his early films, he became a jury member at the Cannes Film Festival in 1995, *Cahiers du Cinema* wrote him up—and in November 2001 he finally became enshrined as "Master of Korean Cinema" at home in South Korea, at the Pusan International Film Festival, the country's biggest and most influential festival. He had his handprint planted into the pavement of PIFF Square, alongside Korean movie luminaries like Kim Ki-young, and had a rather small retrospective—at which, along some of his earlier works, his North Korean productions *Runaway* and *Salt* were shown. That prints were not coming from Pyongyang but from Sheen Films in Los Angeles. Still, the shows were problematic.

In 1999, the Seoul High Court had ruled that *Runaway* was a Northern propaganda movie which could not be screened in the South. The court informed the Pusan Film Festival that a public screening was not permitted. Shin threatened legal action. The festival, which had not printed any info on the film in their catalogue, being aware of the problem, re-scheduled the screening and told only a handful of foreign critics the time it was going to be held—keeping any Korean audience member away. The attendance was accordingly low, only about 10 people.

Salt however got official permission and was announced and the showtime well publicized. Did more people show up for that than for the "secret screening" of *Runaway*? Nope. South Korea's National Security Law, prohibiting Northern propaganda, seems really outdated—South Koreans just don't care about anything Northern!

Shin had a big press conference at the festival and no South Korean journalist asked him any question about his time in the North. At this high-profile event, female critics would rather indulge in lengthy discussions about his presentation of gender relations than ask the obvious. I did, asking what he thought about his time in North Korea. Shin Sang-ok had this to say: "In the North, I had a lot of artistic freedom and unlimited money. Sometimes I miss North Korea. The North Koreans want to show the outside world how great they are by way of their movies. They treat their film workers well, like they did in all socialist countries, they take them seriously and respect them." And what about Kim Jong-il and his involvement in film? "Kim Jong-il is very knowledgeable when it comes to film. He has a very good 'filmmaker's eye.' He advised me a lot on shooting and editing. He's got a vast film library—that's how he learns about the outside world. By watching movies. The trouble is that he can't distinguish between fiction and reality."

Maybe Shin Sang-ok[29] should have stayed there, helped the country reform, and taught Kim Jong-il the difference between the movies and life. The Americans could have easily lived without *Galgameth* and *3 Ninjas*....

Notes

1. *Korean Film Art*, Korean Film Export and Import Corporation, Pyongyang, 1985. This book has no page numbers; therefore, it will be cited in the chapter as simply (*Korean Film Art*).

2. (North) Korea Central News Agency (KCNA), 13 September 2000
3. BBC News (Internet version) on 5 September 2001
4. Lee, Hyanjin: *Contemporary Korean Cinema—Identity, Culture and Politics*, Manchester University Press, Manchester and New York, 2000, page 41
5. Colima is a mythical horse that could leap 1000 rib (250 km / 150 miles). The myth originated in China but was appropriated by the North Koreans in the 1950s. In 1958, Kim Il-sung started the first "Colima movement" for the development of the North Korean economy, a campaign to work harder for the fastest possible progress. More such "Colima movements" followed and today, the Colima horse is considered a symbol of North Korean progress. Countless Colima monuments litter the North Korean cities.
6. *Great Man and Cinema*, Korea Film Export & Import Corporation, Pyongyang, 1998, page 1. Quite a success for a seven-year old. But even if the story is true, the impact of Kim Jong-il's complaints did not last long. Falling snow still went on for decades to accompany heart-rending reunions of people who haven't seen each other for a long time. As of 2000, the snow used in those scenes still looks like cotton wool—though it does stick to heads and shoulders now.
7. *Ibid.*, page 29
8. Im Yoo-hoo, Hong Chan-us, Ri Chol-ho (Editors): *Korean Film*; Korea Film Export & Import Company, Pyongyang, 1998, no page numbers given
9. *Great Man and Cinema*, page 23
10. It's quite usual for North Korean film literature to suddenly omit a film or a name from its records. *Korean Film Art*, for example, was sold with one page glued together to hide a seventies film named *The 14th Winter*. Why? We don't know. But the book was sold in both English and French translation and in all copies of both versions, the pages were glued shut. The glue was of poor quality, though, and didn't resist a short bath of the page in hot water—revealing the hidden content.
11. Kim Jong-il: *On the Art of Cinema*, Foreign Languages Publishing House; Pyongyang, 1989 (reprint from the original, published 11 April 1973), page 2
12. "N Korean movies' propaganda role" on BBC News—World Edition (Internet version), 18 August 2003
13. Tetsuo Nishida: *Kyoto no Yazoo (Fictional Image)*, Hihyoo-Sha, Tokyo, 1988
14. Prior to the crushing of the Czechoslovakian "democratic way of Socialism" by Soviet troops in 1968, Czechoslovakia was home to one of the most daring, wild and sophisticated film industries in Europe. Milos Forman, Vera Chytichlova, Ivan Passer and Juraj Herz were among the most notable directors. The directors fled mostly to the West that year; the technicians mostly stayed on at Barrandov Studios.
15. Kenpachiro Satsuma: *Gojira ga mita kita chosen (North Korea Seen Through the Eyes of Godzilla)*, NESCO, Tokyo, 1988
16. Kim Hyun-hee: *Tears of My Soul*, William Morrow & Co., New York, 1993
17. When I showed *Order No. 027* in Munich in Spring 2000, the inner circle of the Munich taek-won-do scene showed up to see it. When they saw the fight scenes, their jaws dropped almost to the floor, and after the movie they were full of praise for the actors and stunt men and rated their performance as "absolute top level taek-won-do."
18. *The Nation and Destiny* (Parts 1–4) info brochure by Korea Film Export & Import Corporation, Pyongyang, no publication date given
19. *The Nation and Destiny* (Parts 17–32) info brochure by Korea Film Export & Import Corporation, Pyongyang, no publication date given, page 19
20. *Ibid.*, page 1
21. *Ibid.*, inside cover
22. *Korea Herald*, 4 October 2003
23. Nicholas D. Kristof: "Survivors Report Torture in North Korea Labor Camps," *New York Times*, 14 July 1996
24. Not the same Kim Ki-duk who made *The Isle* (2000), *Address Unknown* (2001) and *Bad Guy* (2001).
25. Lee Hyo-sik: Popular South Korean Epic Drama to Air in North Korea," *Korea Times*, 29 June 2004

26. "Korean *Titanic* Amazes Moscow and Hong Kong Audience; To Be Exported to West," The People's Korea: website of the pro–North Korean community in Japan, 2001
27. Choe Sang-hun: "Film, court ruling bring to light 1945 ship tragedy in Korea," *Detroit News*, 25 August 2001
28. Ibid.
29. Shin Sang-ok died on 11 April 2006.

North Korean Film Titles

The following list includes the original Korean titles of the films that have been citied in "A Permanent State of War."

Address Unknown (Suchwiin bulmyeong)
Again to the Front (Tto tashi choson-uro)
Arirang (Arirang)
Bad Guy (Nabbeun namja)
A Bellflower (Torajikkot)
Boy Partisans (Sonyon ildang)
The Defenders of Height 1211 (1211Goji Bangwijadul)
An Emissary of No Return (Doraoji annun milsa)
A Far-Off Islet (Mulri innun sum)
Five Guerilla Brothers (Yugyoktae 5 hongje)
Flower Girl (Kkot panun chyonyo)
A Flower in Hell (Jiokwa)
Forever in Our Memory (Chueon sone yeongweonhari)
The 14th Winter (Yol nebon jjae kyoul)
Hong Kil Dong (Hong Kil Dong)
The Isle (Seom)
Joint Security Area (Gongdong gyeongbi guyeok JSA)
An Jung-gun Shoots Ito Hirobumi (An Chunggun, idungbangmun-ul Ssoda)
Land of Love, aka *The Earth of Love* (Sarangeui Daeji)
Mayumi (Mayumi)
My Happiness (Naeui haengbok)
My Home Village (Nae kohyang)
Myself in the Distant Future, aka *My Look in Distant Future* (Meon hunareui naeui moseub)
Namgang Village Women (Namgangma-euleui Nyeoseongdul)
Nation and Destiny (Choguk-kwa unmyong)
A Naturalized Japanese Woman (Gwuihahan Ilbon-innyeosungpyeon)
Orang River (Oranggang)
Order No. 027 (Myeongryeong 027 ho)
Pulgasari (Bulgasari)
The Road (Gil)

Rose and Wild Dog (Jangmi-wa dulgae)
Runaway (Talchulgi)
Salt (Sogum)
Scouts (Chongchalbyong)
Sea of Blood (Pibada)
The Separation (Heyeeon jekkaji)
The Spinner (Chongbanggong)
Souls Protest (Sara-innun ryonghongdul)
Thaw, aka Snow Melts in Spring (Bomnalui nunseoji)
Unknown Heroes (Irumopnun yongungdul)
Vanished (Jeungbal)
We Are the Happiest (Sesang-e Burumeopeora)
Workers (Rodonggyegeuppyeon)
Yeongsangun

15

Godzilla Goes to North Korea: An Interview with Kenpachiro Satsuma

Johannes Schönherr

KCNA, the official North Korean "news" agency, rails against Japan on a daily basis. The former colonial power has been accused of preparing to colonize Korea again and attacked for not paying reparations for damage inflicted during its colonial reign to the North Korean regime, for not officially apologizing enough for past wrongdoings, and for an alleged ongoing repression of the Korean minority in Japan. In short, in North Korean propaganda Japan has been portrayed as the main enemy Number 2—closely trailing the "aggressive and belligerent" imperialists from the home of all evil, the United States of America.

But hostile rhetoric has never stopped former Dear Leader and current Great Leader Kim Jong-il from having a very soft spot for movies from both the U.S. and Japan. He is said to be especially fond of Francis Ford Coppola's *Godfather* movies; of the *Friday the 13th* teen slasher series; of James Bond (with the possible exception of 2002's *Die Another Day* in which 007 is tortured in a North Korean prison camp—North Korean propaganda strongly condemned that film); of Japan's 48-part *Tora-san* movie series by Yamada Yohji; and of the *Godzilla* entries into the kaiju (monster) film genre.

His love for *Godzilla* was actually so deep that in 1985 he instigated the production of his own *Godzilla*-type movie, *Pulgasari*. And not just *any* production of the domestic Korean Film Studio: When Kim Jong-il wanted Godzilla, it meant that he wanted to get the true and only Godzilla! The original! Of course modified according to his own special needs and purposes but a real Godzilla it had to be ... and so he had his underlings at the Korea Film Studio contact Toho, the Tokyo film production company responsible for the *Godzilla* series. They enlisted not only the special effects team who had been

全世界が待っていた本物の怪獣映画！

―98年全国劇場公開作品・ニュープリント完全版―

プルガサリ
伝説の大怪獣
PULGASARI

15. Interview with Kenpachiro Satsuma (J. Schönherr) 207

working on Godzilla, but also hired the man in the monster's rubber suit, Kenpachiro Satsuma, for the North Korean kaiju effort.

Satsuma had started his career as a suit actor by playing Hedorah, the Smog Monster, Godzilla's foe in Yoshimitsu's Banno 1971 entry *Godzilla vs. the Smog Monster* (*Gojira Tai Hedorah*). After a few more times playing the monster opposing Godzilla, he was hired in 1984 to act in the costume of the monster of monsters itself. He replaced former suit inhabitant Haruo Nakajima for the first time in *Godzilla 1985* (*Gojira*) directed by Koji Hashimoto. Then he was the man inside the monster for six more films, retiring after the "death" of Godzilla in 1995's *Godzilla vs. Destroyer* (*Gojira vs. Destroyah*), directed by Takao Okawara.

When Kim Jong-il hired him for *Pulgasari*, Satsuma had only acted once as Godzilla, and he was still not very fond of being a suit actor. He wanted to be a real actor, show his face and mimic on screen, not just tumble about in a monster suit … read more about his point of view in the interview to follow.

As director of the film, Shin Sang-ok, the biggest talent available in North

Above: Pulgasari is invincible! Opposite: Original Japanese video sleeve for *Pulgasari*.

Korea at the time, was chosen. Shin was a former South Korean director who had operated that country's biggest film studio during the sixties and who had had a major fall-out with the South Korean authoritarian regime of Park Chung-hee in the seventies. Under mysterious circumstances he showed up in North Korea in 1978, shortly after his wife, South Korean actress Choi Eun-hee, had arrived there under equally strange circumstances. In 1986 Shin and Choi fled from North Korea and claimed that they had been kidnapped to serve in the film industry of the ever-ambitious Kim Jong-il. If that claim is true or if they were simply deceived into voluntarily settling in North Korea, future research in Kim Jong-il's archives may prove; they are currently not open to foreign scholars, of course.

I contacted Shin for an interview while in Seoul in the Summer of 2003. Shin declined, saying that he "had already told everything he has to tell" to the international press. Well, he told the international press a lot but there are still many unanswered questions ... which he apparently did not want to discuss.

Godzilla/Pulgasari actor Kenpachiro Satsuma, however, proved to be much more accessible. He is a bright, always friendly fellow who likes to tell stories and who happily agreed to an interview.

Pulgasari joins the battle.

The Interview

On a rainy afternoon in late June 2003, my translator Ayako Karino, a film critic with the English edition of Japan's second-biggest daily *Asahi Shimbun*, and I met up with Mr. Satsuma in front of Kinokunya bookstore in Tokyo's bustling Shinjuku Ward before retreating to a nearby coffee house.

JOHANNES SCHÖNHERR: *How did you get involved in the production of* Pulgasari?

KENPACHIRO SATSUMA: The producer asked me if I would be interested in working on a foreign film. At first it sounded like a film being shot in America, in Hollywood. I was very excited and looked forward to the shooting of that movie. It was just at the last minute, when getting ready for departure, that they suddenly told us that it was a North Korean film. And I didn't know that it was a monster suit film. I thought that I would be in the film as an actor. The moment I heard from Toho it was going to be a suit film in North Korea, I was quite disappointed.

What did you know about North Korea before you went there?

Actor Kenpachiro Satsuma, who played Pulgasari in North Korea's answer to Godzilla (courtesy Johannes Schönherr).

I didn't have a lot of information. I knew it was a dangerous country but I didn't know any details.

On the way to North Korea, you went to Beijing first to do some shooting there.

Yes. It was about a week to ten days that we stayed in Beijing and worked in a studio called Beijing Dian Ying Studios. In order to shoot the climax scene of the film, the destruction of the huge castle, we needed that studio because the studios in North Korea were still in the process of construction. That didn't allow us to make that kind of shoot at the North Korean studios. We had two sets rented at the Beijing Dian Ying Studios and we carried out the climax scene for the film there.

You met Shin Sang-ok first in Beijing during that time?

We didn't meet each other in Beijing, because that part was done by the special effects sequence team. Shin was the general producer of the whole film. I heard that he went to Beijing but when I was there, I couldn't meet him.

So, obviously, at that time the monster suit was already made. Was it made in Japan or did it come from North Korea?

In Japan. It was made by the Godzilla staff.

The old blacksmith puts the finishing touches on little Pulgasari.

15. Interview with Kenpachiro Satsuma (J. Schönherr) 211

Were there drawings and ideas coming from North Korea or was it totally up to the Toho people to create the monster?

It was Shin Sang-ok who called up the art director in Japan and he told him what kind of design he would like and then just left it up to the Japanese designer team to come up with different options on the monster. So, the actual creation of the monster was done by Japanese staff.

How many Toho people went to North Korea for this film?
Fifteen.

When you arrived in North Korea, they first took you to a guest house and you had to stay at that guest house for a few days, I read?

People picked us up from the airport and took us straight to a mansion belonging to Kim Jong-il. It was strange. There were two beds in my room but I was staying there alone. I would sleep on each one every night, taking turns [laughs].

So, you had to stay there for a few days?
About a month. About 33 days.

During all of the shooting?

A rebel soldier at Pulgasari's foot.

I was in North Korea for two months. The first half of this, I stayed at this house. Every day, I had to go to the shooting set from the mansion—which was actually quite far. But I wasn't allowed to stay anywhere else.

And you had some minder who was watching all the time what you were doing?
A person, a so-called interpreter, followed me around all the time. That person did both jobs, presumably—watching over me and interpreting. Those interpreters were very irritating. They were always with me. If those persons were just interpreters, they should have just stuck to translating the language rather than saying "Don't do this, don't do that" all the time. I think, probably the main reason of those people being with us was to watch over us, observing what we were doing. Not so much translating the language.

The shooting was done at the Korean Film Studio?
We didn't use the sets of the Korean Film Studio but there is a hill behind the studio. We just shot on that hill, the hill serving as open set to shoot some of the scenes. We had some of the small props brought from Japan and they

Pulgasari headshot.

15. Interview with Kenpachiro Satsuma (J. Schönherr) 213

were put inside one building. It was a building that the studio had erected for Shin Sang-ok. We did the indoor scenes inside that building. But we didn't use the sets of the film studio.

Shin Sang-ok had his own studio then, Shin Films?

Shin Sang-ok was allowed by Kim Jong-il to have his own name for his film company. That was approved.

Who was the actual director of the film? Was it Shin Sang-ok or was it Chong Gon-jo? Shin Sang-ok always says that he is the director but in the film's credits—even in the foreign releases—a Chong Gon-jo is named as director.

Shin Sang-ok was the director.

Who was Chong Gon-jo? What did he do? Was he an assistant director?

He had a kind of a role of assisting the director. But it was always Shin Sang-ok who was directing. He was always above him, giving him orders. But Shin was very busy a lot of the time. So, I think in the latter half of the shooting, he gave Chong Gon-jo some [free] rein to finish the film.

Pulgasari comes to town.

How was the work on the sets with the North Koreans? Was it very different from shooting Godzilla movies in Japan?

Very different! Extremely different. Initially, we were there only to give advice on how to make the film. At first, we were shocked because they couldn't do what we wanted them to do. But there were of course people on the North Korean side who really liked films and we got to communicate and have a mutual understanding. And it kind of paved its way from there on. In terms of the Japanese staff, we were there only to give technical advice. I was there only to give advice on how to act inside a monster suit. The same goes for the cameraman and all the other staff. But it turned out that the North Koreans were hopeless in terms of doing what they were supposed to. So, we said: "Oh, what the hell, we will do it ourselves." We ended up doing the whole film.

What was it like working with the North Korean actors?

Very friendly, very communicative people. But the special effects people, they were not professional. They were more like boys in charge of props. You don't get professional people there. These people are very much kind of fake. They don't understand the concept of being inside a monster suit and acting. I explained it to them over and over again but they didn't seem to get the point.

Originally, you were supposed to teach the North Koreans suit acting but then you ended up being in the suit all the time yourself?

I did all the acting inside the suit of the grown-up Pulgasari monster, except for one scene. That scene was left for me to do later on. I went back to Japan and the deal was that they would have me return to North Korea to [do] that scene. But probably my fee was quite expensive and ... you have to ask Shin Sang-ok about the details ... but they presumably looked at the amount that that required and said: "No." That's why that scene isn't done right. Well, I was supposed to do that ... now, it isn't a very good scene.

Which scene was that?

That scene was called "Marusan" after Marusan, the hill where it was shot. It was when the rebel troops were fighting against the king's troops. Forcing themselves upon them. That was when Pulgasari comes out from behind and then leads the rebels' troops into the fighting.

Right. At that time, he is not so big yet. He is taller than the height of a regular person. But it's the big surprise for the government when Pulgasari shows up because they didn't know about him.

It's a scene when Pulgasari is going into battle. It's supposed to be a very violent, aggressive scene. But that actor did it really light! It wasn't supposed to be that way—it was supposed to be more violent!

The film was obviously done on a very low budget but on the other hand you have a lot of extras. Can you talk a bit about how they work there on the set?

15. Interview with Kenpachiro Satsuma (J. Schönherr)

The emperor at his court.

I don't know much about that in detail but in terms of the extras, I think, you can get any North Korean people to appear in the film for free. Shin Sang-ok told me that you can have as many people as you want for the extra scenes. The military would go and fetch the people and they would come. So, it wasn't a matter of money at all in that sense.

But in terms of the special effects, we haven't used computer graphics and it may look like low budget but it was a very expensive film for the North Koreans. It was like one of the first films they produced on kind of a blockbuster scale. It was like 200 to 300 million Yen [two or three million US dollars] they spent on the film. That might not sound like much for a Japanese production but for the North Koreans that was a huge amount of money. They were all hoping that this film would be released abroad, in theaters worldwide. It was a huge project and it was a big burden on them to spend so much money on the film.

What was your impression of Shin Sang-ok? He was the supposedly "kidnapped" director working in North Korea. Must have been kind of like strange, I imagine ...

He didn't show any kind of image of the kidnapped director as far as I'm concerned. He was very friendly and he was a very nice person. Very peaceful. But he was extremely busy and he was often absent. But he was the director

Pulgasari caged and set afire.

in charge and he had all the scenes inside his head like which scene comes after this scene. As soon as he appeared, people would go to him and he would be walking around and everybody was following him, asking questions, and he would be walking and doing the job at the same time. A lot of time Shin Sang-ok wasn't there and everybody was waiting for him to come back. He was a very busy person. As I said, he was a very peaceful person on the outside but in terms of work, he was very strict and he had a lot of ideas.

Kim Jong-il is known to be a big film fan. He went to the Korean Film Studio many, many times. They had a list of about 10,000 visits up to 1993 displayed at the Korean Film Studio when I was there. Did you meet Kim Jong-il during the time of the filming? Was he around the sets?

He didn't appear in front of the Japanese people. In the dining room of the mansion, there was a picture of him having dinner at exactly the same seat where I was always sitting. But I didn't come across him.

So, he came to the set but the Japanese could not meet him?

He was probably there. Having lots of meetings and gatherings but probably because we are Japanese, he didn't show himself.

15. Interview with Kenpachiro Satsuma (J. Schönherr)   217

No wall can stop Pulgasari.

What did the North Koreans tell you about Kim Jong-il? You were there before he became head of the state. He was kind of the big movie producer back then ...

He was the number two at the time and nobody, no staff, wanted to talk about him. People at the mansion kept their mouths shut as well. Funniest thing was that all the portraits of Kim Jong-il were removed from the mansion probably because Japanese people were coming. I saw no portraits of Kim Jong-il in the mansion but the spots where they had hung were still visible.

The portrait of Kim Il-sung were also removed?

His photos weren't there, either. I would like to ask you, why do you think they didn't have any of those pictures there?

It might be because there were foreigners staying there. In the rooms of international hotels, you also don't have pictures of the Great Leaders. But in all the rooms where the North Koreans are, in every apartment, in all offices and function rooms, there are always portraits.

After we were allowed to move out of the mansion, we stayed at the Changgansan Hotel. We saw the portraits of father and son there.

That was probably not an international hotel ...

It was very old. The elevator was really rocky. I felt like I would fall out of it.

Pulgasari getting ready to smash the palace.

Did they show you around Pyongyang a lot? Did they do tours with you?
We didn't go on any kind of tourist tours at all.

Was the film all shot at that studio outside of Pyongyang or did you also go to the countryside to shoot scenes?
The special effects were made at the studio only. And in the Beijing studio. The Japanese always had to stay at the studio. The North Koreans went to other places to shoot the rest.

You went back to Japan not long before the film was finished?
Yes. I went back to Japan and then I went to Beijing again to shoot the final fighting sequences when Pulgasari is 20 meters high and destroys the imperial palace. At the Chinese studio, we made a miniature of that huge entrance gate into the imperial palace.

The destruction of the imperial palace was shot before or after going to North Korea?
On the first trip to Beijing, we started that scene. But on the second trip, we did the continuation scenes, especially the collapse of the castle walls and the interior scenes.

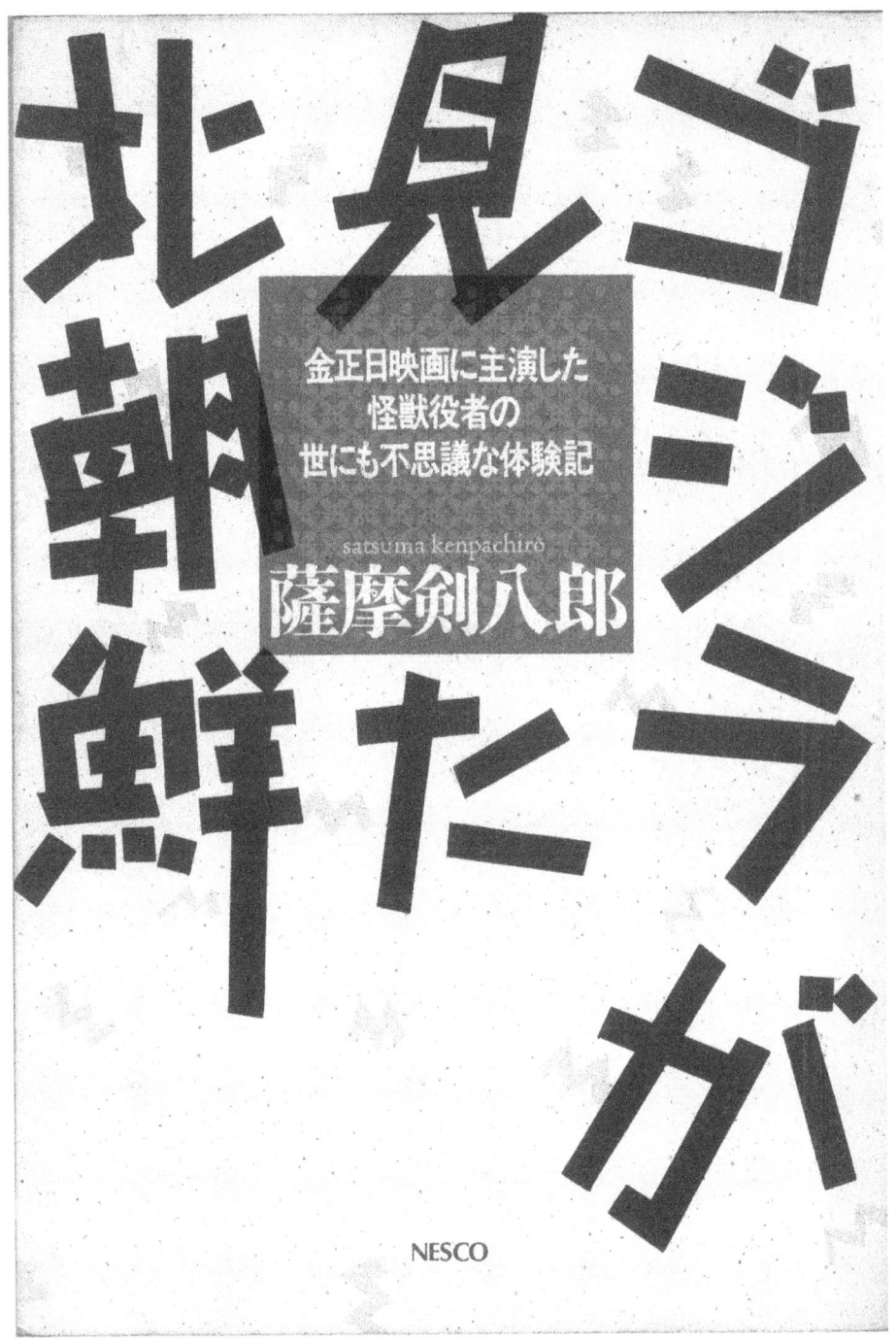

Front cover of Kenpachiro Satsuma's book *North Korea Seen Through the Eyes of Godzilla* (Gojira ga mita kita chosen; published in 1998).

Did you see any North Korean films while you where there?
None at all.

What do you think about Pulgasari *now? Do you like it when you see it?*
It's great! I like it because it is not so detailed. Nowadays all films like that are made with computer graphics and I think it's just too much. The film was very well received in Japan and I got very good comments, especially from the media. In America, too. They said it was better than the U.S. Godzilla film.

In Japan, Pulgasari *was shown in 1998, the same time the American* Godzilla *came out. A lot of people said that* Pulgasari *was more like the real thing.*
The scale of the American Godzilla film was absolutely different. It got a worldwide release and loads of money was pumped into that film. But when *Pulgasari* was being shown in Japan, it was the first ever release of that film in a foreign country. It was first shown in a very tiny theater, Kineteka Omori in Tokyo, but it became a hit. At Kineteka Omori, they extended the screening dates because there were so many people coming to see the film. I heard there was a theater next door showing the U.S. *Godzilla*. But there were more people coming to see *Pulgasari* than the U.S. *Godzilla*.

16

The Winnipeg Wonder: An Interview with Guy Maddin

Matthew Edwards

Guy Maddin needs little introduction. He is one of the most original filmmakers working today. With a résumé filled with such critically applauded films as *Archangel*, *Careful*, *The Heart of the World*, *Dracula: Pages from a Virgin's Diary*, *Cowards Bend the Knee*, and *The Saddest Music in the World*, it is unsurprising that Maddin is recognized in the filmmaking community as a true maverick. So much so that he has become the youngest filmmaker to be awarded the Telluride Lifetime Achievement Award.

I had stumbled across Maddin's films through the brilliant cult favorite *Tales from the Gimli Hospital*, and I was immediately hooked. *Archangel* followed (my personal favorite), and then the underrated *Twilight of the Ice Nymphs* with Shelley Duvall. For the uninitiated, Maddin's films are like lost cinematic features that have recently been unearthed and projected for an unsuspecting audience. Finding inspiration from silent cinema and early talkies, Maddin is unique in that his films hark back to the lost golden era of cinema by employing vintage techniques and working with antiquated cameras that have become redundant through the progression of cinema.

I was lucky enough to meet Guy at the London premiere of *The Saddest Music in the World*, after a question and answer session with the audience. As the audience slowly exited the auditorium, I noticed that Guy had been caught behind the rabble of people as they pushed and shoved their way out. Then, as poor old Guy wandered past, I managed a peanut of a squeak and I thrust a copy of the book *The Films of Guy Maddin* by Caelum Vatnsdal in his general direction, for him to sign. Guy kindly signed the book, and I inquired whether he would be interested in being interviewed for this book. To my surprise he agreed, and handed me his business card.

Originally I attempted to do an interview with Guy via email. Unsurprisingly the whole thing died a sad death, for e-mail interviews are notoriously

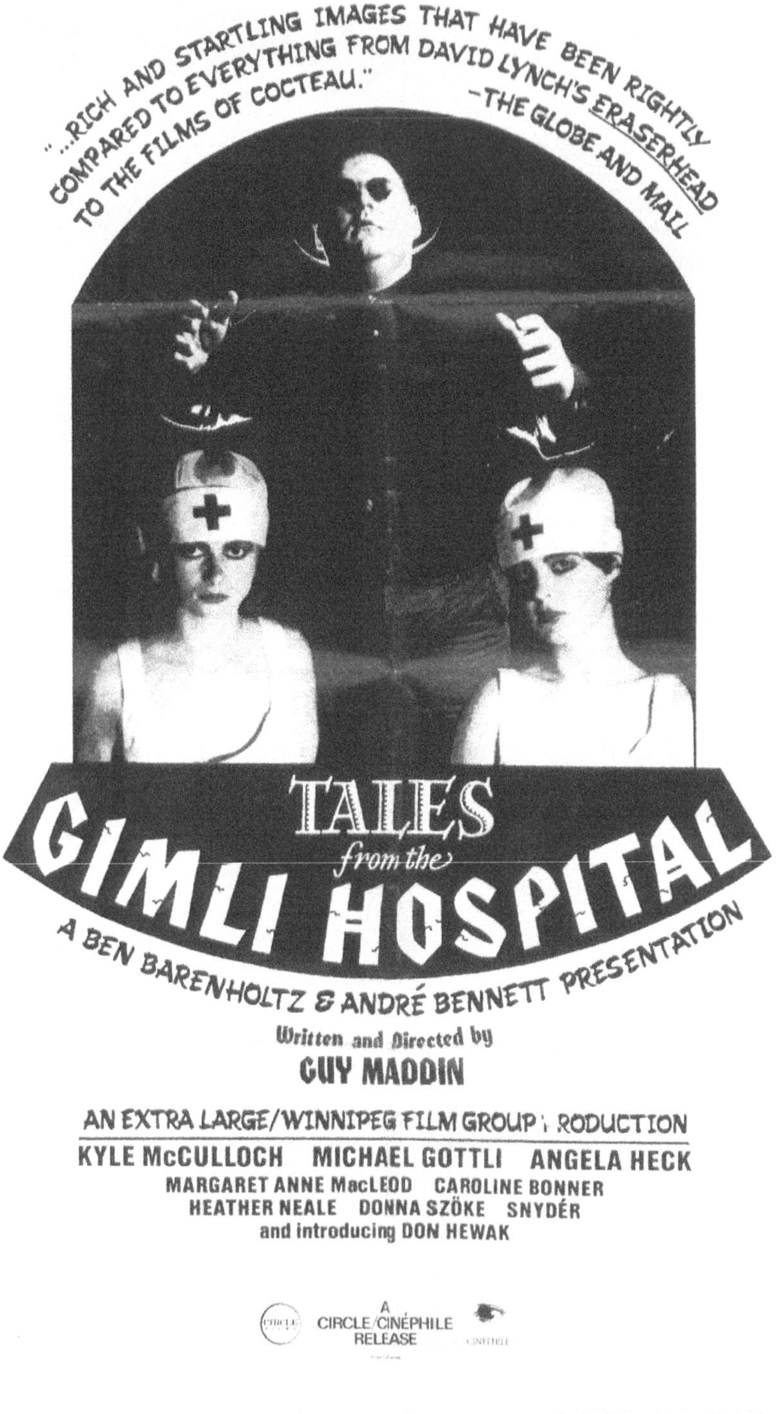

"...RICH AND STARTLING IMAGES THAT HAVE BEEN RIGHTLY COMPARED TO EVERYTHING FROM DAVID LYNCH'S ERASERHEAD TO THE FILMS OF COCTEAU." —THE GLOBE AND MAIL

TALES from the GIMLI HOSPITAL

A BEN BARENHOLTZ & ANDRÉ BENNETT PRESENTATION

Written and Directed by
GUY MADDIN

AN EXTRA LARGE/WINNIPEG FILM GROUP PRODUCTION
KYLE McCULLOCH   MICHAEL GOTTLI   ANGELA HECK
MARGARET ANNE MacLEOD   CAROLINE BONNER
HEATHER NEALE   DONNA SZÖKE   SNYDÉR
and introducing DON HEWAK

A CIRCLE/CINÉPHILE RELEASE

16. Interview with Guy Maddin (Matthew Edwards)

time-consuming for the interviewee. A year later, and despite my folly, I thought I would contact Guy again and ask whether he would be interested in a telephone interview. Again he kindly agreed.

The telephone interview was conducted in September 2005. Guy had unexpectedly spent the day at his vet's, and had just returned with his pet dog in time for the interview. In fact, the dog interrupted the interview at one point when he jumped onto Guy! The poor hound was ejected from the room. That aside, the interview ran smoothly with Guy in top form. With his dry sense of humor and his hilarious anecdotes, I frequently had to suppress my laughter so as not to ruin the recording.

MATTHEW EDWARDS: *You have had no formal training in filmmaking, have you?*

GUY MADDIN: No I haven't. I trained in economics and mathematics, then I kind of rotated hemispheres halfway through my life. I wasn't getting a good job, and I wasn't getting anything rewarding out of maths or economics. Then I met and fell in with a motley crew of book readers and movie watchers when I was twenty-four years old, and suddenly I discovered I had an interest in and knack for absorbing all this stuff. And some of them even played around with film cameras and I felt the need to express myself somehow, preferably as a writer. But I was a good enough reader to know I could never be a good writer. I discovered that some primitive filmmakers like Luis Buñuel, Dali and George Kuchar could really get great effects, the way the Sex Pistols got great effects without knowing how to play their instruments. These guys didn't know how to work their cameras, and yet their work is amazing. So I decided to pick up a camera, just the way a young kid would pick up a guitar and start playing away on it.

How did the making of your first film The Dead Father *lead into the making of* Tales from the Gimli Hospital?

For my first film I wanted to choose something pretty autobiographical, as I didn't want to be accused of being a wanker by anybody. I guess though, if you're too autobiographical you get accused of being a wanking self-absorbed person! I thought I would try and be honest about myself. I tend to make movies about something I'm really ashamed about, a theme embedded into the story, and for the duration of the movie I try and tell people that they too should be ashamed.

The Dead Father was pretty autobiographical. I tried to put onscreen, and failed I think, the feeling I got whenever I dreamt of my father who had died. In my dreams I would see myself with him, it was always nice to see him, and

Opposite: **Promotional poster from Guy Maddin's wonderfully absurd debut feature** *Tales from the Gimli Hospital.*

Something fishy is happening in old Gimli! Actor Kyle McCulloch in *Tales from the Gimli Hosptial*; McCulloch went on to star in further Maddin films, including *Archangel* (1990) and *Careful* (1992) (courtesy Guy Maddin).

he would always come back long enough to desert me again. With *Tales from the Gimli Hospital* I wanted something more autobiographical, but I couldn't think of anything in particular. I wasn't full of imagination. Being a former economist and mathematician, creating stuff was something new to me, but one of my friends suggested I do something about Gimli because it was a strange place. It was our summer home. Full of drunken Icelanders, humorless fisherman who were obsessed with their genealogy and their history. They were proud of their Icelandic heritage. Icelandic Canadians are ludicrously more Icelandic than real Icelanders! So it had a highly mockable subject. My family was Icelandic, so I felt I could turn the gun towards myself. And that always feels better. I don't feel so mean-spirited, when I'm poking fun. I started musing about all things Icelandic that I heard, without really paying attention to it as a kid. I tried to put this onscreen. And I was pleased that *Tales from the Gimli Hospital* irked all my relatives, so mission accomplished!

Do you consider yourself a maverick?

I guess so. I've never really looked up maverick in the dictionary, but I think I know what it means. I guess it means someone who does something

16. Interview with Guy Maddin (Matthew Edwards)

slightly unpredictable or maybe something that doesn't make all that much sense. Or someone who doesn't always make the best career move. That would certainly be me. I'm never really capable of planning ahead. I just kind of do whatever I feel like doing, and try and get away with doing it.

Tales from the Gimli Hospital, Archangel and The Heart of the World rely heavily on imagery and tableaux as their narrative devices. By doing so, you highlight the impact of cinema as a purely visual medium. Relating this in a wider context, do silent films represent cinema at its best?

Not necessarily. There are some pretty bad silent movies. I think potentially you should use whatever you can, depending on your subject matter. I guess the real good artists, and I wouldn't include myself among those, use all the colors on their palette in the right proportion and the right amount. So whether that is sound or audible dialogue or just inter-title dialogue, or music, choreography even with a degree of stylization, all those types of things. So there is no such thing as pure cinema. I know what you're talking about. Andy Warhol's *Empire State Building* or *Blow Job*. I know those things used to be hotly debated at one time. I found out when hanging out with Isabella Rossellini that her father and other Italian film directors, and Renoir, would always argue about the purity of camera moves and camera angles and the

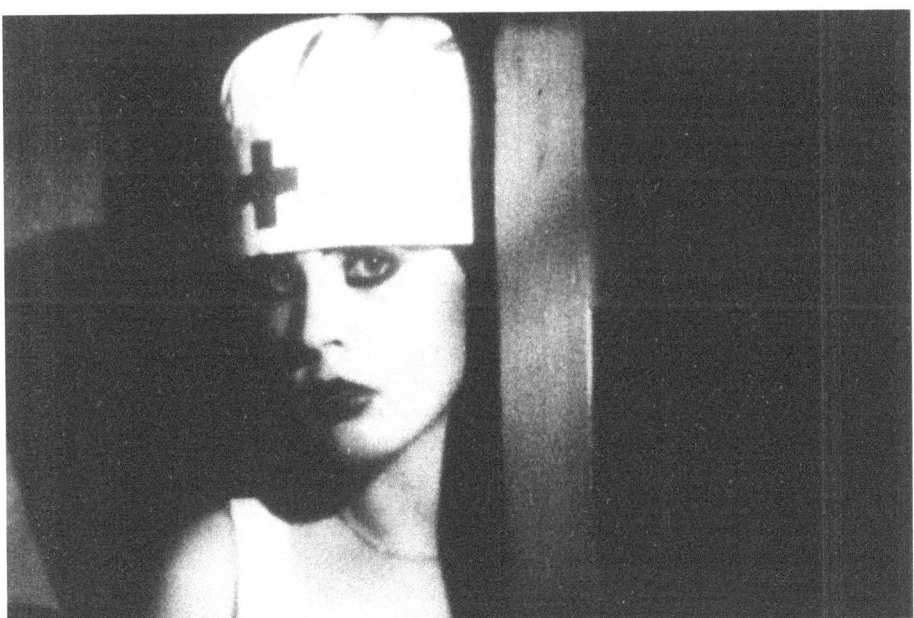

The smallpox epidemic is getting worse! A nurse looks on in *Tales from the Gimli Hospital* (courtesy Guy Maddin).

immorality of an overhead shot. I just think that anything goes, and I try and combine all the elements in the best possible way. I obviously work more in silent film than most people making movies today, but I am also trying to make music, dialogue and movement work together in really interesting ways. For my next project, a dream of mine is to get all those things going as powerfully as possible all at once. I'm trying some different things, although to the untrained eye I guess all my movies are kind of the same.

For your third feature Careful, *you shot the film in bright vivid colors, reminiscent of early two-strip Technicolor. Had you originally conceived* Careful *looking this way, or were you under some degree of pressure from the financiers to infuse some color into the film?*

I had planned to shoot *Careful* in black and white, just because I was still learning how black and white worked. But shortly before shooting I was told that it would have to be in color. I was told the Japanese would buy anything in color! At first I was quite taken aback, but then I decided that I should take a cautious approach to the color. I chose to use two colors at a time usually, sometimes three, sometimes only one when I was feeling really cautious. I painted everything in very saturated colors, then over-exposed it, which then de-saturated [it]. My working name for this process was Represso-vision, a way of repressing the melodramatic fermentation that was going on in all the characters' heads. At least I had some fun finding rationalized justification for using the kind of color that I did.

I think I got over a phobia of using color. I was kind of scared of using it. Ever since seeing *Don't Look Now*, the Nicolas Roeg film where color is so important. This earth shade Venice, then there's this red raincoat running around. It really means a lot. I didn't want any accidental red. I didn't want any red dwarves lurking around in my *mise-en-scene*! I had to be careful to control everything.

Twilight of the Ice Nymphs *should have been your breakthrough movie...*

That was full color, but all of a sudden I wasn't making a movie about caution. So I didn't know what kind of color to have for that. I could see so many ways for that movie. I didn't really have a mischievous banner under which to work, or I wasn't feeling very mischievous. It's the only movie I really ended up feeling depressed when shooting. It shows on the screen, I think.

What went wrong?

Just about everything that could go wrong, did go wrong, short of debilitating accidents! I have been very lucky on all my movies, and things have always gone right for me. I'm glad that everything sort of went wrong on one picture, so I could get it out of the way.

I didn't write the script, my best friend George Toles wrote it. It was the first time I have ever been faced with the prospect of adapting a script that I hadn't written myself. And I didn't know how to do it. George can see his projects a little more verbally than I do, whereas he and I working together have a visual hybrid. I was trying to figure out ways of visualizing these things, and I was having some trouble putting them onto the screen. I was trying to configure what color I should make them. I didn't know how to make these things visual. They didn't seem to have a reason for popping out of the page for me. There was no apparent reason for popping any one way rather than another. I had a lot of trouble there.

I also had a producer who was an unmitigated disaster. He was a stereo salesman who had been elevated by the state to the position of film producer and assigned to me. He's back selling his stereos, thank God. The God stereo salesman and I agreed that we would share everything fifty-fifty, and he would defer to me on all artistic matters. But he interfered continually with a giant philistine oafish face and voice combination. And at the end of it all he ended up with a house, a new car and I ended up $14,000 in the hole! It was a bad extreme.

Did making the acclaimed short The Heart of the World *rekindle your passion for filmmaking?*

I chanced upon my assignment for that accidentally in a way. I had started teaching to earn some money. I was teaching filmmaking and film history at the University, here in Winnipeg. Some of my students were using Super 8 cameras because we didn't have enough 16mm cameras. I noticed how beautiful Super 8 was, and it had never occurred to me to go backwards. I always felt pressure to go forward, to go to 35mm or even 70mm, IMAX or Cinema Scope. Then I discovered just how portable and convenient Super 8 could be, even more than video cameras. They have auto apertures in them, and you don't have to take a meter reading and put on a wide-angle lens on a Super 8 camera. You don't even have to focus. So they have really changed the way the world looks. All of a sudden I was back to making little images that were out of this world. That excited me. It was right around this time that I got the invitation to make a film for the Toronto Film Festival's 25th birthday. I had this long-brewing project in mind to make four- or five-minute versions of long lost films. Like *London after Midnight*, *The Case of Lena Smith*. All these films made by legendary directors that had been lost, and I would do four- or five-minute version of one. At the time I thought, because I couldn't find it, that Abel Gance's film *End of the World* had been lost forever. I think only a mutilated portion of it exists. I had read a one-paragraph plot summary of it, and I had decided to shoot my own version of it, but tailor it to pay tribute to cinema and to the Toronto Film Festival. And *The Heart of the World* resulted from this. I just wrote a feature film script treatment and then filmed it and then cut it down really tightly to five and a half minutes. That's how it came

Anna (Lesley Bais), a state scientist, discovers the world is about to face an apocalypse in *The Heart of the World*. After fending off the advances of two brothers and a corrupt capitalist named Akmatov (played by Greg Klymkiw who acted as producer on *Archangel* and *Careful* and also helped finance *Tales from the Gimli Hospital*), she saves the Earth by becoming the new Heart of the World! (courtesy Guy Maddin).

about. But I was really emboldened by the imagery, and the super primitive imagery of Super 8.

You alternate between making feature-length films and short films. Do short films give you more creative freedom, and more opportunities to be experimental?

I found out very early on that there is a big layoff in between movies and by making short films [during those intervals] you can keep the rust off your eyeballs. If I remain inactive for too long I find myself on the first day of shooting making the very same mistakes I made the very first day I ever picked up a camera. This way I manage to keep in shape, just the way a footballer would have to work out between games. I just like to keep active. It's also a good excuse to get actresses to do nude scenes!

How did you come to adapt the Royal Winnipeg ballet Dracula: Pages from a Virgin's Diary *into a full-length feature?*

Once again, some of the best things I have done come from desperation. I was really broke. I had quit my job at the University because I felt it was pre-

16. Interview with Guy Maddin (Matthew Edwards)

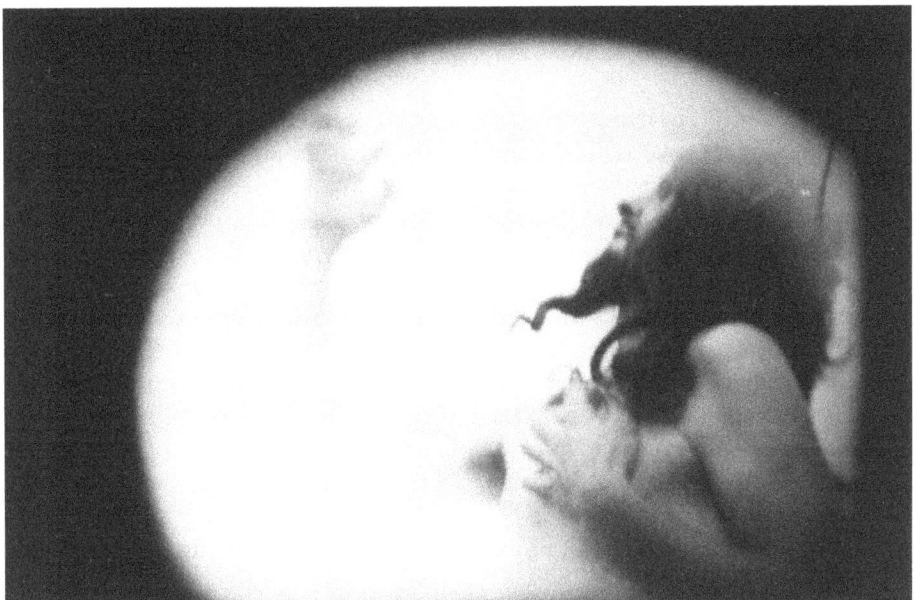

Osip tries to impress Anna. Actor and author Caelum Vatnsdal (who wrote *The Films of Guy Maddin*) in Maddin's *The Heart of the World*. The film was commissioned by the Toronto International Film Festival, to celebrate their 25th anniversary. The short film, a fantastic parody of silent Soviet propaganda films, went on to great critical acclaim, winning a host of awards (courtesy Guy Maddin).

venting me from working full-time on film. But then I didn't have a film to work on. I liked the desperation of that. Sometimes I work better when I'm more desperate. I try harder, I get up earlier and I work longer hours. And I got this really frightening offer to shoot a ballet on Dracula that had already been staged across the continent for the last three years by the Royal Winnipeg Ballet. I watched it for the first time by myself—the choreographer held me by the knee to the neck and steered me around the stage to keep me out of the way of ballerinas that might fly into my face and take my head off. I got to videotape the entire thing for myself, not just to commit it to memory but to experience it close up, like a filmmaker and have a record of it that I could watch on television. I learned during that time that ballet dancers, far from objecting to having their bodies cropped off by a camera making a close-up of them, actually thrived in the close-up situation and had been longing for their close-ups like glorious swans on Sunset Boulevard for a very long time. They put a lot of work into acting with their faces, and even with the tips of their fingers and their toes. A lot of what the dancers do on stage really should be seen in close-up, even at the expense of the rest of their bodies. The ideal situation for watching dance would be to watch it live, but with one of those jumbo television screens above the stage, so that the dancers can get their close-ups as well.

I asked all the dancers what their favorite dance films were, because I was terrified by the project. I had never really watched much ballet, and the few dance films I tried to watch put me to sleep in a hurry. With the exception of big chunks of Michael Powell's *The Tales of Hoffmann*, and maybe *The Red Shoes*, but that's not really a dance film. It's got dancing in it. All the dancers, even the choreographer, said they didn't like dance films. Dance is never represented in the way that they experience it. And what I noticed when I was right on stage videotaping these dancers, is that you could feel the floor giving way whenever they landed near you. You could hear them grunting, straining, you could hear their muscles flexing. You would get sprayed in the face with sweat, and you could hear their panties ripping! That sort of immediacy and that chaos was what dancing was for them. I vowed right then to get the camera onstage and in amongst them, now and then at least, to step inside the choreography so that it broke down. It was an interesting experience to be so terrified of making a movie that even I couldn't watch out of boredom. But then I was actually proud of it by the time I had finished it.

In Dracula *there are obvious nods to such seminal works as F.W. Murnau's* Nosferatu, *Carl Dreyer's* Vampyr, *Benjamin Christensen's* Haxan *and Hammer horror films. It's recognizable that these films have had a certain degree of influence on you.*

I really like *Haxan*. I first saw it years ago with the William Burroughs narration. Pretty funny. I never really watched *Nosferatu*. I made myself watch the Bela Lugosi *Dracula*, as research beforehand. I heard it was boring, but when I watched it with the optional Philip Glass score it really got under my skin. The movie is so slow-moving and the people speak so slowly and hypnotically, and they move across the frame very methodically. But the Philip Glass music is so repetitive and incessant that this to me feels like the real ballet version of Dracula, that it was directed by Tod Browning and completed as a ballet by Philip Glass several decades later and that there was no need to make *Dracula: Pages from a Virgin's Diary*. So I was kind of discouraged at first, but then I convinced myself while reading the Bram Stoker novel that there were a number of things that no movie had ever proceeded with. So I seized on the chance to turn the dials of the movie's concerns towards male jealousy. I got the chance to put myself in the movies because I have been at one time or another a very, very propagandizing male. So I had just started making a movie about male jealousy in the way I think Bram Stoker meant it to be.

Dracula: Pages from a Virgin's Diary *has received a tremendous amount of international recognition and acclaim. When making the film, did it ever seem remotely*

16. Interview with Guy Maddin (Matthew Edwards) 231

conceivable that it would connect so well with audiences?

I was really lucky. It even won an Emmy. It was originally produced for television, so it was eligible for an International Emmy Award. I think it was up against an Elton John special. I can't remember what else it beat, but it used to give me a chuckle out of it. Awards are kind of silly, who knows how they are decided. They seem to go to the wrong people, but this time I was on the winning end so I'm not complaining.

You embraced digital technology with Dracula: Pages from a Virgin's Diary. *That seems a very un–Guy Maddin–esque thing to do.*

I really wanted to hand paint some color onto black and white film, but it just wasn't in the budget to make a film print of the movie. So there was nothing to hand paint the colors onto, so we had to use CGI. I did make sure that the CGI artist who followed my instructions only had an hour to do a ten-hour job, so they had to do it sloppily so it would look kind of wobbly.

What prompted you to develop Cowards Bend the Knee *into a full-length feature? It originally started life as a series of peepshows at the Rotterdam film festival.*

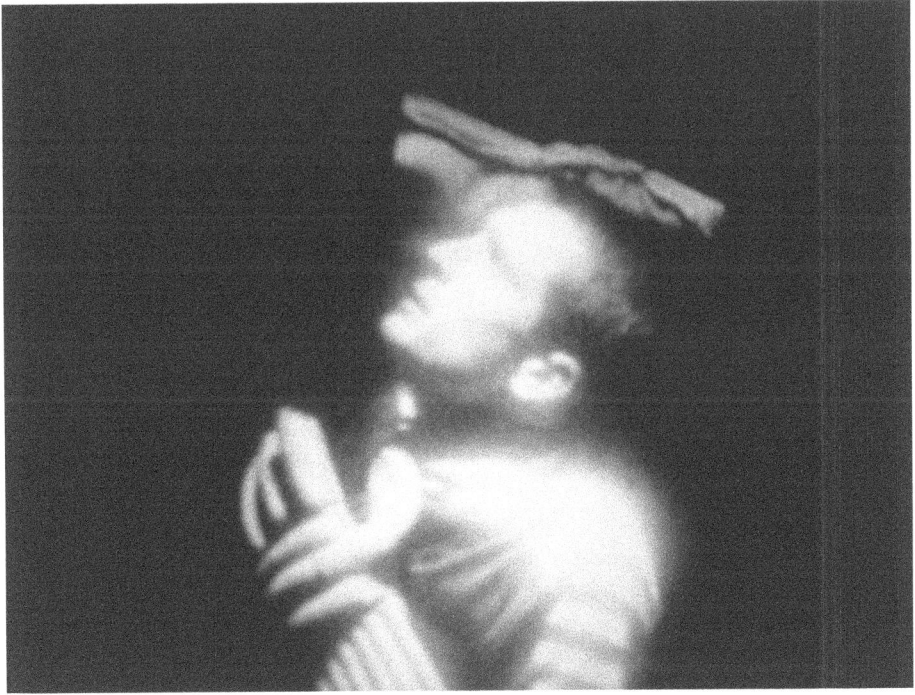

Cowards Bend the Knee **was originally commissioned by the Rotterdam Film Festival, as a series of peepshows. The peepshows were later edited together and released as a feature (courtesy Guy Maddin).**

Cowards Bend the Knee, Maddin's most personal and autobiographical film (courtesy Guy Maddin).

It started out as an installation, but I'm kind of scared of installation art. I would like to give it another shot, but that was my first foray into the world of art galleries. Once again I thought it was best to do something that was autobiographical, and I suppose if you're asking viewers to bend over and look through a peephole then you shouldn't ask them to do it for over an hour. If the length had been twelve minutes or so, or if it wasn't so narrative-driven and they were just a series of images, then you could make it any length you wanted.

I accidentally made a movie that was a lot longer than I intended. I also made a movie with a narrative that was more coherent and a lot more savagely honest about myself than I intended. I surprised myself by making my favorite movie when I originally intended to make a series of images for peepholes. I thank the gallery that commissioned me for they allowed me to release *Cowards Bend the Knee* as a film, so people wouldn't be forced to watch it through peepholes. Whenever anyone tried watching *Cowards Bend the Knee* for more than ten or fifteen minutes through peepholes, they would end up with extraordinarily bloodshot eyes. Or dehydrated eyes, because there was

16. Interview with Guy Maddin (Matthew Edwards) 233

sometimes a wind blowing through the peepholes, and one of my best friends watched about halfway through and he had a hemorrhaged eyeball and a hemorrhage that bled upwards from his eye up onto his temple! It was really hard on viewers. I like to make viewers as comfortable as possible. I was really pleased to get *Cowards Bend the Knee* out there as a film and DVD.

The Saddest Music in the World is perhaps your most accessible piece of work, yet you haven't compromised your vision.

I felt good that I didn't compromise my vision.

Were you deliberately aiming to reach out to a wider audience?

I was aiming to reach a wider audience. One of my producers, Niv Fichman, approached me one day saying he had this script that Kazuo Ishiguro had written many years earlier. Ishiguro had grown tired of finding a producer who could get the picture made. He had decided to ask Niv to find a director that would be willing to re-write it in his own obsessive colors. Niv invited me to that, but he said that he had always been struck by how promising my imagery had been, but something had always stopped me reaching more people. He was also determined to help me remain true to myself. He felt that was possible, and I agreed. Most people always saw me as a non-narrative filmmaker, but my desires have always been to be more narrative than I seem. I've started to have more preview screenings, so thoughtful viewers can make narrative or editing suggestions to make my films more accessible.

I was struck by the similarities between The Saddest Music in the World *and* Archangel. *Is* The Saddest Music in the World *an expansion on some of themes and ideas behind* Archangel?

Yeah, it might have been. A lot of people have started to notice that I have a few themes popping up in my work. There's kind of an amnesia drift rolling through the place. They're all just my own version of *Vertigo* anyway—my favorite movie.

On the subject of Archangel, *tell us about the action sequences. They were extraordinary. How did you film them?*

They were filmed so casually. They really did reinforce my suspicions about how over-fussy filmmaking usually gets. I remember many years ago, but it still sticks in my head, that it was a Friday afternoon and it was time to go to the lake soon. It was time to wrap up shooting, and we still hadn't filmed any of the action sequences. We had a twelve foot–wide fake sky and I remember filming people in front of it fighting. I had hired a bunch of professors, lawyers, doctors and friends of mine—all of the grownups I could trick into being in such a ridiculous enterprise! I dressed them up in toy soldier costumes, men and women alike, and just told them to play fight in a way they might remember doing as children. I should have recorded the sound. They were all growling and yelling *bang* with the fake guns they were pretending to fire. Then it was just a matter of cutting out the stuff that looked really bad, but keeping in the stuff that looked terminally bad. I know right around that time that Kenneth Branagh came out with *Henry V*, and everyone was talking about how wonderful his action sequences were given his budget. Mine was conspicuously a lot lower.

You have just directed a short film about Isabella Rossellini's father. What can you tell us about that?

The film is called *My Dad Is 100 Years Old*. It's a very personal script written by Isabella, best described as a love letter to her dead father. It was a way of massaging audiences into the experience of watching a Roberto Rossellini movie, because Isabella is convinced that Roberto's been forgotten quickly and that the occasion of a centennial will at least bring about a few retrospectives. She wanted to take advantage of that opportunity to say "I love you" to her dead father.

I thought it worked out pretty well, actually. I was really proud, much

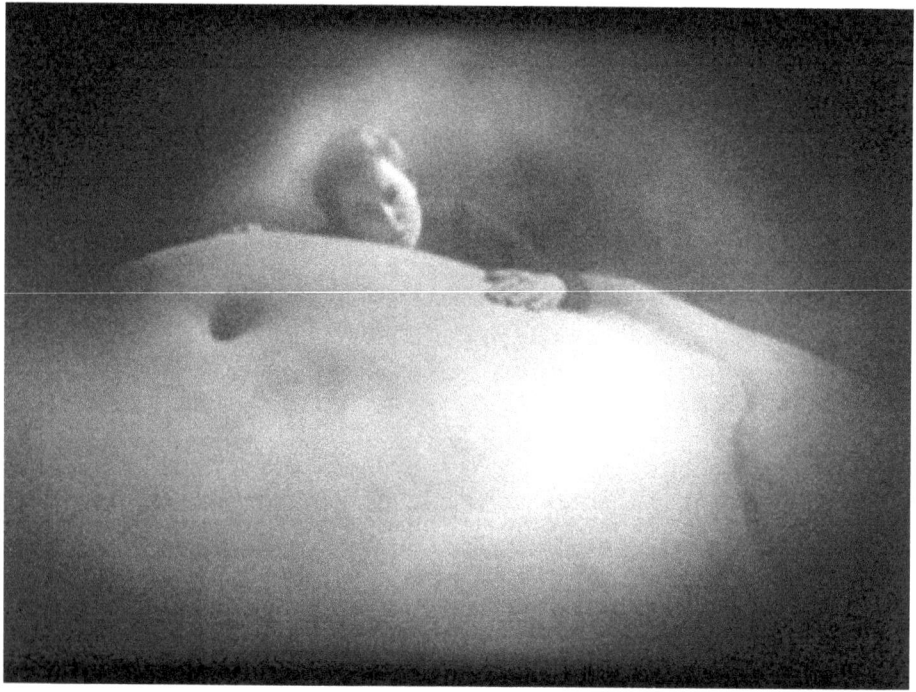

My Dad Is 100 Years Old **was Isabella Rossellini's tribute to her late father, legendary filmmaker Roberto Rossellini. Directed by Maddin, the film has received critical acclaim from audiences and critics. However, it has not been to everybody's liking. Isabella Rossellini's sister has labeled the film disrespectful (courtesy Guy Maddin).**

like I was with *Dracula: Pages from a Virgin's Diary*. I had a real assignment here. I was very worried about misrepresenting Isabella or coming across as someone who was trying to show up Roberto, or imitating him badly. So, I just decided to be as true to Isabella's feelings, as far as I understood them, and made no attempts to imitate anything. I just filmed the movie. I filmed an Isabella Rossellini movie, not a Guy Maddin movie.

Tell us about your latest film Brand Upon the Brain.

It's a companion piece to *Cowards Bend the Knee*. I shot it in a similar way, and it's a prequel or sequel. I'm not sure which. It's only partially edited right now. I shot it in Seattle, so I didn't use any of the same cast. I shot it under this great arrangement from a Seattle Utopian film company called The Film Company, which is the only not-for-profit film production studio in the world. They invite filmmakers to make features. Each filmmaker is only paid $4,000, but they receive a free low-budget movie. The only condition is that they have to use an all–Seattle cast and crew. The script didn't have to be approved or anything. I was writing the script while I was still flying in the airplane to Seattle, drawing on huge chunks of my own past. I'm pleased with the script, although I didn't get a chance to work on it as much as I wanted

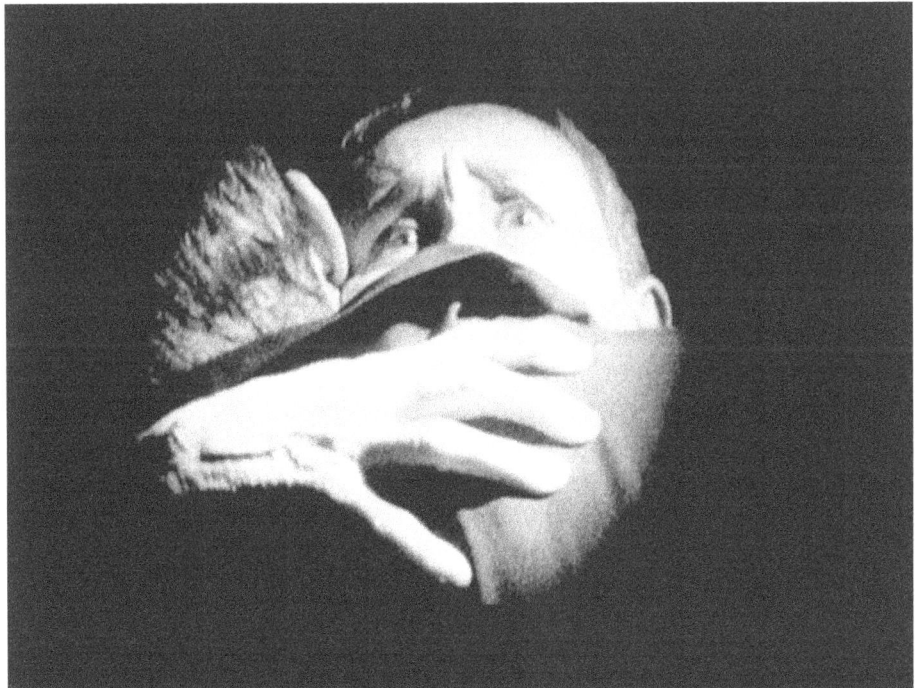

Scene from Maddin's *Brand Upon the Brain* (courtesy Guy Maddin).

Maddin's latest feature, *Brand Upon the Brain* (courtesy Guy Maddin).

to. So editing is taking a lot longer.

How influential has George Toles been on your career?

I wouldn't have been doing this at all if I had never met George. He is the guy that really got me to switch hemispheres, back when I first met him in 1980. He got me reading books, something I was too lazy to do as a kid. He got me watching movies. I like to think that I have helped him too. He's a professor and he always saw himself as more of a critic, than a creator. I got him to help me on some of my earlier attempts at creating things. He discovered he had a creative streak. So did I. We're best friends. We both still try and improve, even though I'm in my forties. I still feel really young, because we both feel we have just begun this filmmaking thing, as we came so late to it.

Tell us about The Drones.

They are finally fading from memory. In the early days of filmmaking I had this inseparable group of friends. There were four of us. George wasn't one of them, he was my best friend. The Drones were made up by my actor friend Kyle McCulloch, who starred in *Tales from the Gimli Hospital*, *Archangel* and *Careful*, my house painting partner Ian Handford whose grandfather delivered me on the day I was born, and John Harvie, a guy who walks around in spats; he's a barrister here in Winnipeg. He is an amazing expert on all things Austro-Hungarian. He is a buff of things long gone and forgotten, but he incarnates them. We used to drive around, pick up girls and puzzle them as to what decade they were really living in. We would take them out to goat fields and serenade them. It was surprising how successful we were, considering how obnoxiously affected we really were. It was a real tight-knit little group. The four of us on four wheels, driving around and casting really self-centered spells wherever we went. I prized the break-up of The Drones. We broke up as soon as we got together. We had been hanging out for about a year, before we decided to call ourselves The Drones. We named ourselves after the P.G. Wodehouse characters. We set up some sort of constitution where we would have to eat fish every Friday, and drink out of hip flasks. I forget the entire list of strictures we made up, as the four of us were never in the same room together after that night. We are all very high-tempered people. There have been reconciliations where three Drones have been together at one time. I have a hunch that maybe, at best, the four will be together at one Drone's funeral.

About the Contributors

About the Editor

Matthew Edwards is a writer from Cheddar, United Kingdom. His work has appeared in *Naked, Headpress, Venue, Eastern Cult Cinema* (under the pseudonym Kim Kiyamo), *Jade Screen, JC World, Screen Power, Necronomicon,* and *Twisted Visions*. He is currently based in Japan, where he is teaching English on the JET Programme.

Contributors

Mark Edwards is a student at the University of Plymouth. When not studying, he spends his time sitting in caves in Cheddar, Somerset and Australia. This is his first article published, and is largely down to the fact that his brother is the volume's editor. It's not what you know, it's who you know.

Maitland McDonagh—Born in New York City, Maitland McDonagh misspent her youth prowling Times Square grind houses in search of horror, exploitation and mondo movies, and has been writing about them ever since. She has appeared in documentaries ranging from Sky Television's *Illuminations* series (2000) to *100 Scariest Movie Moments* (2004). The senior movies editor of *TV Guide Online,* she earned an MFA in film history, theory and criticism from Columbia University, has taught film at the City University of New York and is the author of *Broken Mirrors/Broken Minds: The Dark Dreams of Dario Argento* (1990), *Filmmaking on the Fringe: The Good, the Bad and the Deviant Directors* (1995) and *The 50 Most Erotic Films of All Time.* She has contributed essays to *Zombie* (1999), *The Time Out Book of New York Walks* (2000), *Fantasy Females* (2001) and *The Last Great American Picture Show: New Hollywood 1967–1976* (2004) and written for dozens of publications in the United States and Europe.

Jasper Sharp was raised in the rural idyll of Devon, England, and has lived in Japan, Montreal, Amsterdam and Finland. As well as acting as co-editor for the website *Midnight Eye,* his writings on film have appeared in numerous countries, from the U.S. and Russia to Malaysia, in magazines such as *SFX, Japan: People, Power, Opinion* and the book anthology *24 Frames: The Cinema of Japan and Korea.* He has conducted interviews and provided audio commentaries for a number of DVD releases, and also worked on the Douglas Adams computer game *Starship Titanic.* He is currently based in Bath, United Kingdom.

Johannes Schönherr, originally from Leipzig, East Germany, joined the Kino im Komm cinema collective in Nuremberg in 1983—a small movie house showing art films: every member had to learn everything about running a theater. He created a network of similar theaters across Europe to import films from the U.S. and the UK and arranged European tours for American underground filmmakers while studying film history at Erlangen University. In 1992, he enrolled in the Cinema Studies department of New York University from which he received an MA in 1994. For a time he ran the Lighthouse Cinema on New York's Lower East Side. In 1999, he went to North Korea for the first time, helping to arrange for a 2000 European tour of North Korean feature films, and was a guest at the 2000 Pyongyang International Film Festival. His book *Trashfilm Roadshows: Off the Beaten Track with Subversive Movies* was published in 2002. Johannes is currently living in Beppu, Japan.

Marcus Stiglegger, Ph.D., is a lecturer of film studies at the University of Mainz, Germany. He has published books on Abel Ferrara, Popcinema and Westerns, as well as transgressive cinema, and is the editor of the cultural magazine *Ikonen*: www.ikonenmagazin.de. Contact: ikonenmagazin@hotmail.com

Bibliography

Carter, Angela. *The Bloody Chamber and Other Stories*. London: Vintage, 2006.
Cronin, Paul (editor). *Herzog on Herzog*. New York: Faber and Faber, 2002.
Curry, Christopher Wayne, and John W. Curry. *A Taste of Blood: The Films of Herschell Gordon Lewis*. New York: Creation Books, 1999.
Evans, Owen, and Graeme Harper. *Studies in European Cinema: 1.1*. Bristol, United Kingdom: Intellect, 2004.
Flint, David. *Babylon Blue: An Illustrated History of Adult Film*. New York: Creation Books, 1999.
Freud, Sigmund. *The Interpretation of Dreams*. London: Penguin Books, 1991.
Gallant, Chris. *The Art of Darkness–The Cinema of Dario Argento*. Godalming, United Kingdom: Fab Press, 2002.
Hardy, Phil (editor). *The Aurum Film Encyclopedia*. London: Aurum Press, 1985.
Hiller, Jim. *American Independent Cinema: A Sight and Sound Reader*. London: British Film Institute, 2001.
Hunter, Jack. *Eros in Hell*. New York: Creation Books, 1998.
Jones, Alan. *Profondo Argento*. Godalming, United Kingdom: Fab Press, 2004.
Kerekes, David (editor). *Creeping Flesh: The Horror Fantasy Film Book*. London: Headpress, 2003.
Kim, Suk. *North Korean Review, Vol. 1*. Jefferson, North Carolina: McFarland, 2005.
Lee, Hyanjin. *Contemporary Korean Cinema–Identity, Culture and Politics*. Manchester and New York: Manchester University Press, 2000
LoBrutto, Vincent. *Stanley Kubrick*. New York: Faber and Faber, 1997.
Maddin, Guy. *From the Atelier Tovar: Selected Writings*. Toronto, Canada: Coach House, 2003.
Mathews, Tom Dewe. *Censored: What They Didn't Allow You to See, and Why: The Story of Film Censorship in Britain*. London: Chatto & Windus, 1994.
McDonagh, Maitland. *Broken Mirrors, Broken Minds*. London: Sun Tavern Fields, 1991.
Mendik, Xavier, and Stephen Jay Schneider. *Underground USA: Filmmaking Beyond the Hollywood Canon*. London: Wallflower Press, 2002.
Mes, Tom. *Agitator. The Cinema of Takashi Miike*. Godalming, United Kingdom: Fab Press, 2003.
____, and Jasper Sharp (editors). *The Midnight Eye Guide to New Japanese Film*. Berkeley, California: Stone Bridge Press, 2005.
Palmer, Randy. *Herschell Gordon Lewis, Godfather of Gore*. Jefferson, North Carolina: McFarland, 2000.

Popple, Simon, and Joe Kember. *Early Cinema: From Factory Gate to Dream Factory.* London: Wallflower Press, 2004.
Pym, John (editor). *Time Out Film Guide: Twelfth Edition.* London: Penguin Books, 2004.
Schneider, Stephen Jay (editor). *Horror Film and Psychoanalysis: Freud's Worst Nightmare.* Cambridge, United Kingdom: Cambridge University Press, 2004.
Schönherr, Johannes. *Trashfilms Roadshows: Off the Beaten Track with Subversive Movies.* London: Critical Vision, imprint of Headpress, 2002.
Schreck, Nikolas. *The Satanic Screen: An Illustrated Guide to the Devil in Cinema.* New York: Creation Books, 2001.
Vatnsdal, Caelum. *Kino Delirium: The Films of Guy Maddin.* Winnipeg: Arbeiter Ring Publishing, 2000.
Yoshinaga, Masayuki. *Bosozoku—Japan's Biker Gangs.* New York: Trolley Books, 2003.

Sources and Resources

A list of additional useful magazines, websites and publishers dedicated to the discussion of cult and world cinema. Also included are a number of DVD distributors from whom you can obtain some of the more obscure titles that have been covered in this book.

Amaranth Films
http://www.amaranthfilms.com
Director Paul Hills' production company. The website offers further information on his films, projects currently in development and how to obtain his films.

British Film Institute
http://www.bfi.org

Dark Dreams
http://www.darkdreams.org
A comprehensive website dedicated to Italian horror master Dario Argento.

Fab Press
Book publisher, United Kingdom.
http://www.fabpress.com

Film Threat
http://www.filmthreat.com
This on-line journal contains news and information on cult, underground and independent cinema, as well as a wealth of reviews and interviews.

Film International
Bi-monthly magazine, Intellect Publishing, United Kingdom.

Headpress
Book publisher, United Kingdom.
http://www.headpress.com

Herschell Gordon Lewis
Official website
http://www.herschellgordonlewis.com

Ikonen Magazine
On-line film magazine.
http://www.ikonen-magzin.de

Intellect Books
Book Publisher, United Kingdom.
http://www.intellectbooks.co.uk

Neil Jordan
Official website
http://www.neiljordan.com

Midnight Eye
http://www.midnighteye.com
Seminal website dedicated to Japanese film that includes many reviews and interviews. Highly recommended.

Phil Mulloy
Official website.
http://www.philmulloy.com

Salvation Films
Film distributor, United Kingdom.
http://www.salvation-films.com
Salvation Films has a large collection of Euro-horror titles. Their catalogue also includes a number of Japanese Pink Cinema titles, including Takahisa Zeze's *Raigyo*.

Screen Edge
Film Distributor, United Kingdom.
http://www.screenedge.com
Screen Edge has released Paul Hills' *The Frontline* on DVD. They have also released a handful of Pink Cinema titles, including Hisayasu Sato's *The Bedroom*.

Senses of Cinema
On-line film journal.
http://www.sensesofcinema.com

Sight and Sound magazine
London. United Kingdom.
Popular monthly magazine with a strong emphasis on Independent and World Cinema.

Thundercrack!
http://www.thundercrackthefilm.com
Thundercrack!'s official website, created by Melinda McDowell. There you can also purchase the Special Edition DVD release of *Thundercrack!*

Dante Tomaselli
Official website.
http://www.horrorthemovie.com

Index

About Love Tokyo 133
Adachi, Masao 54, 55, 56
Address Unknown 203
Adultery Mother Daughter 57
ADV Films 197
The Adventures of Galgameth 169, 202
Affleck, Ben 44
Again to the Front 149
Ai ni Tsuite, Tokyo see *About Love Tokyo*
Ai No Corrida see *In the Realm of the Senses*
A.K.A. Serial Killer 55
Akira 127
Alcantud, Miguel 108
Alice in Wonderland 7
Alice, Sweet Alice 113, 124
Amado, Norberto López 106
Amenabar, Alejandro 104
An American Werewolf in London 13
The Amityville Horror 109
Ampo Treaty 54
Anarchy in Japansuke 58
An Chunggun, idungbangmun-ul Ssoda see *An Jung-gun Shoots Ito Hirobumi*
Andrews, Joceline 29
Angeli, Michael 170
An Jung-gun Shoots Ito Hirobumi 162, 163, 165, 167
Antonioni, Michelangelo 99
Aoyama, Shinji 58
April 25 Film Studio of the Korean People's Army 143, 184
April 26 Children Film Studio 143
Archangel 221, 224, 225, 228, 233, 236
Ardman Animation 74
Arduous March 189, 190
Argento, Dario 95–101, 102, 113, 243
Arirang 198
Armani 197
Arts Council of England Lottery Department 93
Asadal 147
Asahi Shimbun 209
Asakura, Daisuke 56

Athénée Français Cultural Centre 57
Autobiography of a Flea 61
AV (Adult Video) 50, 51, 56, 60
Ayako, Karino 209

Babelsberg Studios 189
Bad Guy 203
Baghdad 170
Baker, Rick 13
Bakuhatsu! see *Detonation*
Balaguero, James 106–109
Balanescu, Alex 80, 85
Balun, Chas 123
Baraku Emperoru see *Godspeed You! Black Emperor*
Barandov Film Studio 167, 202
Barron, Brian 141
Barron, David 29
Bava, Mario 98, 113
BBC 90, 141, 166, 202
BBC World Service 166
BBC2 80
The Beast Must Die 97
The Bedroom 58, 244
Begotten 20
Behind the Green Door 61
Beijing 210, 218
Beijing Dian Ying Studios 210
La Belle au bois Dormant 14
A Bellflower 180, 181, 182, 184, 192
Ben-Hur 44
Benson, Moira 63, 71
Bentham, John 27
Bentley, James 103
Berlin Film Festival 54, 169
Berlin Wall 189
Best Is My Country 188
BFI (British Film Institute) 38, 80, 94, 243
Bias, Lesley 228
Bing 63, 64, 65, 67, 69
The Bird with the Crystal Plumage 96, 98
The Black Emperors 127–134

Black Snow 55
Blackwood, Algernon 97
The Blair Witch Project 42
Blampied, Anthony 101
Blockbuster Video 45
Blodgett, Mookie 63
Blood Feast 40, 41, 42, 44, 45, 47, 48, 49
Blood Feast 2 41–47, 49
The Bloody Chamber 6, 7, 17
Bloody Conference 167
Blow Job 225
Bluebell Films 29
Bomnalui nunseoji see *Thaw*, aka *Snow Melts in Spring*
Boso-zoku 126, 127
Boston Kickout 21–25, 27, 29, 32, 35, 36
Bottin, Rob 13
Botto, Juan Diego 110
Bournemouth & Poole College of Art and Design 25
Boyle, Danny 21, 127
Boy Partisans 148
Brady, Francie 5
Branagh, Kenneth 234
The Brand Upon the Brain 235, 236
Brez, Michael 11
Bright, Matthew 7, 13
British Arts Council 75
British Cinema 1, 2, 5–13, 15–39, 72–94
British Screen 38
Broken Mirrors/Broken Minds: The Dark Dreams of Dario Argento 95, 101
Brooklyn 113
The Brothers Grimm 7, 11
Browning, Tod 230
Bubble Years 56
Bulgasari see *Pulgasari*
Bunka Gekijô 50
Bunuel, Luis 223
Burst City 127
Burroughs, William 230
Bush, George W. 199
The Butcher Boy 5
Byong-Cho, O. 151, 152

Cabinet of Dr. Caligari 105
Café Flesh 61
Cahiers du Cinema 200
The Calendar Girls 22
California 48
Camera d'Or Prize 57
Campbell, Ramsey 108
Cannes Film Festival 27, 57, 169, 200
Cannon 14
Cannon, Danny 36, 37
Cannon, Roy 37
Careful 221, 224, 225, 228, 236

Carpenter, John 13
Carter, Angela 6–10, 12, 14–17
The Case of Lena Smith 227
Cassidy, Elaine 103
Cat O' Nine Tails 98
Catholic Nun Runa's Confession 53
CGI 12, 13, 85, 231
The Chain 92
Chambers, Marilyn 61
Chang-bum, Kim 177, 179
The Changeling 124
Changgansan Hotel 217
Chang-sun, Park 174, 177
Chang-wook, Park 143
Channel 4 36, 90, 93
Channel 5 37
Chan-us, Hong 202
Charisma 58
Le Chat Botté 14
Chicago 48
Chikan Densha see *Train Pervert*
Chikan Densha Hitozuma-Hen: Okusama Wa Chijo see *Tandem*
Children's Palace (North Korea) 139
Cho, Eiju 126
Choe Hyon see *Nation and Destiny*
Choguk-kwa unmyong see *Nation and Destiny*
Chol-ho, Ri 202
Chollima 153, 202
Chol-suk, Ri 194
Chongbanggong see *The Spinner*
Chongchalbyong see *Scouts*
Chongryon Film Studio 177
Choson Ilbo 174
Christensen, Benjamin 230
The Christies 94
Chueon sone yeongweonhari see *Forever in Our Memory*
Chul-woo, Lee 200
Chung-hee, Park 165, 170, 208
Chunhyang 198
Chun-song, Kim 199
Chytichlova, Vera 202
Le Cinque Giornate 98
Cinema Vérité 132, 134
Le Cirque de Corée 174
Clerks 25
Clinton Administration 199
Cocteau, John 51
Color Me Blood Red 40, 48
Colt, Zebedy 61, 62
Columbia University 95
Committee of Japanese Film Production 54
The Company of Wolves 2, 5–19
Confessions of a Trickbaby, AKA *Freeway 2*, 7, 13

The Conformist see *Cowboys*
Contemporary Korean Cinema 142, 202
Cooper, Leroy 29
Coward's Bend the Knee 221, 231–235
Cowboys 73–77
Crazy Thunder Road 127
Creepers see *Phenomena*
Creeping Flesh 1
Cronenberg, David 20, 59
The Crying Game 5
Cure 58
Curtis, Dan 97

Dae-jung, Kim 136, 165, 196, 197, 199
Dae-sik, Pak 149
The Daily Mail 74
Dali, Salvador 223
Damiano, Gerard 61
Danchi Tsuma Hakuchū No Furin see *Tenement Wife Midday Adultery*
Dandong 143
Dante, Joe 13
Dark Shadows 97
Darkness 106, 107, 108, 109, 110, 111
Darwinian 31, 38
Dawn of the Dead 112
Dead by Dawn Film Festival 45
The Dead Father 223
Deep Red 96, 98
Deep Red Magazine 123
Deep Throat 61
*The Defenders of Height 12*11, 149, 150
The Defiance 62
Democratic People's Republic of Korea (DPRK) 136, 182, 199
Desecration 112–118, 121, 124
DeToledo, Tedi 29
Detonation 127
Detroit Times 203
Deuce 96, 98
The Devil in Miss Jones 61
The Devil Inside Her 62
The Devil's Backbone 103–106
The Devil's Cleavage 67
Devil's Ecstasy 62
The Devil's Playground 62
DiCaprio, Leonardi 200
Die Another Day 205
Digital Film(making) 1, 31, 39, 42
A Dirty Western 62
Disney 7, 14, 73
Diva 17
Do I Love You 11
Dog Star 58
Dogma 31
Dong-ho, Kim 198
Dong-min, Chon 149

Don't Let It Bring You Down 57
Don't Look Now 6, 226
Doo-young, Lee 198
Doraoji annun milsa see *An Emissary of No Return*
Dracula 230
Dracula: Pages from a Virgin's Diary 221, 228–231, 234
Dracula: Prince of Darkness 11
The Dragons 126
Drew, Robert 132
Dreyer, Carl 230
The Drones 236
Dublin 17
Dune 14

Earls Court 41
East Hastings 127
Eaton, Marion 63, 69
Ebert, Roger 96
Edinburgh 45
Ego 10
Eiffel Tower 174, 176
Eirin 51
The Elephant Man 14
Ellinger, Mark 67, 71
Emanuelle 53
An Emissary of No Return 166
Emmerich, Roland 197
Emmy 231
Empire State Building 225
The End of the Affair 5, 85
End of the World 227
Enigma 23
Enquist, Stephen 109
Eraserhead 20, 39
Eung-suk, Kim 174, 176
Eun-hee, Choi 166–170, 208
Eureka 58
Evil Dead 17, 20, 112, 119, 120
The Exorcist 119, 124
Expensive Tastes 62
Extreme Indulgence Woman—Pleasure Deep Within 53
The Eye of the Storm 86

f# a# ∞ 127
Fab Press 1, 243
Fahrenheit 9/11 133
Falcon Crest 97
Family Guy 74
Fangoria 99, 123
A Far-Off Islet 184, 185
Farewell to the Land 133
Fata Morgana 133
The Feature Film Company 235
Feature Film List 140, 142

February 8 Film Studio of the Korean People's Army 143
Feire, Daniel 108
Fellini, Federico 99
Ferrara, Abel 20
Fichman, Nic 233
Fictional Image 166, 202
Figgis, Mike 31
Film Council 38, 72, 93
Film Four 20, 37
Film Quarterly 101
Film Threat 1, 243
Fire Festival 133, 134
Fisher, Terence 11
5 Guerilla Brothers 159, 160, 161
Flanagan, Fionnula 103
Flesh Gordon 61
Florida 46
The Flower Girl 159–163, 165, 168
Forced Entry 62
Foreman, Milos 202
Ford, W Boyd 43
Forever in Our Memory 193–196
Fort Lauderdale 43
42nd Street 97, 98
Four Devils 56, 57, 60
Four Flies on Grey Velvet 98, 99
The 14th Winter 202
Freeway 7, 13
Freud, Sigmund 10, 14
Freudian 6, 7, 8, 10, 13, 18
Frid, Jonathan 97
Friday the 13th 14, 205
Friedman, David F. 40, 43, 48, 49
The Frontline 20, 21, 23–35, 37, 39, 244
Fulci, Lucio 113
The Full Monty 22
Funshutsu Jūgosai Baishunpu see *Gushing Prayer—A 15 Year-Old Prostitute*
Furin Haha Musume see *Adultery Mother Daughter*
Furst, Anton 18
Fuwafuwa to Beddo no see *No Love Juice: Rustling in Bed*

Gance, Abel 227
Gate of Flesh 53
German Expressionism 18
Giannini, Giancarlo 110
Gibson, Mel 108
Gigli 44
Gil see *The Road*
Gillis, Jamie 61, 62
Gil Son, Om 163
The Girl Barber 153
Gi-song, Li 149, 150
Goblin 96, 119

Glasnost 181
Glass, Philip 230
The Godfather 205
Godspeed You! Black Emperor 126–134
Godspeed You! Black Emperor (Canadian Instrumental Post-Rock Band) 127, 134
Godzilla 168, 169, 197, 205–210, 214, 219, 220
Godzilla (1998) 197, 220
Godzilla vs. Destroyer 207
Godzilla vs. the Smog Monster 207
Gojira see *Godzilla*
Gojira ga mita kita chosen 202, 219
Goijra Tai Hedorah see *Godzilla vs. the Smog Monster*
Goijra vs Destroyah see *Godzilla vs. Destroyer*
Goldcrest 39
Golden Torch 182, 187, 193
Gómez, Carmelo 106
Gongdong gyeongbi guyeok JSA see *Joint Security Area*
Gon-jo, Chong 213
Gorbachev, Mikhail 181
The Gore Gore Girls 41
Gorezone 123
Gornick, Lisa 11
Granada 27
Grandinetti, Dario 107
Great Man and Cinema 154, 160, 165, 202
Greenaway, Peter 85
Grizzly Man 133
The Gruesome Twosome 44, 48
Guinea Pig 51
Gunro Films 132
Gushing Prayer—A 15 Year-Old Prostitute 55
Gwuihahan Iibon-innyeosungpyeon see *A Naturalized Japanese Women*

The Hague 167
Hak, Pat 161
Hall, Terri 62
Halloween 114, 115, 119, 124
Hammer Horror 11, 18, 230
Hammond, Robert 23
Handford, Ian 236
Haneda Airport 178
Hanoi 139
Hansel and Gretel 7
Harbin 163
Hardy, Robin 6
Harlan, Veit 190
The Harry Allen Mystery 29
Hartevelt, Renée 58
Haruo, Nakajima 207
Harvie, John 236
Haxan 230
Headpress 1, 243

The Heart of the World 221, 225, 227–229
Hedorah 207
Hellraiser 122
Hell's Angels 126
Henry V 234
Hentai Telephone Onanie see *Don't Let it Bring You Down*
Heroes and Villains 14
Herschell Gordon Lewis' Grimm Fairy Tale 49
Herz, Juraj 202
Herzog, Werner 20, 133
Heyeeon jekkaji see *The Separation*
High Noon see *Cowboys*
High School Guerrilla 55
High Spirits 14
Hills, Paul 2, 20–39, 243, 244
Himatsuri see *Fire Festival*
Hirohito, Emperor 144
Hiroshima 126, 144
The History of the World 93
Hitler, Adolf 189
Hoffman, Dustin 23
Hollywood 1, 2, 5, 7, 12, 17, 20, 23, 24, 75, 88, 92, 112, 119, 125, 155, 209
Holmes, John 61
Hong Kil Dong 171–174
Hong Kong 166, 173, 174
Hong-sik, Kang 145
Hooper, Tobe 114
Horror 112, 114–118, 121, 124
Horror Whore 62
Ho-sun, Kim 198
Hotel 31
The Howling 13
Hoxha, Enver 151
Hradshin Castle 176
Hulme 27, 28
Hwanung 146
Hyanjin, Lee 142, 202
Hye-gyong, Kim 191
Hye-young, Kim 170
Hyonjesan District 145
Hyo-sik, Lee 203
Hysteric 58
Hyuk, Ahn 191
Hyun-hee, Kim 170, 202

I Brought a Vampire Motorcycle 25
Id 10
Ik-gyu, Choe 155, 157, 160, 161
Ik-sung, Ri 193
Imaoka, Shinji 60
Immortal Classics 155, 157, 187
Impulse 108
In Cold Blood 97
In Dreams 5, 7, 13
In the Realm of the Senses 51

Inchon 148
The Infernal Desire Machines of Doctor Hoffman 14
Inferno 99, 101
In-hak, Jang 190
Insatiable 62
The Interpretation of Dreams 14
Interview with the Vampire 5
Intolerance 82, 83, 85 93
Intolerance II: The Invasion 82–85
Intolerance III: The Final Solution 85, 89
Inzetsu Fujin–Kairaku No Oku see *Extreme Indulgence Woman–Pleasure Deep Within*
IPC 6
IRA 5
Irish Cinema 5, 6
Irumopnun yongungdul see *Unknown Heroes*
Ishiguro, Kazuo 233
Ishii, Sogo 127
Ishii, Teruo 127
The Isle 143, 203
Itami, Jûzô 55
Ito, Hirobumi 162, 163, 167

Jaeckin, Just 53
James, Henry 104, 106
Jangmi-wa dulgae see *Rose and Wild Dog*
Japan–American Security Pact 54
Japanese Anime 74
Japanese Cinema 50–60, 126–134
Japanese Nouvelle Vague 56
Japanese Pink Cinema (*Pinku Eiga*) 50–60, 243, 244
Jeepers Creepers 122
Jersey Devil 124
Jeungbal see *Vanished*
Jintai Mokei No Yoru see *Night of an Anatomical Dummy*
Jiokwa see *A Flower in Hell*
Jogakusei Gerira see *High School Guerrilla*
Johnson, Rick 63
Joint Security Area 143
Jong-il, Kim 136, 153–156, 160–171, 174, 181, 184, 188–190, 194, 196, 197, 199–202, 205, 208, 210, 213, 216, 217
Jong-mo, Ri 187
Jong-suk, Kim 154
Jordan, Neil 2, 5–19, 85, 243
Joyce, James 17
Jôyoku No Tanima see *Valley of Lust*
Juche 150–153, 160, 161, 164, 190, 194
Judge Dredd 37
Jukyusai No Chisu see *A 19 Year Old's Map*
Jun, Edoki 197
Jun, Ri 167
Jung-gun, An 162, 163, 167
Jung-hwa, Kim 182, 183

Jung-sun, Ho 188
Jun-gyong, Choe 188

Kabe No Naka No Himegoto see *Skeleton in the Closet*
Kaiju 168, 197, 205, 207
Karlovy Vary Film Festival 162, 163, 167, 181
Katō, Akira 53
Kawase, Naomi 57
KBS 198
Kennedy, Pres. John F. 96
Kerwin, William 47
Khabarovsk 154
Kidman, Nicole 103
Kil-duk, Kim 143
Kil-in, Kim 141, 171, 172
Kill Bill 40, 45
Killing Words 107, 108
Ki-mo, Jung 174, 176
Kineteka Omori 220
King Tangun 146
Ki-young, Kim 201
Kkot panun chyonyo see *Flower Girl*
Klimovsky, Andre 101
Klymkiw, Greg 228
Kohlberg, Stanford 48
Koibito-tachi Wa Nureta see *Lovers are Wet*
Koizumi, Juzohiro 199
Koji, Hashimoto 207
Kojong, Kim 198
Kokkuri 58
Kokuei 56
Kolberg 190
Kon, Satoshi 57
Konuma, Masaru 53
Korea Herald 190, 202
Korea Times 198, 203
Korean Central News Agency (KCNA) 142, 184, 202, 205
Korean Film Art 146, 150, 153, 161, 202
Korean Film Export and Import Corporation 140, 142, 150, 152, 197, 202
Korean Film Studio 142–145, 154, 155, 205, 212, 213, 216
Korean People's Army 135, 137, 184, 200
Korean People's Revolutionary Army (KPRA) 145, 147, 157
Korean War 147–150, 174, 175, 182, 183, 199
Koryo Dynasty 168
Kristof, Nicholas D. 203
Krupinski, Renny 29
Kubrick, Stanley 109
Kuchar, George 63, 67–69, 223
Kumashiro, Tatsumi 53
Kuroi Yuki see *Black Snow*
Kurosawa, Kiyoshi 58

Kwon-teak, Im 198
Kyoto 126
Kyoto no Yazoo 202
Kyu, Ahn 191, 192
Kyung-soon, Jo 180, 181

Lam, Ringo 20
Land of Love 142
Landis, John 13
Lang, Fritz 12
Lansbury, Angela 6, 11, 16, 17
The Last Emperor 133
The Last Empress 198
Leaving Las Vegas 31
Lee, Spike 97
Leesley, Geoffrey 29
Legend, Johnny 47
Leicester Square 17
Leon the Pig Farmer 25, 39
Lessons in Darkness 133
Lewis, Herschell Gordon 2, 40–49, 121, 243
Library of Congress 99
Lift yr skinny fists, like antennas to heaven! 127
Little Dieter Needs to Fly 133
Little Orphan Dusty 62
Little Red Riding Hood 6, 7, 10, 14
Lolita Vibrator Torture 58
London 21, 28, 41
London After Midnight 227
Lone, John 133
Lone Ranger 75
Long, Tim 62
Lopez, Danny 121
Lord, Paul 29
Lost 29
Lovecraft, H.P. 97
Lovelace, Linda 61
Lovers Are Wet 53
Lucas, George 12
Lucid Dreams 10
Lucky Pierre 43
Lugosi, Bela 230
Lycanthropy 9, 10
Lynch, David 20, 38, 39

M1 28
Machen, Arthur 97
Mad in Tokyo 29
Madden, John 22
Maddin, Guy 2, 221–237
Man Bites Dog 20
Maná, Laura 107
Manchester 25, 28, 202
Manchester University Press 202
Manchuria 145, 166, 168

The Manchurian Candidate 17
Manhattan 177
Mann, Alakina 103
Manson, Charles 96
El Mar 105
Marathon Man 23
Marles, Steve 29
Martinez, Fele 109
Marusan 214
Marylebone Station 37
Maslon, Jim 46, 47
Mayumi 170
McCabe, Patrick 5
McCourt, Emer 21
McCulloch, Kyle 224, 236
McDowell, Curt 63, 67, 68, 69, 70,
McDowell, Melinda 2, 63, 65, 67–71
McKnight, Sharon 62
McNamara, Sean 170
Medusa 63, 64, 65, 69
Megyaku: Naked Blood see *Naked Blood*
Meike, Mitsuru 60
Meon hunareui naeui moseub see *Myself in the Distant Future*
Metropolis 12
Metzger, Radley 1, 61, 62
Michael Collins 5
Midnight Eye 1
Mi-hwa, Park 176
Miike, Takashi 1, 20, 51
Mindan 178
Mission Impossible 2, 23
Mitchell Brothers 61
Miyazaki, Hayao 74
Moistening Housewife: Panty-less Apron 55
Molyneux, Neil 29
Momma, Takashi 139
Mona Lisa 5
Mona Lisa (painting) 47
Mona, the Virgin Nymph 61
Montreal 127
Moon Child 51
Moonshine Mountain 46–48
Morgan, Jacky Lee 42–45, 47
Moscow International Film Festival 168
Moss Side 28
Mount Paektu 146, 147, 154, 191
Moviola 99
MTV 90, 112
Mulloy, Phil 2, 72–94, 243
Mulri innun sum see *A Far-Off Islet*
Munich 202
Murder She Wrote 17
Murnau F.W. 18, 230
Museum of Modern Art (New York) 200
My Best Fiend 133
My Dad Is 100 Years Old 234

My Happiness 182–184, 192
My Home Village 145, 146, 151, 154, 160, 161
Myeongryeong 027 ho see *Order No. 027*
Myong-mun, Kim 190, 192
Myself in the Distant Future 190–193

Nabbeun namja see *Bad Guy*
Nae Kohyang see *My Home Village*
Naeui haengbok see *My Happiness*
Nagasaki 144
Nairobi 31
Nakata, Hideo 59
Naked Blood 58
The Nameless 103, 106–109, 111
Namgang Village Women 149
Namgangma-euleui Nyeoseongdul see *Namgang Village Women*
Narai Film Company 199, 200
Nation and Destiny 184–189, 202, 203
National Film School 25, 37
A Naturalized Japanese Woman 188
Nawa to Chibusa see *Rope and Breasts*
New Jersey 113, 119, 124
New Line 95, 96
New York 48, 69, 96, 97, 201
The New York Times 191, 192, 203
Nicholson, Jack 120
Night Dreams 62
Night of an Anatomical Dummy 58
Night of the Living Dead 124
Night Porter 98
A Nightmare on Elm Street 95
Nikkatsu 51–54
9/11 90
A 19 Year Old's Map 133
Nintendo 190
Nishimura, Shogorō 53
NME (New Musical Express) 127
No Love Juice: Rustling in Bed 59, 60
Noar, Amanda 29, 34
Noriega, Eduardo 104
North, Howard 62
North Carolina 46
North Korea 135–220
North Korea Seen Through the Eyes of Godzilla 169, 202, 219
North Korean Cinema 135–220
North Korean State Circus 174
Nosferatu 230
Not of This Earth 97
Nudes–A Sketchbook 67

The Ocean 125
Ock-hee, Kim 182
Odeon 17, 94
Official Detective 97
Okasareta Byakui see *Violated Angels*

OL No Rabu Jûsa see No Love Juice
Oldfield, Mike 119
Olin, Lena 109
Olivier, Laurence 23
Ollson, Erik 29
Olympic Games 170
The Omen 124
Omorashi Okusan Noopan Kappôgi see Moistening Housewife: Panty-less Apron
On the Art of the Cinema 163–165, 202
1211 Goji Bangwijadul see The Defenders of Height 1211
Open Your Eyes 104
The Opening of Misty Beetoven 62
Orang River 148, 149
Oranggang see Orang River
Order No. 027 174–176, 202
Oscars 93
Osco, Bill 61
Ôshima, Nagisa 51
The Others 103–106
Otomo, Katsuhiro 127
Outrage! see Cowboys
Owens, Eamonn 5
Oxford Street 21

Paco Plaze 108, 109
Pagan Films 53
Palace Pictures 6, 15, 17
Palestinian liberation movement 55
Pan Horror 97
Panmunchon 148
Paquin, Anna 109
Paris 174, 176
Paris, Henry 61, 62
Parry, Martin 29
Passer, Ivan 202
The Passion of Christ 108
Patterson, Sarah 11, 16
Perestroika 181
Perfect Blue 57
Perrault, Charles 7, 14
Le Petit Chaperon Rouge 14
Phantasm 124
The Phantom of Terror see The Bird with the Crystal Plumage
Phenomena 95, 96
Phillips, Vincent 29, 33, 34
Pi 20
Pibada see Sea of Blood
Ping, Deng Xiao 181
Plan 9 from Outer Space 116
Play Dead 36, 37
Poe, Edgar Allan 97
The Poet 21–25, 29, 33, 35
Poltergeist 114, 115
Pope, F.X. 62

The Possession 62
Powell, Michael 230
Prague 176
Pratt Institute 113
Prior, Eric 109
Pulgasari 143, 168, 169, 174, 197, 199, 200, 205–220
Pulse 58
Pusan 148
Pusan Film Festival 198, 200
Puss in Boots 7, 14
Pyle, Maggie 63
Pyongyang 135–139, 143, 145, 147, 148, 163, 166, 168, 182, 183, 184, 187, 190–193, 196–202, 218
Pyongyang Film Festival of Non-Aligned and Other Developing Countries 135–139, 141, 143, 154, 182, 187, 193
Pyongyang International Cinema House 135, 136, 138, 139
Pyongyang University of Dramatic and Cinematic Arts 151, 165

Quay, Brothers 101

Raigyo 58, 243
Ravensbourne College of Art 86
Raving Beauties 21, 22, 39
Rea, Stephen 11, 13
Reagan, Ronald 62
Red Army 145
The Red Army/PFLP: Declaration of World War 55
The Red Shoes 230
Reems, Harry 61, 62
Reich, Sidney 48
Remember to Keep Holy the Sabbath Day see The Ten Commandments
The Resurrection of Eve 61
The Return 86
Revenge in the Tiger Cage 166
Riley, Michael 29
Ring 59
Rio, Vanessa Del 61
Risueno, Ana 108
River Taedong 135
The Road 171
Robin Hood 171
Rochester 48
Rodonggyegeuppyeon 204
Roeg, Nicolas 6, 226
Roman Gekijô 50–53, 55
Roman Porno 51–54
Romeo and Juliet 179
Rope and Breasts 53
Rorita Baibu Seme see Lolita Vibrator Torture

Rose, Felissa 117, 125
Rose and Wild Dog 165
Rosenberg, Stuart 109
Rossellini, Isabella 225, 234, 235
Rossellini, Roberto 234, 235
Rotterdam 52, 231
Rotterdam Film Festival 231
Roxy 96
Royal College of Art 86
Royal Road 10
Royal Winnipeg Ballet 228, 229
Rue Morgue 123
Runaway 168, 201
Rustling in Bed see No Love Juice
Ryokushô Renzoku Shashatsuma see A.K.A. Serial Killer
Ryong-gu, Yun 148, 149

The Sad Mafioso 127
The Saddest Music in the World 221, 233
Sadeghi, Afshin 136
Sagawa, Issei 58
St. Paule, Irma 121
Sakamoto, Rei 60
Sakhalin Island 170
Saki 97
Sakura, Moe 60
Salt 168, 201
San Francisco 69
Sandweiss, Ellen 123, 125
Sanford, Christie 120
Sang-bok, Pak 171
Sang-hun, Choe 203
Sang-ok, Shin 165–171, 174, 181, 182, 197, 200, 201, 203, 205–220
Sang-soo, Choe 168
Sano, Kazuhiro 56, 57
Santiago de Compostela 110
Saraba Itoshiki Daichi see Farewell to the Land
Sara-innun ryonghongdul see Souls Protest
Sarangeui Daeji see Land of Love
Satan's Playground 117, 119–121, 123–125
Satô, Hisayasu 56, 58–60, 244
Satô, Toshiki 56, 57, 59
Satsuma, Kenpachiro 169, 202, 205–220
Saunders, Andrew 37
Sayadian, Stephen 61, 62
Scott, Dougray 23
Scouts 149, 174
Scream 42, 116, 122
Screaming Mimi 99
Screen Actors Guild 47
Screen Edge 20, 26–29, 31, 57–59, 243
Scudder, Ken 63
Sea of Blood 155–158, 160, 161, 165
Second Name 108, 109

Secrets 29
Seidan Botandoro see Hellish Love
Seizure 97
Seki, Kôji 56
Selby, David 97
Selwyn 97
Senses of Cinema 1
Seom see The Isle
Seoul 170, 172, 176, 178, 197–201, 208
The Separation 174, 177
Serial Mom 47
Sesang-e Burumeopeora see We are the Happiest
Seven Gods of Fortune 60
Sex Pistols 223
Sex Séance 62
Sex Wish 62
The Sexlife of a Chair 74, 81
Shadow of China 133, 134
Shaft 180
Shakespeare in Love 22
Shall We Dance 59
Sheen, Simon 169, 170
Sheen Films 201
Shichifukujin see Seven Gods of Fortune
Shimbashi Station 50
Shin Film 165, 166, 168, 213
The Shining 109, 114, 115, 120, 124
Shinjuku 128, 209
Shinto 103
Shisenjô No Aria see The Bedroom
Shi-Tennô see Four Devils
Shûdôjo Runa No Kokuhaku see Catholic Nun Runa's Confession
Sight and Sound 1
Simm, John 21, 32, 36
The Simpsons 74, 91
The Sixth Sense 106
Skeleton in the Closet 54
Sleepaway Camp 117
Sleeping Beauty 14
SN21 Enterprise 197
Snow White 7, 11, 13
Sogum see Salt
Sole, Alfred 113
Something Weird Video 46
Sone, Chusei 53
Songun 194
Son-hui, Jang 168
Sonyon ildang see Boy Partisans
Souls Protest 199, 200
The Sound of Music 74, 87, 90
Sound on Film 80, 85
South Korean Film 135–204
South Park 74, 91
Southern Culture on the Skids 47
Spanish Civil War 105

Spanish Mystery Thrillers 103–111
Sparkle's Tavern 67
The Spinner 151, 152
Sprinkles, Annie 61, 62
Stalin, Joseph 145, 150
Stallone, Sylvester 37
Star Wars 12, 14
Statue of Liberty 177
Stevenage 33, 36
Stoker, Bram
Stone, Oliver 97
The Story of O 53
Strode, Dennis 29
Suchwiin bulmyeong see Address Unknown
Suh-hae, Choi 168
Summer of Sam 97
Sung, Kim Il 135, 141, 145–148, 150–152, 154, 157, 160–164, 167, 168, 181–183, 189–191, 194, 196, 199, 200
Sung-chu, Kim 145
Sunshine Policy 196, 199
Suô, Masayuki 59
Super Ego 10
Super Size Me 133
Suspiria 99, 100, 101, 119
Suzaku 57
Suzuki, Seijun 53
Sykes, Eric 103
Syng-man, Rhee 145, 148

Tabisuru Pao-Jiang-Hu see The Wandering Peddlers
Taboo: The Single and the LP 67
Taek-won-do 175, 202
The Taking of Christina 62
Takita, Yôjirô 59
Talchulgi see Runaway
Tales from the Gimli Hospital 221–225, 228
The Tales of Hoffmann 230
Tama, Rumi 54
Tampopo 55
Tanaka, Noboru 53
Tandem 58
Tarantino, Quentin 25
Tarzan 56
A Taste of Blood 48
Tears of My Soul 202
Ted Bundy 13
The Ten Commandments 74, 77–79, 91, 92
Tenebrae 99
Tenement Wife Midday Adultery 58
Terri's Revenge 62
La Terza Madre 101
Tesis 104
Tetsuji, Takechi 54, 55
Tetsuo 20
Tetsuo, Nishida 166, 202

Texas Chain Saw Massacre 114, 119, 124
That's Nothin see Cowboys
Thaw 177–181, 184
They 106
They're Watching Us 106
The Thing 13
The Third Mother 101
38th parallel 145, 147, 198
33 Video 36, 37
Thomas Brothers 70
Thou Shalt Not Adore False Gods see The Ten Commandments
Thou Shalt Not Bare False Witness see The Ten Commandments
Thou Shalt Not Commit Blasphemy see The Ten Commandments
Thou Shalt Not Kill see The Ten Commandments
3 Ninjas 170, 171, 202
Through the Looking Glass 62
Thundercrack!, 2, 61–71, 244
Time Code 31
Times Square 96, 97
Timpone, Tony 123
Tiptoes 13
Titanic 199, 200
Titanic (1997) 200
Tito, Marshall 150, 151
Toho Studio 169, 197, 205, 209, 210
Tokyo 50, 52–54, 56, 57, 126, 130–133, 177, 178, 180, 200, 202, 205, 209, 220
Tôkyô Emanieru Fujin see Tokyo Emanuelle
Tokyo Emanuelle 53
Tokyo Olympics 54
Tokyo X Erotica 58
Toles, George 226, 227, 236
Tomaselli, Dante 2, 3, 112–125, 244
Torajikkot see A Bellflower
Tora-san 205
Toro, Guillermo Del 105, 106
Toronto Film Festival 227, 229
Total Media Corporation 54
Train Pervert 58
Trainspotting 21
True Detective 97
Tse-tung, Mao 148, 150
Tto tashi choson-uro see Again to the Front
Tubular Bells 119
Tucker, Christopher 12, 14
Turn of the Screw 104, 106
TV Ontario 79
28 Days Later 127
Twilight of the Ice Nymphs 221, 226
Twin Town 23
2000 A.D. 37
2001 Maniacs 43, 44, 47
Two Thousand Maniacs 40, 42–44, 47, 48, 49

Udine Far East Festival 52
Ueno, Toshiya 60
Ukishima Maru 201
Un-bong, Ham 149
Unknown Heroes 184
Until We Sleep 29
Urban Gothic 21, 37
Uroboros 110

V–Cinema 54
Valley of Lust 56
Vampyr 230
Vanilla Sky 104
Vanished 170
Vatnsdal, Caelum 221, 229
Versace 197
Vertigo 233
Video Nasty 45
Vietnam War 54, 62
Villaronga, Agusti 105
Villaverde, Xavier 110, 111
Villefranche 29
Violated Angels 55
Vision du monde 111
Vraney, Mike 46, 47

Wakamatsu, Kôji 54, 55
Wakamastu Pro 55
The Wandering Peddlers 133
Warhol, Andy 225
Warner, David 11, 16
Washington DC 99, 199
Watcher in the Attic 53
Water Power 62
Waters, John 47
Watson, Callum 27, 29
We Are the Happiest 152, 153
Wells, Professor Paul 80, 85
Wheel of Time 133
When the Bell Chimed 13, 110, 111
When the Last Sword Is Drawn 59
The White Diamond 133
White House 199
The Wicker Man 6
Wiene, Robert 105
The Wild Blue Yonder 133
William Morrow & Co 202

The Winds of Change 80
Winnipeg 221, 227, 236
Winslet, Kate 200
Winterbottom, Michael 31
The Wizard of Gore 44
Wodehouse, P.G. 237
Wolf-Alice 6
Won-jun, Yu 175, 177
Wood, Ed 116
Wood, Thomas 47
Woolley, Stephen 19
Wolves/Werewolves 5–19, 97
The World Today 166
World War II 103, 105, 144, 145, 167, 189, 193, 199
Wun-kyu, Nah 198

Yakuza 126, 130
Yanagimachi, Mitsuo 127–134
Yaneura No Sanposha see *Watcher in the Attic*
Yanggak Islet 135
Yanqui u.x.o 127
Yasukuni Shrine 199
Year of the Yahoo 46
Yeongsangun 165
Yi Dynasty 198
The Yin Yang Master 59
Yohji, Yamada 205
Yol nebon jjae kyoul see *The 14th Winter*
Yonggari 197
Yong-kwan, Lee 198
Yoo-hoo, Im 202
Yoshimitsu, Banno 207
Yoshinaga, Masayuka 127
Yoshiyuki, Yumi 60
Young Americans 36
Young-ho, Kim 182
Yugyoktae 5 honje see *Five Guerilla Brothers*
Yuji, Tajiri 59, 60
Yume Nara Samete see *Perfect Blue*

A Zed and Two Noughts 85
Zeze, Takahisa 51, 56, 58, 59, 60, 243
Ziehm, Howard 61
Zog (s) 78, 82–84

www.ingramcontent.com/pod-product-compliance
Ingram Content Group UK Ltd.
Pitfield, Milton Keynes, MK11 3LW, UK
UKHW021844140426
5217IPUK00022B/1585